BRITISH VCs
OF
WORLD WAR 2

A STUDY IN HEROISM

Also by John Laffin

Military

Brassey's Battles: 3,500 Years of
   Conflict, Campaigns and Wars from
   A–Z
War Annual 1
War Annual 2
War Annual 3
War Annual 4
War Annual 5
War Annual 6
War Annual 7
Middle East Journey
Return to Glory
One Man's War
The Walking Wounded
Digger (The Story of the Australian
   Soldier)
Scotland the Brave (The Story of the
   Scottish Soldier)
Jackboot (The Story of the German
   Soldier)
Tommy Atkins (The Story of the
   English Soldier)
Jack Tar (The Story of the English
   Seaman)
Swifter than Eagles (Biography of
   Marshal of the RAF Sir John
   Salmond)
The Face of War
British Campaign Medals
Codes and Ciphers
Boys in Battle
Women in Battle
Anzacs at War
Links of Leadership (Thirty Centuries
   of Command)
Surgeons in the Field
Americans in Battle
Letters from the Front 1914–18
The French Foreign Legion
Damn the Dardanelles! (The Agony of
   Gallipoli)
The Australian Army at War 1899–1974
The Israeli Army in the Middle East
   Wars 1948–1973
The Arab Armies in the Middle East
   Wars 1948–1973

Fight for the Falklands!
On the Western Front: Soldiers' Stories
   1914–18
The Man the Nazis Couldn't Catch
The War of Desperation: Lebanon
   1982–85
Battlefield Archaeology
The Western Front 1916–17: The Price
   of Honour
The Western Front 1917–18: The Cost
   of Victory
Greece, Crete and Syria 1941
Secret and Special
Holy War: Islam Fights
World War 1 in Postcards
Soldiers of Scotland (with John Baynes)
British Butchers and Bunglers of World
   War 1
The Western Front Illustrated
Guide to Australian Battlefields of the
   Western Front 1916–1918
Digging Up the Diggers' War
Panorama of the Western Front
Western Front Companion
We Will Remember Them: AIF
   Epitaphs of World War 1

General

The Hunger to Come (Food and
   Population Crises)
New Geography 1966–67
New Geography 1968–69
New Geography 1970–71
Anatomy of Captivity (Political
   Prisoners)
Devil's Goad
Fedayeen (The Arab-Israeli Dilemma)
The Arab Mind
The Israeli Mind
The Dagger of Islam
The PLO Connections
The Arabs as Master Slavers
Know the Middle East
Fontana Dictionary of Africa since 1960
   (with John Grace)
Hitler Warned Us
Aussie Guide to Britain

and other titles, including novels

BRITISH VCs
OF
WORLD WAR 2

A STUDY IN HEROISM

JOHN LAFFIN

A Budding Book

This book was first published in 1997 by
Sutton Publishing Limited

This edition first published in 2000 by Budding Books, an imprint of
Sutton Publishing Limited
Phoenix Mill · Thrupp · Stroud · Gloucestershire · GL5 2BU

A catalogue record for this book is available from the British Library

ISBN 1-84015-107-2

Typeset in 10/12pt Plantin Light.
Typesetting and origination by
Sutton Publishing Limited.
Printed in Great Britain by
Redwood Books, Trowbridge, Wiltshire.

CONTENTS

List of Plates

Between pages 70 and 71

RAF VCs

Acknowledgements

A book such as this is not written without assistance from recognized authorities on the VC, the families of VC winners, organizations, libraries, regimental headquarters and museums and not least from VC winners themselves. Some people supplied information and answered my questions, others provided photographs and other illustrations. On this particular subject, VC winners, I did not expect anybody to require a reproduction fee or indeed any fee beyond the cost of a print. I had thought that pride in 'possession' of a VC winner and a natural desire to see him in a definitive book would be sufficient – and it was. Most people connected to a VC winner were enthusiastic about my book and eager to see that he was given adequate mention in it. I was sent personal information as well as further details that clarified the citation of a VC award. Most regiments, elements of the Royal Navy and of the Royal Air Force are inordinately proud of their VC winners, as a visit to any Services museum readily illustrates. VCs are always prominently displayed.

I was surprised that a few museums sought to make a profit out of a VC winner by asking for a reproduction fee, especially in relation to those whose awards were posthumous.

The first person I must thank is Mrs Moira Few, widow of Major Jack Anderson VC, DSO, who gave me much help in relation to her husband; also Captain Philip Gardner VC, MC, honorary secretary of the Victoria Cross and George Cross Association; Lieutenant-Colonel Eric Wilson VC and Captain Richard Annand VC. Mrs Didy Grahame MVO, secretary of the VC and GC Association, was also most helpful. I owe particular thanks to Chaz Bowyer, the world's leading authority on air/war VCs (see Bibliography). Others to whom I am indebted include: Lieutenant-Colonel C.D. Darrach DL, Royal Hampshire Regiment; Major W.H. Reeve, Royal Norfolk Regiment Association; Major E. Green, Staffordshire Regiment; Lieutenant-Colonel Neil McIntosh MBE, Green Howards; Lieutenant-Colonel S.F. Groves, Irish Guards; Captain D.J. Lee, Royal Anglian Regiment (Lincolnshire); Brigadier K.A. Timbers, Royal Artillery Historical Trust; Major R.D. Cassidy MBE, Royal Green Jackets; Lieutenant-Colonel A.W. Scott Elliott, Argyll and Sutherland Highlanders; Lieutenant-Colonel T.C.E. Vines, Prince of Wales Own Regiment of Yorkshire; Major J. McQ. Hallam, Lancashire HQ Royal Regiment of Fusiliers; Clem Webb and Alan Morris, London Scottish; Don Kearney (formerly Drum Major), Irish Guards; Cliff Housley, Sherwood Foresters (Nottingham and Derbyshire Regiment); David Fletcher, the Tank

Museum; Stephen Shannon, Durham Light Infantry; P.V.J. Elliott, Royal Air Force Museum; Kate Thaxton, Norfolk Museum Service; Richard Lewis, National Library of Wales; T. O'Hanlon, *London Gazette*; Bridget Spiers, Whitehall Library, Ministry of Defence; Dr Linda Washington, Head, Department of Printed Books, Imperial War Museum; Rector M. Bossy, Stonyhurst College; Mrs S.A. Riseborough, Her Majesty's Stationery Office; Dr Gwyn Bayliss, Imperial War Museum; Canon Lisle Ryder. A special word of thanks to two friends, Claude Woodroffe, a wing commander RAF in the war and Dr Brian Davies, a major of Gurkhas during the war.

Without exception, the photographs of VC winners were taken during the war, obviously so in the case of the posthumous awards. Many appeared in *The Bronze Cross*, published in 1945. The prints have come from a variety of sources, several from family members. Interestingly, most of them said that they preferred not to have their names in the book; 'the glory belonged to my grandfather', one of them eloquently said. I am grateful to these unnamed people.

I must also record my gratitude to my wife, Hazelle, for her seemingly endless typing and retyping of this lengthy book and for her always helpful and constructive criticisms and queries – 'Do you suppose that all your readers will know what a PIAT is?' Well, no, perhaps not. Of course, *she* knew; Hazelle is herself an authority on matters of military history and with me she has visited many places where VC exploits took place and cemeteries where VC winners are buried.

Most importantly, I am grateful to Sir Roden Cutler VC for his Foreword to my book. Sir Roden, who is Deputy President of the Victoria Cross and George Cross Association, is the only Australian artilleryman to be awarded the Victoria Cross. His citation, gazetted on 28 November 1941, is unusually detailed and, again unusually, it covers a long period – no less than 18 days. It makes stirring reading. Sir Roden's exploits are stated to have taken place in Syria. The area of Merdjayoun-Damour is actually in Lebanon, but the fighting of June-July 1941 is officially known as the Syrian campaign.

Lieutenant Arthur Roden Cutler, 2/5th Australian Field Regiment AIF. 19th June to 6th July 1941, at Merdjayoun-Damour area, Syria.

For most conspicuous and sustained gallantry during the Syrian Campaign and for outstanding bravery during the bitter fighting at Merdjayoun when this artillery officer became a byword amongst forward troops with which he worked.

At Merdjayoun on 19th June, 1941, our infantry attack was checked after suffering heavy casualties from an enemy counter-attack with tanks. Enemy machine gun fire swept the ground, but Lieutenant Cutler with another artillery officer and a small party pushed on ahead of the infantry and established an outpost in a house. The telephone line was cut and he went out and mended this line under machine gun fire and returned to the house, from which enemy posts and batteries were successfully engaged. The enemy then attacked this outpost with infantry and tanks, killing the Bren gunner and mortally wounding other officers. Lieutenant Cutler and another manned the anti-tank rifle and Bren gun and fought back, driving the enemy infantry away. The tanks continued the attack but under constant fire from the anti-tank rifle and Bren gun eventually withdrew. Lieutenant Cutler then personally supervised the evacuation of the wounded members of his party. Undaunted he pressed for a further advance. He had been ordered to establish an outpost from which he could register the only road by which the enemy transport could enter the town. With a small party of volunteers he pressed on until finally with one other he succeeded in establishing an outpost right in the town, which was occupied by the Foreign Legion, despite enemy machine gun fire which prevented our infantry from advancing. At this time Lieutenant Cutler knew the enemy were massing on his left for a counter-attack and that he was in danger of being cut off. Nevertheless, he carried out his task of registering the battery on the road and engaging enemy posts. The enemy counter-attacked with infantry and tanks and he was cut off. He was forced to go to ground, but after dark succeeded in making his way through enemy lines. His work in registering the only road by which enemy transport could enter the town was of vital importance and a big factor in the enemy's subsequent retreat.

On the night of 23rd–24th June he was in charge of a 25-pounder sent forward into our forward defended localities to silence an enemy anti-tank gun and post, which had held up our attack. This he did and next morning the recapture of Merdjayoun was completed. Later at Damour on 6th July, when our forward infantry were pinned to the ground by heavy hostile machine gun fire Lieutenant Cutler, regardless of all danger, went to bring a line to his outpost when he was seriously wounded. Twenty-six hours elapsed before it was possible to rescue this officer, whose wounds by this time had become septic necessitating the amputation of his leg. Throughout the Campaign this officer's courage was unparalleled and his work was a big factor in the recapture of Merdjayoun.

Abbreviations
and a few military terms

AFC	Air Force Cross
AIF	Australian Imperial Force (the volunteer army prepared to serve anywhere in the world)
AK	Knight of the Order of Australia
AMF	Australian Military Forces (the home defence army)
BEF	British Expeditionary Force
BEM	British Empire Medal
Besa	Type of machine gun
Bren	Type of machine gun
CB	Commander of the Bath
CGM	Conspicuous Gallantry Medal
CQMS	Company Quarter Master Sergeant
CSM	Company Sergeant Major
DCM	Distinguished Conduct Medal
DFC	Distinguished Flying Cross
DFM	Distinguished Flying Medal
DSC	Distinguished Service Cross (Navy)
DSO	Distinguished Service Order (all Services)
GBE	Knight Grand Cross of the Order of the British Empire
GC	George Cross
KAR	King's African Rifles
LRDG	Long Range Desert Group
MC	Military Cross
MID	Mention in Despatches
MM	Military Medal
MTB	Motor Torpedo Boat
MVO	Member of the Victorian Order
NCO	Non-Commissioned Officer
OC	Officer Commanding
PIAT	Projectile Infantry Anti-Tank
POM-POM	Rapid firing 20 mm cannon
RA	Royal Artillery
RAAF	Royal Australian Air Force
RAF	Royal Air Force
RAFVR	Royal Air Force Volunteer Reserve
RAMC	Royal Army Medical Corps

RAN	Royal Australian Navy
RAOC	Royal Army Ordnance Corps
RCAF	Royal Canadian Air Force
RCNVR	Royal Canadian Naval Volunteer Reserve
RM	Royal Marines
RN	Royal Navy
RNR	Royal Navy Reserve
RNVR	Royal Navy Volunteer Reserve
RNZAF	Royal New Zealand Air Force
SAAF	South African Air Force
SBS	Special Boat Service
Spandau	Type of machine gun
TD	Territorial Decoration
VC	Victoria Cross
WAAF	Women's Auxiliary Air Force
WOI and WOII	Warrant Officers Class I and II (senior to an NCO, junior to an officer)

Note: Many servicemen are described in this book as having a Bar to a decoration, for instance, MC and Bar, DFC and Bar, DSC and Bar. A Bar is not an inferior award, as many people imagine, but a second award of the same decoration; that is, the serviceman had won two MCs, two DFCs or two DSCs. On three occasions since the inception of the VC three servicemen have won the award twice. They are designated as VC and Bar.

Author's Preface

The Bravest of the Brave

I saw my first Victoria Cross at the age of eight and the sight of this famous decoration filled me with excitement. Boys of the late 1920s and early 1930s knew a lot about the Cross because we saw former warriors of the First World War wearing it on ceremonial occasions and on parade. Moreover, as a voracious reader, I encountered gallant VC winners in numerous works of war fiction. 'Tim Carew VC', a daring and indomitable young Royal Navy officer, made a deep impression on me.

The occasion on which I had my first close look at the decoration was in Sydney, Australia, on an Anzac Day, 25 April, the greatest day of the year in Australian national life. On this day, ever since 1915, Australians have commemorated the sacrifice of their sons and daughters in the country's wars. In Australia, as in all parts of the old British Empire, VC winners were given pride of place in any parade and it was said that even generals saluted them. Although I never actually saw this happen, it was true, even if the gesture was not an officially required act. The salute was offered as a courtesy by a senior officer to a brave man.

My father, who had been a young officer during the First World War, knew some VC winners personally and on special occasions, such as Anzac Day, when the veterans came together at reunions, I was introduced to them. It meant a lot to me at school to be able to boast that I had met Joe Maxwell VC, MC and Bar, DCM. In 1932, when Maxwell published his book *Hell's Bells and Mademoiselles* he sent my father an autographed copy, which made me the envy of my friends. Arthur Hall VC was another friend of my father. While Joe Maxwell's fame as the second most decorated Australian soldier of the First World War made him court publicity, Arthur Hall remained a truly modest man.

When I became a soldier myself in 1940 I met several VC winners who had enlisted for a second war. They hardly had occasion to wear decorations and medals – they were required only for rare formal events – but they always wore their Service ribbons. That of the VC, 1½ inches wide, officially crimson in colour but actually nearer to claret, took pride of place near the centre of the chest. So rare was this ribbon with its tiny replica of the Cross fixed in its centre that there was no mistaking it. It set the wearer apart from other men, at least among all those who had any knowledge of awards for bravery.

One of the VC winners I met at this time, when we were instructors in a training battalion, was Sergeant Albert ('Alby') Lowerson, whose citation gives some idea of one type of exploit which could result in the award of the VC during the First World War. It is a model against which to measure outstanding exploits of the Second World War.

For most conspicuous bravery and tactical skill on 1st September 1918, during the attack on Mont St. Quentin, north of Peronne [France] when very strong opposition was met with early in the attack and every foot of ground was stubbornly contested by the enemy. Regardless of heavy enemy machine-gun fire, Sergeant Lowerson moved about fearlessly directing his men, encouraging them to still greater effort and finally led them on to the objective. On reaching the objective he saw that the left attacking party was held up by a strong post heavily manned with twelve machine-guns. Under the heaviest sniping and machine-gun fire, Sergeant Lowerson rallied seven men as a storming party, and directing them to attack the flanks of the post, rushed the strong-point and by effective bombing captured it, together with the twelve machine-guns and thirty prisoners. Though severely wounded in the right thigh he refused to leave the front line until the prisoners had been disposed of [sent to the rear, not killed!] and the organisation and consolidation of the post had been thoroughly completed. Throughout a week of operations his leadership and example had a continual effect on the men serving under him, while his prompt and effective action at a critical juncture allowed the forward movement to be carried on without delay, thus ensuring the success of the attack. [*London Gazette*, 14 December 1918]

Alby paid a heavy price for his VC exploit and other outstanding acts of courage, being wounded four times during his two years at war. He was never again truly fit, and although his service during the Second World War was not arduous, he died in 1945 at the age of 49.

During the Syrian campaign of June–July 1941, Jim Gordon, a corporal of my own battalion, was awarded the VC in recognition of a similar act of sustained courage to that of Alby Lowerson, and he was equally unassuming about his decoration.

In 1957 I came to know as a friend Richard Wakeford who, as a lieutenant of the Hampshire Regiment, had won the VC in Italy in 1944. His citation appears elsewhere in the book. Another self-effacing man, Richard died prematurely as a result of wounds received during his VC exploit. Another VC winner of my acquaintance, Philip Gardner, Royal Tank Regiment, though as modest as Wakeford, accepted as a gift a special number plate for his car – VC 128. Its significance was that his VC was the first of the war to be awarded to a Londoner – Gardner came from Sydenham – and the 28th award of the war. Much later, he became honorary secretary of the Victoria Cross and George Cross Association, probably the most exclusive association in the world and one with an ever declining membership. Older members die but there are fewer opportunities for younger servicemen to win the VC. We should be grateful for this since it indicates fewer sustained wars.

As a lifelong military historian I have dealt with many facets of war: strategy, tactics and leadership, victories and defeats, weapons and logistics, wounds and illnesses, the planning, course and outcome of every kind of military encounter from patrols to major battles. However, the aspect of war and conflict which has interested me most is the behaviour of men in battle, with all that this means in terms of their reaction to stress and tension, to fear and the mastering of fear, to exhaustion, hardship and hunger. Above all, I have been interested in the mental and physical reactions of individuals to the terrifying, traumatic and at times numbing experience of battle.

This word – battle – is not a satisfactory one when explaining and discussing military active service. It suggests tremendous noise and smoke, the rattle of machine-gun fire, the grinding of tank tracks and the roar of aircraft. But a battle is not always like this and the term has a much wider application. Some high decorations, including the VC, have been awarded for valorous conduct when the enemy was 'present' but not actually in sight. The citations for Lieutenant Peter Roberts and Petty Officer Thomas Gould, both of the Royal Navy, for remarkable acts of courage, illustrate the point (q.v.). Their exploit took place, under conditions of indescribable tension, in the murky depths of the Mediterranean, away from what we conventionally think of as 'battle.'

During the Second World War, 1939–45, members of the British armed forces were awarded 106 Victoria Crosses. In order of Service: Royal Navy, Royal Marines, Royal Naval Reserve and Royal Naval Volunteer Reserve – 23 awards, of which 8 were posthumous; the Army – 61 awards, of which 33 were posthumous; the Royal Air Force – 22 awards, of which 11 were posthumous.

It is significant that almost half of the awards were awarded posthumously. Put another way, during the Second World War the chances of performing an act of courage considered worthy a VC and of living to receive it were 50–50.

This book is not a mere list of citations for VC awards. Each gallant deed or exploit needs to be looked at in the context of the war and the land, sea or air campaign in which it was won. In what way did any particular exploit affect the outcome of a larger action? Was it more difficult to win a VC in a jungle campaign than in a desert? What made the award of VC for submarine or aerial action different from those earned on the ground or at sea – for assuredly they *were* different.

The system of bravery decorations of all kinds is a strange world to many people who have had no Service experience and no family history of participation in war. But even if they know nothing of all the lesser decorations they are aware that the Victoria Cross is something special.

Over the years I have been asked many questions about the VC and the justification for its award. Here are some of them:

- Who decides that a VC should be awarded?
- How is a courageous exploit evaluated?
- How brave does a man have to be to win the VC?
- If a VC is recommended and then not awarded is the man concerned informed about it and is it possible for him – or his family if he was killed – to appeal against the decision?
- Why is the VC so very highly regarded? This question is often accompanied by the comment that the value placed on a VC exploit is 'disproportionate' when compared with other outstanding examples of leadership and courage.

I answer all these questions and many others in this book, which deals with the 106 VC awards to the United Kingdom armed forces of the Second World War. Collectively, another 76 awards were made to the armed forces of Australia, New Zealand, South Africa, Fiji, Canada, India and there was one to the King's African Rifles. This one I have included in my analytical appraisal because the recipient was a British sergeant seconded to the KAR. For reasons of space, and for that reason alone, the book covers only the UK awards. However, to make a comparison or to emphasize some aspect of VC history some of the awards to the 'Old Empire' are mentioned as are a few from the First World War.

No military decoration in the world has the prestige of the Victoria Cross and none is harder to 'win'. In the 140 years between 1856 and 1996 only 1,353 Crosses were awarded, including three second awards of the VC. This is a remarkably small number considering that awards cover the armed forces of the entire British Empire (later the British Commonwealth) and take in two world wars of great conflict-intensity and innumerable smaller wars and campaigns in many countries.

The German Iron Cross was issued in millions, even the Iron Cross First Class, which was roughly equivalent to the Victoria Cross. Similarly, the French Médaille Militaire and Croix de Guerre were lavishly bestowed. The United States' Medal of Honor, sometimes wrongly called Congressional Medal of Honor, which ranks second only to the Victoria Cross in rarity of award, has nevertheless been rather liberally bestowed.

Of the really superior awards, only the Victoria Cross carries on it or its clasp the name and rank of the recipient *and* the date of the exploit for which the decoration was awarded. The Medal of Honor has the name of the recipient but not the date of his brave exploit, except in the case of the Air Force awards. The Continental decorations bear neither name nor date. This is a pity for such information personalizes a decoration and proves that *this* supreme award was made to *this* particular individual.

The German (or Prussian) Iron Cross and the French Croix de Guerre have the same soldierly simplicity as the Victoria Cross, but they were too frequently awarded to make them as special as the VC and they carry no details of the recipient or his act of courage. The US Medal of Honor is more ornate in design and includes a golden eagle with wings displayed.

It is a remarkable paradox that the bronze Victoria Cross is the plainest of all British decorations and intrinsically the cheapest; at one time the bronze in a VC was worth three pence. Yet among servicemen it is the most highly prized. Many people outside the old British Empire have found this puzzling but, of course, they were not brought up with the VC tradition that is so firmly in place in the British and Commonwealth consciousness.

The monetary value of a Victoria Cross can only be assessed accurately by what it might bring when sold at one of the great London auction houses. In 1952 Leading Seaman James Magennis, the only VC winner from Ulster during the Second World War, was forced through poverty to sell his decoration for £75, though not at auction. Magennis, a diver, had left the Navy in 1949 and worked in a circus for £40 a week, escaping twice daily from a locked iron trunk at the bottom of a water tank. Still poor, he died in Halifax in 1986 at the age of 66.

The first VC of the Second World War to be offered in the salerooms was that of Company Sergeant Major Stanley Hollis of the Green Howards, the only man to be awarded a VC on D-Day, 6 June 1944. His widow reluctantly offered the VC for auction at Sotheby's in order to get some money 'to make ends meet', as she said. The sale of the VC, with seven other medals belonging to Hollis, took place on 4 March 1982 and raised £32,000. In October the same year the VC posthumously awarded to Private James Stokes of the King's Shropshire Light Infantry in 1945, sold for £16,000.

A record figure for a Second World War VC was reached in October 1987 when that awarded to Petty Officer Thomas Gould in 1942 was sold at Sotheby's for £48,000. It was bought by the Association of Jewish Ex-Servicemen. In the same sale the VC awarded to Flight Lieutenant Rex Warneford in 1915 for shooting down a Zeppelin was listed but withdrawn just before the auction. The Fleet Air Arm Museum paid £55,000 for it, a price above the estimate.

The only Battle of Britain VC, to Flying Officer James Nicolson, was sold for £110, 000 at a Glendinnings' auction, London, in 1987.

In November 1988 the VC and 10 other medals belonging to Lieutenant-Commander Ian Fraser RN were sold at Sotheby's auction for £33,000. Fraser, commander of a midget submarine, blew up a Japanese heavy cruiser in Johore Strait in July 1945.

In June 1990 a new record price for a VC was reached when that awarded to Lieutenant W.B.R. Rhodes-Moorhouse in 1915 was sold at Sotheby's for £126,500. All the money went to RAF and other charities.

Some people might think that putting a price on decorations for bravery is objectionable but they rarely finish up in speculators' hands. Most are bought by Services museums for safe-keeping in perpetuity or by collectors who are not only well-informed about medal history but value their purchases for the bravery that they represent. Obviously, some collectors are wealthy.

Another measure of the VC's importance is that when a citation is published in the *London Gazette* it generally takes precedence over all other announcements, including elevations to the peerage, and it is printed in larger type. Truly, the VC, as an award for the bravest of the brave, is very special indeed – just as Queen Victoria intended it to be. The original royal warrant quotes her own words about the new decoration, 'We are desirous that it should be highly prized and eagerly sought after by the officers and men of our Naval and Military Services.' Britain had no Air Force in her lifetime but she would have been equally pleased to have inspired airmen with her Cross.

We can never know to what extent officers and men had in mind the possibility of being awarded a VC when they went into action but my feeling, as a one-time soldier myself, is that the vast majority had more urgent matters on their hands than to give a thought to a possible decoration. The citations for those who did win the VC makes this abundantly clear.

THE VICTORIA CROSS

Lieutenant A.R. Cutler on the day of his investiture with the VC. Australian War Memorial photograph. Negative number 134905.

Foreword

Sir Roden Cutler
VC, AK, KCMG, KCVO, CBE,
formerly of the Australian Imperial Force
and Deputy President of the Victoria Cross
and George Cross Association*

It is a privilege to be able to write a foreword to a book concerning the gallantry of my Victoria Cross comrades who served in the Royal Navy, the British Army and the Royal Air Force during the tumultuous years of the Second World War, 1939–45. Some awards were not gazetted until long after the war, an indication of the difficulty in obtaining adequate evidence of some exploits.

John Laffin points out that every one of the 11 VCs awarded to British soldiers during the campaigns in Burma and India was posthumous and that of all the crosses won throughout the war 50 per cent were posthumous. This was a tragic loss of good men, many of them very young.

As I write this foreword 31 Victoria Cross winners are still living, only 12 of them from Britain. However, through *British VCs of World War 2: A Study in Heroism* the spirit of every man not only survives but another generation is able vicariously to make their acquaintance and to learn something not only of their bravery but the arduous and dangerous circumstances of the campaign or battle, on land, on sea or in the air during which they won their supreme award.

They offered their lives, as did their comrades in arms who did not win any decoration, in the name of service and sacrifice and for a cause in which they believed. In his new book John Laffin pays them a tribute which they richly deserve.

---

* The Association's President is Her Majesty the Queen.

CHAPTER ONE

'Some Signal Act of Valour'

The Victoria Cross owes its origin to Queen Victoria who instituted it in 1856, possibly at the suggestion of Prince Albert, the Prince Consort. The Crimean War was in progress and the VC was seen as a means of rewarding an officer or man of the Army and Navy who might perform 'some signal act of valour or devotion to his country in the presence of the enemy'. The word 'signal' was unfortunate because generations of journalists have read it as single when writing articles about the VC. Others do not comprehend that signal means outstanding, though the significance of the word was clear enough to the Victorians.

But not everything about the decoration was clear and there were many misunderstandings, amendments and changes. We do not even know precisely what form the new superior decoration was supposed to take. The oldest surviving reference appears in a letter which the Secretary of State for War, Lord Panmure, wrote to Queen Victoria on 3 January 1856: 'Lord Panmure submits two drawings of "the Victoria Cross" and a piece of metal showing the size of it. The cross, however, will not be so thick or heavy.'*

No doubt much discussion followed and Victoria would have exchanged views with Albert. It was decided that the new Cross would be made of the bronze extracted from Russian cannons captured at Sebastopol during the Crimean War, 1854–6. Once the Queen had approved the sample Cross, Hancocks, the noted London medal-makers, were asked to produce 106 Crosses. The Cross was to have carried the words *for the brave*, but Queen Victoria asked that the motto should be *for valour*. She considered that 'for the brave' would lead to the inference that only those men who were deemed brave received the Cross and hence that the majority of men would not be seen as brave.

The general public had read about the new Cross but they first saw it on 26 June 1857 when the Queen presented the first awards – 61 of them – before a large crowd in Hyde Park. According to *The Times* reporter, everybody who followed recipients of the decoration in order to get a look at it was disappointed. The reporter himself was most unimpressed:

---

* Panmure's comments are to be found in the Royal Archives, G4/65. In December 1966 a Victoria Cross was found in a copper casket beneath the foundation stone of the Royal Victoria Hospital, Netley, Hampshire, when the building was being demolished. Queen Victoria opened the military hospital four months after the Victoria Cross was instituted. It is possible that the unnamed buried VC was the prototype.

The greatest anxiety was manifested on the part of the people to see the Cross of Valour men as they dispersed and left the ground and [each man's] course could be traced by the group that followed him, anxious to get a glimpse of the Cross, with which all found more or less fault at the very first. Than the Cross of Valour nothing could be more plain and homely, not to say coarse-looking. It is a very small Maltese Cross, formed from the gun-metal of ordnance captured at Sebastopol. In the centre is a small crown and lion, with which latter's natural proportions of mane and tail cutting the cross much interferes. Below these is a small scroll which shortens three arms of the cross and is utterly out of keeping with the upper portions bearing the words 'For Valour.' But even with all the care and skill which distinguishes Mr Hancock the whole Cross is, after all, poor looking and mean in the extreme.

This turgid, convoluted prose, expressing such a hostile opinion, did nothing to make the Cross popular. The palace and the War Office had no public relations or publicity experts in those days. Had they done so the press and public would have been briefed about the essential thought behind the Cross – that it should not be coveted for its intrinsic or ornamental value. It was *meant* to be simple, but this *The Times* reporter did not understand.

It is possible, though, that his report was influenced by *The Times'* editorial policy which opposed anything done or said by Prince Albert. The same piece makes the first known allusion to the design of the Cross being the work of Prince Albert. M.J. Crook, who has thoroughly researched the origins and history of the Cross, suggests that *The Times* report might well have been malicious and prejudiced.

Undeniably, compared with the great distinctions of the day such as the Most Noble Order and Most Ancient Order of the Thistle and the Most Noble Order of the Garter, the Victoria Cross looked commonplace. Because of its humdrum bronze colour it may have appeared inferior to the various British campaign medals, nearly all of which were of silver, but *The Times* reporter was prejudiced, even jaundiced, when he described it as 'poor looking and mean'. It was neither. It had a simple dignity and strong design, and this must have been as evident then as it is today.

The Victoria Cross is a bronze cross pattée, 1½ inches in diameter with raised edges.* On the obverse is a lion passant gardant upon the royal crown and below, on an arc scroll are the words *For Valour*. The reverse also has raised edges and in the centre is the date on which the valorous act took place. The Cross is suspended from its clasp by an integrated plain V. The clasp is ornamented with laurel leaves and on the back of the clasp is the name, rank, regiment, ship or squadron of the recipient. The ribbon was

---

* The bronze from the captured Russian guns ran out in 1942. Since then the medal-makers have supplied the bronze.

originally blue for the Navy but in 1920 this gave way to the claret-crimson which became uniform for all three Services.*

From the beginning there was much confusion about the status of the Victoria Cross. One official document referred to it as 'the Order of the Victoria Cross' and the Queen herself had to stress that it was not an Order. Even then some senior officers called it the Order of Valour and others the Victoria Medal. Because no proper procedure had been laid down for selecting potential recipients, the confusion was compounded. One generous colonel submitted the names of 31 NCOs and men so that they would have the satisfaction of knowing that their gallantry had been recognized; only two were approved.

Queen Victoria, Edward VII and George V carefully read through the citations and sometimes suggested changes or deletions. For instance, Victoria had a complaint about the citation for Captain H.M. Jones which stated that his act of valour had occurred 'during a panic' of the troops around him. Her comment had the weight of censure: 'It will be desirable if those words are omitted.' And they were left out of the *London Gazette*'s publication of the VC award.

In November 1918 George V upbraided the War Office for the use of the words 'Hun' and 'pill-box' in the citation of Lieutenant Charles Smith Rutherford. A general responded to the King, saying that Hun had already been changed to enemy for publication but that pill-box was a universal expression. He himself knew of no other term to describe, well, a pill-box. But he could have used blockhouse, which is actually what the Canadian lieutenant had captured, not a pill-box. The rectangular blockhouse of reinforced concrete looked like a giant brick or block, while a smaller construction, whether square, round or octagonal in shape, resembled the boxes in which chemists supplied their pills. Soldiers reckoned that a blockhouse was more difficult to capture than a pill-box because it was more heavily defended by machine guns.

During the Second World War the original citation for Lieutenant Charles Upham's VC stated that his courage on the island of Crete in 1941 had been all the more remarkable because throughout the entire period he had been suffering from diarrhoea. Before the text was sent to King George VI for his approval diarrhoea was changed to dysentery. Diarrhoea is a symptom of dysentery but it was not a quibble over medical definitions that brought about the word change – diarrhoea was considered too coarse a word for a VC citation.

Many exploits which resulted in the award of the VC during its first 60

---

* M.J. Crook says that it is an 'awkward fact that, so far as English heraldry is concerned there is no appropriate term which identifies unambiguously the shape of the Victoria Cross'. He means that strictly speaking it is not a Maltese Cross, a cross pattée (paty) or cross formée (formy). However, there are authorities who favour each of these terms. The matter is so complex that every recognized authority has written copiously about it.

years would later have merited nothing more than a minor decoration, such as the Military Medal or even a Mention in Despatches, which bestows no actual medal at all. During the South African (Boer) War of 1899–1902 many a VC was granted for rescuing a comrade 'under fire'. Sometimes the fire came from only a few enemy rifles at long range, and the rescue was carried out on horseback. These were indeed brave acts but the standard of valour required for the award of a VC during the two great wars was far, far higher. This was largely because fighting was so much more intense, more frequent and more dangerous, with very large numbers of men involved. In a very real sense recommendations for the VC had to compete with one another for attention.

The path along which a recommendation had to travel was strewn with hurdles. It began with the serviceman's immediate commander, who would forward his statement about the act of courage – though the man himself could submit a claim to his CO. It then moved slowly upwards along the military chain of command to the area commander-in-chief, who placed it before a board of officers. Should these gentlemen regard it with favour the area C-in-C sent it to the Horse Guards in Whitehall from whence it made its way to the commander-in-chief of the Army. The recommendation, with its various endorsements and comments attached, now went to the War Office. Here it came under the scrutiny, in the VC's early years, of Mr Edward Pennington, a senior clerk who studied it to see that the recommendation complied with the terms stated in the royal warrant. Even then the file had to return to the War Office, which sent it to the palace for the royal signature.

Over the decades many changes were made to the warrant and its conditions were not always followed. For a long period two witnesses to an heroic act were required, preferably officers. Later three witnesses were thought necessary.

For some students of VC history as well as for many other people the powerful humanitarian motivation which inspired acts of heroism was justification enough for granting the decoration. However, I believe that the matter is much more complex. For instance, a soldier rescuing a comrade on the battlefield may not actually be putting his own life at risk in doing so. In thousands of cases a soldier has risked his life to rescue a comrade but for few of them was a VC awarded. What made some of these acts of bravery worthy of the supreme VC when others were rewarded with the lesser DCM, MM or a Mention in Despatches?

Philip Gardner

The heroism of Acting Captain Philip Gardner, who had already been awarded the MC, on the morning of 23 November 1941, near Tobruk in Libya, illustrates the degree of danger faced and valour displayed in order to be awarded the VC for saving life in the Second World War:

Captain Gardner was ordered to take two tanks to the assistance of two armoured cars of the King's Dragoon Guards which were out of action and under fire in close proximity to the enemy. He found the two cars halted two hundred yards apart, being heavily fired on at close range and gradually smashed to pieces.

Ordering the other tank to give him covering fire, Captain Gardner manoeuvred his own close up to the foremost car. He then dismounted in the face of intense anti-tank and machine-gun fire and secured a tow rope to the car. Seeing an officer lying beside it with his legs blown off, he lifted him into the car and gave the order to tow. The tow rope, however, broke and Captain Gardner returned to the armoured car, being immediately wounded in the arm and leg. Despite his wounds he lifted the other officer out of the car and carried him back to the tank, placing him on the back engine louvres and climbing alongside to hold him on. [It would have taken Gardner longer to get the dangerously wounded officer and himself into the tank through the turret.] While the tank was being driven back to safety it was subjected to heavy shell fire and the loader was killed. The courage, determination and complete disregard for his own safety displayed by Captain Gardner enabled him, despite his own wounds, and in the face of intense fire at close range, to save the life of a fellow officer, in circumstances fraught with great difficulty and danger. [*London Gazette*, 10 February 1942]

The various people who saw Gardner's action on the ground and those who had to assess it away from the battlefield had no hesitation in agreeing that this life-saving exploit could only adequately be rewarded with the VC rather than the MC, the lesser alternative.

Frederick Dobson

It is interesting to read General Sir Douglas Haig's note on a recommendation for the VC for Private Frederick Dobson of the Coldstream Guards. On 28 September 1914 at Chavanne, Aisne, in France, Dobson twice volunteered to go out under heavy fire to bring in two wounded men. This venture meant that he had to cross much open ground in full view of the enemy. Dobson crawled out and found one of the men dead and the other wounded. He dressed the wounds and then crawled back to return with a corporal and a stretcher. They put the wounded man on to it and dragged him to safety.

Haig wrote: 'I fully appreciate the bravery but I am not in favour of this coveted award being granted for bringing in wounded officers or men in European warfare.' The reference to European warfare is important. Haig knew, as did every soldier, that the Germans would not decapitate, blind, castrate, disembowel or torture a wounded prisoner as enemies in Africa,

India and other theatres of war might do. Two months later General Sir John French, at that time Haig's superior, also made an observation about VCs awarded for saving life on the battlefield:

> I am in agreement with the view that the VC should not be awarded for the rescue of wounded in the case of officers unless under very exceptional circumstances. As regards men, I think it should be awarded but in making recommendations, I have to be guided by the facts of the case. For instance, the rescue of wounded men lying exposed to fire between two trenches, or in a retreat, where a rescue has to be made on the sole initiative of the non-commissioned officer or private are cases in which recommendations would be given. I am willing to be guided by any ruling which may be given as no doubt the present system tends to lack uniformity.

French was correct in this observation – uniformity was totally lacking. Private Dobson was awarded the VC but other brave soldiers who showed equal or greater courage were not. There was a much higher chance of being awarded the VC early in the First World War, partly because the MM had not yet come into existence and also for the reason that nobody yet knew that the war would last four more years with thousands of men performing acts of outstanding valour.*

Nigel Leakey

Evaluating an act for which a VC has been recommended has always been difficult and especially so in a borderline case. When one of the evaluating authorities imposes his own subjective assessment on a recommendation the situation is even more problematic. Fortunately for his peace of mind – assuming that he has survived – the serviceman concerned is usually unaware of what is going on in the rarefied atmosphere of the War Office, obviously not in the case of someone killed performing his heroic act.

On 19 May 1941 near Colito, Abyssinia, Sergeant Nigel Leakey of 1st/6th Battalion King's African Rifles, was a member of a company which had established a bridgehead against strong Italian opposition. The enemy made a sudden counter-attack with tanks, whose fire was withering. Sergeant Leakey jumped on to one of the tanks, wrenched open the turret and shot the entire crew except for the driver, whom Leakey forced to drive to cover. Leakey then led three other men in stalking the rest of the tanks. He jumped on one of them and killed a member of its crew before he himself was killed. The Italians were defeated in the action and Leakey was almost wholly responsible.

---

* The references for French and Haig come from PRO files WO 32/7463, WO 32/7483 and WO 32/4993.

Since Swahili was the language of the King's African Rifles, the recommendation that he be awarded a high decoration came from men who spoke only that language and they duly signed it with their thumb prints. It was then translated by Swahili-speaking British officers. The recommendation began its long climb. The chief of the Imperial General Staff and others approved it but the influential Military Secretary, Lieutenant-General A.N. Floyer-Acland, did not. He wrote: 'Sergeant Leakey certainly displayed great gallantry but I regard his action as of the spontaneous nature, lacking the elements of long sustained courage and endurance which tell of the highest form of self-sacrifice.'

In effect Floyer-Acland was saying that Leakey's valour had been too brief; I would have asked him 'How brief is too brief? For how many minutes and seconds does a man have to perform heroically to be worthy of the VC?' I would also have reminded him that many a soldier of the first great war captured a German machine-gun post in an act of 'spontaneous nature' which lasted only half a minute but for which he was awarded the VC.

King George VI agreed with Floyer-Acland that Leakey's act did not warrant a VC but the case was resubmitted in 1945 with the backing of General Sir Alan Cunningham, who had commanded in the East African campaign. By now, with the fighting in Africa long over, Leakey's supporters were able to furnish further evidence of his exploit. They knew that his courage had been sustained. Floyer-Acland, regarded as a bottleneck by his peers, was no longer military secretary and King George VI now readily approved the award. It was gazetted on 15 November 1945. Leakey's body has never been recovered so he is commemorated only on the East Africa Memorial, Nairobi, Kenya.

Nigel Leakey's full citation shows why his actions in May 1941 warranted the award of the VC:

On the 19th May 1941, at Colito, Abyssinia, two companies of the 1st/6th The King's African Rifles successfully crossed the Billate River in the face of strong enemy [Italian] opposition and established a precarious bridgehead without hope of immediate reinforcement.

Throughout the operation Sergeant Leakey had been supporting the crossing with 3in. mortar fire and having expended his ammunition he went forward to see what he could do.

Suddenly the enemy launched a surprise counter-attack with medium and light tanks which emerged from the bush, threatening to overrun the two companies of the 1st/6th The King's African Rifles. Advancing from the rear, one of these tanks was bearing down on the troops, who had no anti-tank weapons for their defence.

With complete disregard for his own safety and in the face of withering machine-gun fire from the enemy's ground troops and from the tanks in front, Sergeant Leakey leaped on top of the tank which was coming in from behind our position and wrenched open the turret. With his revolver he shot the commander of this tank and the crew, with the exception of the driver, whom he forced to drive into cover.

Having failed to get the cannon of this tank to fire he dismounted, calling out, 'I'll get them on foot!' and charged across ground which was being swept by machine-gun and shell-fire from the other enemy tanks, which were advancing and causing casualties to our infantry.

In company with an African CSM and two other Askari he proceeded to stalk these tanks. The first two tanks passed but Sergeant Leakey managed to jump onto the third tank and opened the turret and killed one of the crew before the fourth tank opened fire with a machine-gun and shot him off the tank.

Sergeant Leakey throughout the action displayed valour of the highest order, his determination and his initiative were entirely responsible for breaking up the Italian tank attack. By his own individual action he saved what would have developed into a most critical situation, for had the Italian tanks succeeded the result would have been the loss of a most valuable bridgehead which would have had far-reaching results in the subsequent operations. The superb courage and magnificent fighting spirit which Sergeant Leakey displayed, facing almost certain death, was an incentive to the troops who fought on with inspiration after witnessing the gallantry of this NCO's remarkable feat and succeeded in retaining their positions in the face of considerable odds.

J.H. Edmondson

It is interesting to note General Floyer-Acland's assessment of the action in which Corporal J.H. Edmondson 2/17th Battalion, AIF, lost his life. During the night of 13/14 April 1941 at Tobruk, Libya, John Edmondson was a member of a party which counter-attacked Germans who had broken through the Australians' barbed wire defences. Edmondson was severely wounded but he continued to advance and went to help his lieutenant who was in difficulties – he had his bayonet through a German soldier who, in his death throes, was clasping him fiercely around the legs while another German was attacking the lieutenant from behind. Despite his own serious injuries, Edmondson went to his rescue and killed both of the enemy. Soon after this tremendous effort he died of his wounds.

In due course, a recommendation that Edmondson be awarded the VC reached General Floyer-Acland. He wrote:

In offering my opinion with recommendations for the Victoria Cross I am guided to a great extent by the answer to the question of whether the act was of a spontaneous nature and of short duration or a long sustained effort of great courage and determination. In this case the act [the

Edmondson exploit] was evidently of the spontaneous character. On the other hand, it is fair to assume that Edmondson would have realised that having been wounded in the stomach, his chances of survival were negligible unless he immediately refrained from further activity and received early medical attention. Not to mention the pain he must have been suffering, there is a definite element of very courageous self-sacrifice in this case and, taking all circumstances into account, I am prepared to advise the award of the Victoria Cross.

King George VI approved the award on 29 June 1941 and it was gazetted on 4 July. Edmondson, who was 27 when he died, is buried in Tobruk Cemetery, North Africa. It is difficult to understand why Floyer-Acland had to debate with himself – as he obviously did – over the Edmondson award.

How many other senior military officers and civilian officials made a principle of questioning the merit of a 'spontaneous act' as being worthy of the VC it is impossible to tell, but it is reasonable to assume that some were influenced by the Floyer-Acland attitude. It is also reasonable to assume that Floyer-Acland had not adequately studied the royal warrant under which the VC is awarded. Had he done so he would have found no reference to 'spontaneous acts', under any circumstances of war, as being unworthy of the VC.

A great merit of the VC, at least as stated in the original royal warrant, is that 'neither rank, long service, wounds nor any other considerations than the merit of conspicuous bravery should be considered'. One clause of the warrant ordained that when a large number of men had performed 'a gallant and daring act' in which all had been equally brave and distinguished the officers present could select by ballot one of their number for a VC recommendation, that similarly non-commissioned officers (or petty officers) could choose one of their number and two seamen or private soldiers would be selected by their comrades. This did not necessarily mean that the decoration would be awarded but the clause stated that the admiral or general officer commanding would 'in due manner confer the decoration as if the acts were done under his own eye'.

The VC, unlike any other decoration, has a small financial accompaniment. Under the original warrant all other rank VC winners would receive a pension of £10 a year. And there was a penalty for bringing shame upon the decoration by any holder convicted of treason, cowardice, felony or 'any other infamous crime'; in such an eventuality the Cross was forfeit and the name of its recipient expunged from the list of heroes. In all, eight men lost their VC under this penalty, the last in 1908.

Among those disgraced was Midshipman Edward St John Daniel, who won his VC for three acts of bravery during the Crimean War. He received the decoration at an investiture in India in September 1859 and the following year he shook hands with Queen Victoria at a levee in St James's Palace. She commented that she was 'much impressed' by him.

In 1860 Daniel was twice reprimanded for being absent without leave and finally, having been found drunk, he was court-martialled. His punishment was relatively light: he was dismissed from his ship, HMS *Wasp*, and placed at the bottom of the Lieutenants' List. Then in June 1861, on HMS *Victor Emmanuel*, his captain placed him under arrest for 'taking indecent liberties' with some junior officers. He jumped ship in Corfu and thus became a deserter. The paperwork to bring about Daniel's forfeiture was handled by the same Mr Pennington whose job it was to pass judgment on the admissibility of VC awards under the royal warrant. On 4 September 1861 Queen Victoria, who a year earlier had been so much taken by young Mr Daniel, signed the Warrant of Forfeiture that made him the first winner of the VC – and the only officer – to forfeit his award. It read:

Whereas it has been reported unto us that Edward St. John Daniel late a Lieutenant in Our Navy, upon whom we have conferred the decoration of the Victoria Cross, has been accused of a disgraceful offence, and having evaded inquiry by desertion from Our Service, his name has been removed from the list of officers of Our Navy – know ye therefore that we are pleased to command that the said Edward St. John Daniel shall no longer be entitled to have his name enrolled in the Registry of persons on whom we have bestowed the said decoration, but shall be and he is hereby adjudged and declared to be henceforth removed and degraded from all and singular rights, privileges and advantages appertaining thereto.

Daniel emigrated to Australia and then to New Zealand, where he served as a private in the wars against the Maoris. When his regiment was disbanded he became a constable in the New Zealand Armed Constabulary. On his death in May 1868 his comrades gave him a military funeral. According to an obituary notice in the *West Coast Times* he was 'much respected'.

On forfeiture, his VC was supposed to be returned to the War Office but Daniel kept it. It turned up in a Sotheby's sale on 21 March 1988, where it sold for £19,800. Apparently the people bidding for it at the auction did not consider Daniel's Cross to have been dishonoured. It is one of the most famous Crosses in the history of the decoration.

In my opinion no offence committed after the award of a VC should ever lead to its forfeiture. No form of disgrace should cancel out the valour for which a man has been decorated. In 1920 King George V expressed strong views against forfeiture and it was discontinued in practice.

Originally, no provision was made for posthumous awards of the VC so some of the greatest acts of heroism went unrecognized. Also, no VC was actually conferred in cases of officers and men who had been awarded the VC but had died before it could be bestowed. The award stood and was published in the *London Gazette* but next of kin were given nothing tangible.

King Edward VII put this right in 1902 when he ordered that VCs awarded to soldiers and sailors who had been killed should be delivered to their family. He must have felt strongly about the matter because the change to the system was made retrospective, so that relatives of VC heroes as far back as the Crimean War received their awards. The King also authorized the award of posthumous VCs to men killed during their award-exploit.

All servicemen know that many outstandingly courageous acts are not recognized by the VC or by any other decoration. This is because nobody has survived to bring such an act to the notice of the authorities. During some battles on land an entire company might be wiped out. It is possible that before this happened some soldier displayed prodigious valour, but who could know? Similarly, some officers and men of a warship may have displayed great courage and self-sacrifice – on HMS *Hood*, perhaps, when this battleship was torpedoed in the North Sea on 24 May 1941. Of the crew of 1,419 men only three survived and they had been in no position to witness episodes of courage. No doubt many a fighter pilot displayed qualities worthy of a VC award only to be shot down before he could return to base. In any case, a fighter pilot is necessarily alone, so who could witness his bravery over enemy territory? For this very reason, during the Second World War only one fighter pilot was awarded the VC.

Until the 1990s a great anomaly existed in the decoration's award. If a serviceman was posthumously recommended for the VC and the recommendation was 'failed' he could not, under the regulations, be awarded a lesser decoration posthumously. During the Second World War the only recognition his family could receive for his gallantry was a Mention in Despatches, presented on a small certificate that could be framed. Also, a bronze oak leaf was affixed to the ribbon of the War Medal. We will never know how many men would have been downgraded from the VC to a lesser decoration – such as the DSO, MC, DCM, DFC, DFM, DSC, DSM – had they lived. This no longer happens but the many changes made to bravery awards following reviews in 1955, 1974, and 1991 are beyond the scope of this book.

Of all the anomalies and discrepancies which come to light in studies of VC citations the most striking is that the description of a VC action in a citation can differ from that which appears in an official history of a campaign or battle of a Service unit. This is because some citations were written up third-hand, even fourth-hand, by an officer or official who was not himself present at the scene but had testimony from several sources. It was his task to mould this material into a citation.

Undoubtedly the literary skill of the citation-writer sometimes influenced the level of a decoration. An authoritative source on this is Colonel Rowland Feilding, who during the First World War commanded two separate infantry battalions. Feilding said, 'Recommendations have to be couched in the flamboyant language of the Penny Dreadful and the result is that the most deserving cases get cut out by the authorities, far behind the line . . . who have no personal first-hand knowledge of the man or the conditions upon which they pass judgment.'

Feilding told of a man whom his CO had recommended for the Military Medal, the lowest level of decoration for bravery. The recommendation was not approved and the CO, who was disappointed because the man concerned deserved recognition, tried again. This time he wrote his recommendation in the most extravagant language he could dream up. The fruits of his efforts astounded him: the soldier was awarded the VC.

Said Feilding, 'The most difficult place to win fighting distinction is the fighting line itself. I have known good men eating their hearts out through want of recognition. A ribbon is the only prize in war for the ordinary soldier. I wish that this form of reward did not exist, seeing that ribbons must be distributed by men, not by gods. If they were given by God, how many an iridescent breast would cease to sparkle – and the contrary!'*

While I have reservations about some of the VCs awarded during the First World War, I have no difficulty in accepting that all those of the Second World War were hard earned and well merited. That some warriors who deserved the VC did not get it does not detract from the valour of those who did.

Lloyd Allan Trigg

One might expect that witnesses to an exploit which could attract a recommendation for a VC would have to be of the same nationality as the man being proposed for the VC, or at least from an allied army. The VC awarded to Flying Officer L.A. Trigg DFC was remarkably different. Trigg was an officer of the Royal New Zealand Air Force and as such ought not to appear in this book, since it concerns only British awards, except that the circumstances of his award are so unusual that they make VC history.

In August 1943 Trigg, flying a Liberator over the Atlantic, attacked a U-boat on the surface and sank it, but the German deck-gunners shot down Trigg's aircraft. Trigg and his crew perished and there were no Allied witnesses to his exploit. However, several U-boat survivors were picked up and told of the 'amazing courage' of the enemy pilot who had sunk them. On the evidence of their statements as witnesses and following rigorous questioning, Trigg was posthumously awarded the VC. Interestingly, his citation, gazetted on 2 November 1943, makes no reference to what his German victims had said about his exploit. The prose clearly comes from a British hand and there is some justifiable speculation – 'There could have been no hesitation or doubt in his mind.' The eternally interesting factor is

---

* Colonel Feilding, who was writing to his wife, was awarded the DSO, scant enough recognition for fully four years of outstandingly successful service as an infantry battalion commander.

that the recommendation came from the men whom Trigg had been trying to destroy.

Flying Officer Lloyd Allan Trigg, DFC (NS 413515) No 200 Squadron RNZAF missing, believed killed

In recognition of most conspicuous bravery. Flying Officer Trigg had rendered outstanding service on convoy escort and anti-submarine duties. He had completed 46 operational sorties and had invariably displayed skill and courage of a very high order.

One day in August 1943 [11 August] Flying Officer Trigg undertook, as captain and pilot, a patrol in a Liberator although he had not previously made any operational sorties in that type of aircraft. After searching for 8 hours a surfaced U-boat was sighted. Flying Officer Trigg immediately prepared to attack. During the approach, the aircraft received many hits from the submarine's anti-aircraft guns and burst into flames, which quickly enveloped the tail. The moment was critical. Flying Officer Trigg could have broken off the engagement and made a forced landing in the sea. But if he continued the attack, the aircraft would present a 'no deflection' target to deadly accurate anti-aircraft fire, and every second spent in the air would increase the extent and intensity of the flames and diminish his chances of survival.

There could have been no hesitation or doubt in his mind. He maintained his course in spite of the already precarious condition of his aircraft and executed a masterly attack. Skimming over the U-boat at less than 50 feet with anti-aircraft fire entering his opened bomb doors, Flying Officer Trigg dropped his bombs on and around the U-boat where they exploded with devastating effect. A short distance further on the Liberator dived into the sea with her gallant captain and crew. The U-boat sank within 20 minutes and some of her crew were picked up later in a rubber dinghy that had broken loose from the Liberator.

The Battle of the Atlantic has yielded many fine stories of air attacks on underwater craft but Flying Officer Trigg's exploit stands out as an epic of grim determination and high courage. His was the path of duty that leads to glory.

The Royal Navy VCs

CHAPTER TWO

Surface Ships VCs

Bernard Armitage Warburton-Lee

It was probably inevitable that the first Victoria Cross of the Second World War should go to the Navy – and as early as April 1940. The war in the air had yet to reach the level of fighting that might produce the supreme valour required for a VC award and on land the belligerent armies were still getting into position while the 'phoney war' was keeping hostilities to a minimum.

But at sea British warships of all kinds, including armed merchantmen acting as convoy escorts, were busy from the beginning of the war, as was the German Navy. One of the theatres of naval warfare was Norway. Early in the war Hitler had told his subordinates that he would prefer a neutral Norway but stated that if the Allies (France had not yet surrendered) planned to enlarge the scope of hostilities he would pre-empt them. He had not definitely decided to attack but discussion in Britain – some of which was published in the newspapers – about a perceived German threat to Norway caused Hitler to order plans for an invasion.

He gave the task to General von Falkenhorst and on 1 April, after Falkenhorst had had a month to prepare, Hitler made his decision: Norway and Denmark would be overrun. German ships began to move on 7 April and on that same day the Royal Navy left port to mine Scandinavian waters. On 9 April Captain Bernard Warburton-Lee, commanding 2nd Destroyer Flotilla, was ordered to Narvik. His mission was to prevent enemy troops from landing there, but they landed the same day and Warburton-Lee was now told to sink or capture their transports. He was commanding HMS *Hardy* and he led *Hotspur, Havock* and *Hunter*. Joining them quickly was *Hostile*.

From the pilot station at the entrance to Ofotfiord, Warburton-Lee found out that at least six large destroyers and a submarine had been sighted heading for Narvik. The true situation, in fact, was that the British flotilla was steaming towards 10 enemy ships. Warburton-Lee signalled the Admiralty that he intended to attack at dawn high water and this was approved. On the receipt of further intelligence, the Admiralty cautioned Warburton-Lee and said: 'You alone can judge whether attack should be made. We shall support whatever decision you take.'

Warburton-Lee's audacious attack took the Germans completely by surprise. HMS *Hardy* torpedoed one German destroyer, *Schmidt*, blew the stern off a second and sank or badly damaged several transports. The ship's guns left the destroyer *Roeder* a wreck. Warburton-Lee withdrew *Hardy* to allow *Havock* and *Hotspur* to take her place. Narvik harbour became a place of panic and confusion while Warburton-Lee took his destroyers a short distance down the fiord, where he discussed the situation with his subordinate commanders. With torpedoes still to be fired, he returned to Narvik and led his ships in line past the harbour entrance while they shelled some targets and torpedoed others.

Then Warburton-Lee gave the order to head for the open sea. He was too late. Three enemy destroyers loomed out of the mist from another fiord and soon after this two others appeared dead ahead. Steaming at 30 knots, the British ships fought a running battle as Warburton-Lee hoisted the signal *Keep on engaging the enemy*.

A shell, bursting on her bridge, decided *Hardy*'s fate. Every officer and man on board was killed or wounded and the destroyer kept on steaming without a commander or steersman until Lieutenant G.H. Stanning staggered to his feet and took the wheel. Further salvoes hit *Hardy* and caused so much damage that Stanning beached the ship. The desperately wounded Warburton-Lee was floated towards the shore but died on the way. Norwegians looked after the survivors until a destroyer sent from Britain rescued them.

HMS *Hardy* was not the only victim. The Germans sank *Hunter* and seriously damaged *Hotspur* though *Hostile* and *Havock* were able to take her in tow and rescue her. Now the Germans held the advantage but they did not exploit it and the three surviving destroyers of Warburton-Lee's flotilla got away. On the way out of the fiord *Havock* sank a German ammunition ship.

Aged 45 when he died, Warburton-Lee had served in destroyers during the First World War and they had remained his great naval love. His signal, *Keep on engaging the enemy*, became instantly famous and his posthumous VC was gazetted on 7 June 1940. His exploit had the effect of setting the standard of service and sacrifice expected of naval officers and their crews in the ever widening theatre of war.

Captain Bernard Armitage Warburton-Lee, RN, Captain (D), 2nd Destroyer Flotilla, HMS *Hardy*

For gallantry, enterprise and daring in command of the Force engaged in the first Battle of Narvik, on the 10th of April 1940. On being ordered to carry out an attack on Narvik, he learned from Tranoy that the enemy held the place in much greater force than had been thought. He signalled to the Admiralty that the enemy were reported to be holding Narvik in force, that six Destroyers and one Submarine were there, that the channel might be mined, and that he intended to attack at dawn, high water. The Admiralty replied that two Norwegian Coast Defence Ships might be in

German hands, that he alone could judge whether to attack, and that whatever decision he made would have full support. Captain Warburton-Lee gave out the plan for his attack and led his Flotilla of five Destroyers up the Fjord in heavy snowstorms, arriving off Narvik just after daybreak. He took the enemy completely by surprise and made three successful attacks on warships and merchantmen in the harbour. The last attack was made only after anxious debate on the Flotilla withdrawing, five enemy Destroyers of superior gun-power were encountered and engaged. The Captain was mortally wounded by a shell which hit *Hardy*'s bridge. His last signal was 'Keep on engaging the enemy.'

Lieutenant Stanning was awarded the DSO and several other members of HMS *Hardy*'s crew, as well as some officers and men from *Hostile, Hotspur, Havock* and *Hunter*, were decorated.

Gerard Broadmead Roope

While Warburton-Lee's VC was the first to be gazetted it was not the first to be won. That honour went to Lieutenant-Commander Gerard Roope, commanding the destroyer HMS *Glowworm*. Though only 35 in 1940, he was known to the Navy as 'Old Ardover', because he changed course violently when this was necessary, without regard to the comfort of his men. He was imbued with the 'attack spirit', so common among naval officers trained during the First World War and its aftermath. It was 10 July 1945 before the *London Gazette* carried his VC citation.

The late Lieutenant-Commander Gerard Broadmead Roope, RN

On the 8th April 1940, HMS *Glowworm* was proceeding alone in heavy weather towards a rendezvous in West Fiord when she met and engaged two enemy destroyers, scoring at least one hit on them. The enemy broke off the action and headed north, to lead the *Glowworm* on to his supporting forces. The Commanding Officer, whilst correctly appreciating the intentions of the enemy, at once gave chase. The German heavy cruiser, *Admiral Hipper*, was sighted closing on the *Glowworm* at high speed and an enemy report was sent which was received by HMS *Renown*. Because of the heavy sea, the *Glowworm* could not shadow the enemy and the Commanding Officer therefore decided to attack with torpedoes and then to close in order to inflict as much damage as possible. Five torpedoes were fired and later the remaining five, but without success. The *Glowworm* was badly hit; one gun was out of action and her speed was much reduced, but with the other three guns still firing she closed and rammed the *Admiral Hipper*. As the *Glowworm* drew away, she opened fire again and scored one hit at a range of 400 yards. The

Glowworm badly stove in forward and riddled with enemy fire, heeled over to starboard and the Commanding Officer gave the order to abandon her. Shortly afterwards she capsized and sank. The *Admiral Hipper* hove to for at least an hour picking up survivors but the loss of life was heavy, only 31 out of the *Glowworm's* complement of 149 being saved.

Full information concerning this action has only recently been received and the Victoria Cross is bestowed in recognition of the great valour of the Commanding Officer who, after fighting off a superior force of destroyers, sought out and reported a powerful enemy unit, and then fought his ship to the end against overwhelming odds, finally ramming the enemy with supreme coolness and skill.

Roope's VC award was five years late because nobody other than the Germans knew about *Glowworm's* end. The destroyer's survivors knew, but any references they may have made in their letters from captivity were censored. The only officer to survive the sinking was Lieutenant Robert Ramsay, the torpedo officer, who, on his repatriation, described Roope's courage. Members of the crew supported Ramsay's account. Ramsay himself was awarded the DSO and three of the crew received the CGM.

For a destroyer of 1,345 tons to attack and ram a battleship of 10,000 tons took superb navigation, with much determination and great courage. The *Admiral Hipper* was forced to return to Germany for repairs. In retrospect, one might speculate whether the loss of 117 British seamen was commensurate with the damage to the *Admiral Hipper*, especially as nobody would have criticized Roope had he turned away from certain destruction; but, like Warburton-Lee, he had been brought up with the naval imperative to *Keep on engaging the enemy.*

Richard Been Stannard

Yet a third VC was won in Norwegian waters; it was also the first awarded to an officer of the Royal Naval Reserve (RNR). On 14 April 1940 the British commenced Operation Maurice as part of their Norwegian campaign. The objective was to make a landing at Namsos, the timber port north-east of Trondheim and about 50 miles from the mouth of Namsenfiord. Namsos was selected because it had a good anchorage and a railhead and the British planners were satisfied with their choice. Part of the naval force consisted of two flotillas each of four armed trawlers, manned almost entirely by RNR officers and men. Their duty was to patrol the fiords for enemy submarines but the German Stuka dive-bombers made their mission impossible by daylight.

Commanding HMS *Arab* was Lieutenant Richard Stannard, whose VC citation, gazetted on 16 August 1940, records an exploit that was richer in its diversity than many others.

Lieutenant Richard Been Stannard, RNR, HMS *Arab,* **for outstanding valour and signal devotion to duty at Namsos**

When enemy bombing attacks had set on fire many tons of hand grenades on Namsos wharf, with no shore water supply available, Lieutenant Stannard ran *Arab's* bows against the wharf and held her there. Sending all but two of his crew aft, he then endeavoured for two hours to extinguish the fire with hoses from the forecastle. He persisted in this work till the attempt had to be given up as hopeless.

After helping other ships against air attacks, he placed his own damaged vessel under shelter of a cliff, landed his crew and those of two other trawlers, and established an armed camp. Here those off duty could rest while he attacked enemy aircraft which approached by day, and kept anti-submarine watch during the night. When another trawler nearby was hit and set on fire by a bomb, he, with two others, boarded *Arab* and moved her 100 yards before the other vessel blew up.

Finally, when leaving the fiord, he was attacked by a German bomber which ordered him to steer east or be sunk. He held on his course, reserved his fire till the enemy was within 800 yards, and then brought the aircraft down.

Throughout a period of five days *Arab* was subjected to *31* bombing attacks and throughout Lieutenant Stannard's continuous gallantry in the presence of the enemy was magnificent and his enterprise and resource not only caused losses to the Germans but saved his ship and many lives.

Promoted to lieutenant-commander, Stannard was awarded the DSO three years later to add to his VC. He died in Sydney in 1977.

Edward Stephen Fogarty Fegen

In 1940 the Royal Navy was desperately short of warships for convoy escort. Many of its fighting ships were continuously occupied either in the Mediterranean or in home waters and until more destroyers could be turned out by the yards few could be spared to protect the convoys. Yet the convoys were bringing much needed food and supplies for Britain's war economy.

In the early years of the war the protection of convoys was left largely to armed merchantmen. Among the best known was HM Armed Merchant Cruiser *Jervis Bay*. The *Jervis Bay*, a vessel of 14,000 tons with a crew of 254, had been completed as a passenger liner in 1922 and in 1939 was armed with eight primitive hand-operated 6-inch guns and two 3-inch anti-aircraft guns.

In November 1940, at the height of the convoy escort shortage, *Jervis Bay* was the sole escorting vessel for a westbound Atlantic convoy of 38 ships, returning to Canada and the US for further supplies. This task was out of all proportion to the *Jervis Bay*'s strength. In command was Commander (acting Captain) Edward Fegen, aged 49, a seaman of vast experience and an officer of the old school, steeped in the stoic spirit of the Royal Navy. Fegen's unusually brief citation explains what happened when the *Jervis Bay* sighted the German pocket battleship *Admiral Scheer*.

The late Commander (acting Captain) Edward Stephen Fogarty Fegen, RN

For valour in challenging hopeless odds and giving his life to save the many ships it was his duty to protect. On the 5th November 1940, in heavy seas, Captain Fegen, in His Majesty's Armed Merchant Cruiser *Jervis Bay*, was escorting thirty-eight merchantmen. Sighting a powerful German warship he at once drew clear of the convoy and made straight for the enemy and brought his ship between the raider and her prey so that they might scatter and escape. Crippled, in flames, unable to reply, for nearly an hour *Jervis Bay* held the Germans' fire. So she went down but of the merchantmen all but four or five were saved.

The citation, announced on 17 November and gazetted on 22 November, only 19 days after the *Jervis Bay*'s crew so gallantly gave battle to the *Admiral Scheer*, needs to be filled out. The period between the exploit and the award is one of the shortest in VC history, for reasons which will become apparent.

When the powerful *Admiral Scheer*, captained by Theodor Krancke, came into view the skippers of the ships in convoy knew what to do. The convoy commodore and Captain Fegen had already ordered them to make smoke in an emergency, such as that which was now upon them, and to scatter. As prearranged, to provide some kind of cover, the ships dropped floats from which smoke billowed up.

Fegen would have had in mind the time of day – just after five in the evening. If he could buy time for his charges they might disappear into the darkness. He manoeuvred to present a head-on target to *Admiral Scheer*'s guns rather than a broadside one and *Jervis Bay*'s own gunners opened fire. They had little chance of reaching *Admiral Scheer* with their shells but the gunners kept on serving their guns. *Admiral Scheer*'s great guns hit *Jervis Bay* with one salvo after another. With one arm smashed and his bridge ablaze, Fegen went to the after bridge to exercise command from there, but his ship's steering gear, radio and rangefinder were wrecked, the engines had lost much of their power and there were fires everywhere. Fegen returned to the main bridge but nobody knows what happened to him after that.

The gunners stayed in action, firing bravely but futilely at the German battleship. Nobody mentioned surrender and when the *Jervis Bay*'s ensign was shot away a sailor found another and nailed it to the flagstaff as high as he could climb. He was never identified but the ensign was still flying when the burning wreck sank at 8 p.m. The engagement itself lasted only 22 minutes – rather longer than the *Admiral Scheer*'s officers would have expected.

Captain Sven Olander and the crew of the neutral Swedish ship *Stureholm* had observed the one-sided but remarkable battle from a distance. Olander did not want to compromise his nation's neutrality but he had been profoundly moved by the gallantry of the *Jervis Bay*'s crew and consulted with his own crew about saving the survivors from the water. Unanimously, officers and men backed him and Olander steamed in close for a rescue, which was accomplished, Olander taking the survivors to a British port. *Stureholm* rescued 3 officers and 68 men, but Fegen was not among them.

Admiral Scheer caught the tanker *San Demetrio* and shelled her but later some of the ship's survivors boarded their badly damaged ship and managed to get her back to England. Of the convoy 30 other ships escaped, 27 of them to Britain, 3 to Canada. *Admiral Scheer* sank 5 ships but might well have destroyed several times that number had not Captain Krancke become obsessed with finishing off the defiant *Jervis Bay*.

There were many witnesses to describe the *Jervis Bay*'s fight, including her own survivors. Captain Olander spoke publicly about it and news of the act of impossible and dramatic heroism travelled around the world. Even more importantly, it quickly reached King George VI, who took the initiative in pressing for a VC for Captain Fegen. It was the King who insisted on an early announcement, on the grounds that the Germans could learn nothing from it that they did not already know. Tactfully, though, no mention was made of the Swedish rescuers.

The story of Captain Edward Fegen and the *Jervis Bay* is surely one of the best known episodes of the Second World War. A writer in *The Times*, on 19 November 1940, commented that 'if ever a ship deserved the VC that ship is surely the *Jervis Bay*'. The *Jervis Bay* has the VC because she and her captain are inseparable in history.

Thomas Wilkinson

HMS *Li Wo* was an unlikely man o' war and for a Royal Navy warship she had an unlikely name. But then she had not been a warship in peace time, merely a three-decker Yangtze river-boat with a flat bottom designed for shallow waters. She had carried passengers on unhurried journeys to the Upper Yangtze and later she operated on the delta but *Li Wo* had never ventured into the open sea. Her British captain, Thomas Wilkinson, had comfortable quarters on board and enjoyed the status and social life that his job brought him.

When war against Japan seemed imminent the Royal Navy took over *Li Wo*, mounted a single 4-inch gun, two machine guns and a depth-charge thrower on her deck and appointed Wilkinson as a temporary lieutenant

RNR to be her commander. Even with the white ensign flying the 1,000-ton craft hardly looked aggressive. To the Japanese enemy she must have seemed nothing more than easy target practice.

Wilkinson, a 42-year-old who had served as a young seaman aboard a troopship during the First World War, was ordered to take *Li Wo* to Singapore in company with HMS *Fuk Wo*, another converted river-boat, under Lieutenant N. Cooke RNR. Wilkinson's crew numbered 84 and its make-up reflected the difficulties of the British in the Far East as they faced the might of Japan. Many of the seamen aboard *Li Wo* were survivors of ships already sunk, but there were soldiers and airmen as well as an elderly civilian.

Singapore harbour was no haven and Japanese planes frequently bombed it. Wilkinson and Cooke were ordered to head for Batavia. They were bombed south of Singapore Straits and found some shelter near an island where the two ships separated. Wilkinson's VC citation describes what happened the next day.

The late Temporary Lieutenant Thomas Wilkinson, RNR

On 14th February, 1942, HM Ship *Li Wo*, a patrol vessel of 1,000 tons, formerly a passenger steamer on the Upper Yangtse River, was on passage from Singapore to Batavia. Her ship's company consisted of eighty-four officers and men, including one civilian; they were mainly survivors from His Majesty's Ships which had been sunk, and a few from units of the Army and the Royal Air Force. Her armament was one 4-inch gun, for which she had only thirteen practice shells, and two machine-guns.

Since leaving Singapore the previous day, the ship had beaten off four air attacks, in one of which fifty-two machines took part, and had suffered considerable damage. Late in the afternoon, she sighted two enemy convoys, the larger of which was escorted by Japanese naval units, including a heavy cruiser and some destroyers. The Commanding Officer, Lieutenant T. Wilkinson, RNR, gathered his scratch ship's company together and told them that, rather than try to escape, he had decided to engage the convoy and fight to the last, in the hope that he might inflict damage upon the enemy. In making this decision, which drew resolute support from the whole ship's company, Lieutenant Wilkinson knew that his ship faced certain destruction, and that his own chances of survival were small.

HMS *Li Wo* hoisted her battle ensign and made straight for the enemy. In the action which followed, the machine guns were used with effect upon the crews of all ships in range, and a volunteer gun's crew manned the 4-inch gun, which they fought with such purpose that a Japanese transport was badly hit and set on fire.

After a little over an hour, HMS *Li Wo* had been critically damaged and was sinking. Lieutenant Wilkinson then decided to ram his principal target, the large transport, which had been abandoned by her crew. It is known that this ship burnt fiercely throughout the night following the action, and was probably sunk.

HMS *Li Wo*'s gallant fight ended when, her shells spent, and under heavy fire from the enemy cruiser, Lieutenant Wilkinson finally ordered abandon ship. He himself remained on board, and went down with her. There were only about ten survivors, who were later made prisoners of war.

Lieutenant Wilkinson's valour was equalled only by the skill with which he fought his ship. The Victoria Cross is bestowed upon him posthumously in recognition both of his own heroism and self-sacrifice, and of that of all who fought and died with him.

The attack made by the high-sided river-boat on a Japanese fleet and its convoy must have been one of the most astonishing sights of the war. After the war Temporary Sub-Lieutenant Donald Stanton, the only surviving officer, gave more details of the fight against impossible odds. He had been responsible for the organization of the ship and in the final action he served as a member of the volunteer 4-inch gun crew, who handled their weapons with great courage. Stanton was awarded the DSO while the CGM went to Acting Petty Officer Arthur Thompson, the gun-layer. His citation noted that he had laid (aimed) the weapon 'with coolness and effect, showing the utmost skill, courage and resource throughout the action. In a brave company his conduct was outstanding.'

Thompson and Stanton were following the example of their skipper who had done all that British naval tradition demanded of him and much more. Wilkinson's VC was gazetted on 17 December 1946, more than a year after the war had ended. The *Li Wo*'s battle had not been fully known until Lieutenant Stanton and the other survivors returned to Britain to tell their tale.

Frederick Thornton Peters

Oran, Algeria, was a vital port for the logistical support of the Allied armies in Africa. It was held by Vichy French forces, who collaborated with the Nazis, and in November 1942 it became the focus of Centre Task Force in Operation Torch, a major Allied landing. Oran was well protected with coastal guns and lay in a defensible basin ringed by hills, but opposition was overcome within two days.

That Operation Torch proved a victory was due to the courage of men such as Acting Captain Frederick Peters, who had been awarded the DSO and DSC during the First World War. Out of the Navy between 1919 and 1939, Peters quickly rejoined at the outbreak of hostilities and before long was commanding a flotilla of destroyers protecting convoys. While engaged on this work he was awarded a Bar to his DSC.

Noted for his dedication and determination, Peters was selected for an extraordinary mission – to lead two ships into Oran harbour and capture it. The vessels were not exactly warships, merely two US Coastguard cutters presented to Britain by the American government and named HMS *Walney* and HMS *Hartland*. They would be facing shore batteries as well as Vichy destroyers, cruisers and submarines. *Walney* and *Hartland* were to carry US Rangers who would disembark at the quay and capture enemy HQ and the batteries and possibly a cruiser. Considering the great size of the Operation Torch forces employed at Algiers, Casablanca and elsewhere it is surprising that two small 'destroyers' and their soldiers were expected to capture Oran harbour. It was truly a mission improbable.

Peters's VC citation, gazetted on 18 May 1943, is brief but graphic.

The late Acting Captain Frederick Thornton Peters DSO, DSC, RN

For valour in taking HMS *Walney*, in an enterprise of desperate hazard, into the harbour of Oran on the 8th November 1942. Captain Peters led his force through the boom towards the jetty in the face of point-blank fire from shore batteries, a Destroyer and a Cruiser. Blinded in one eye, he alone of the seventeen Officers and Men on the bridge survived. The *Walney* reached the jetty disabled and ablaze, and went down with her colours flying.

In the citation Peters is referred to as 'the late' but he did not die during the exploit. The citation was incomplete and should have continued to describe what happened when Peters took the *Walney* alongside a French warship. The US Rangers threw grapnels to hold the two ships together and then, firing their Tommy guns, they stormed the Vichy ship. In turn, *Walney* was hit again and again until her boilers blew up. Then she capsized and sank. With most of her crew dead or dying, HMS *Hartland* also blew up.

The wounded Peters and some 10 men reached shore on a Carley float or hanging on to it. A Vichy admiral interrogated Peters but not surprisingly got nothing from him. Many local people had seen the one-sided battle and when Allied soldiers swept through the streets of Oran it was they who told them that Peters and his men were in prison. When the troops released him from captivity the cheering populace showered him with flowers. On 13 November a special aircraft with Peters aboard was scheduled to leave Gibraltar for England where, it was said, Peters was to see the Prime Minister, Winston Churchill, about another special mission.* The aircraft crashed during take-off and Peters was killed.

---

* This could well have been so. Between August 1940 and July 1941 Peters was CO of a school near Hertford where special agents were trained. Among his students were Kim Philby and Guy Burgess who later became infamous as traitors.

Robert St Vincent Sherbrooke

The most direct route between Britain and the Soviet Union was by convoy around the northern tip of Norway to Murmansk. But it was a terrible journey for the ships in the convoy and for their escort vessels, for they faced appalling weather as well as the ever-present risk from German U-boats, surface raiders and aircraft. During the period June 1941 to September 1943 more than one-fifth of all supplies moved to Murmansk by convoy was lost. In one convoy, PQ–17, 21 of 33 ships were sunk.

On 22 December 1953 Convoy JW51B left Loch Ewe for Russia. The 14 supply ships carried, among other cargo, more than 200 tanks, 2,000 vehicles and 120 warplanes. The convoy began its journey escorted by a relatively weak force which handed over on Christmas Day to the 17th Destroyer Flotilla under Captain R. St Vincent Sherbrooke DSO. Sherbrooke himself was in HMS *Onslow* and he led *Obedient, Orwell, Obdurate* and *Achates*.

It was the northern midwinter and daylight hours were short but a U-boat spotted the convoy in the Barents Sea and reported the sighting to the heavy cruiser *Admiral Hipper* – the very ship which Lieutenant Commander Gerard Roope VC had rammed more than 30 months earlier. The pocket battleship *Lutzow, Admiral Hipper* and six destroyers, all under Admiral Kummetz, sailed from Altenfiord on New Year's Eve to intercept. HMS *Obdurate* was the first British ship to come under fire.

The vastly experienced Sherbrooke, aged 42, had foreseen such an attack and had made plans to meet it. Turning stern-on, the convoy would steam at full speed away from the enemy ships while the destroyers would not only guard the supply ships' rear but head straight at the enemy as if about to make a torpedo attack.

Sherbrooke's VC citation of 12 January 1943, describes what happened.

Captain Robert St Vincent Sherbrooke DSO, RN

Captain Sherbrooke, in HMS *Onslow*, was the Senior Officer in command of the destroyers escorting an important convoy bound for North Russia. On the morning of 31st December, off the North Cape, he made contact with a greatly superior enemy force which was attempting to destroy the convoy. Captain Sherbrooke led his destroyers into attack and closed the enemy. Four times the enemy tried to attack the convoy, but was forced each time to withdraw behind a smoke screen to avoid the threat of torpedoes, and each time Captain Sherbrooke pursued him and drove him outside gun range of the convoy and towards our covering forces. These engagements lasted about two hours, but after the first forty minutes HMS *Onslow* was hit, and Captain Sherbrooke was seriously wounded in the face and temporarily lost the use of one eye. Nevertheless he continued to direct the ships under his command until further hits on his own ship compelled him to disengage, but not until he was satisfied that the next Senior Officer had assumed control. It was only then that he agreed to leave the bridge for medical attention and until the convoy was out of danger he insisted on receiving all reports of the action.

His courage, his fortitude and his cool and prompt decisions inspired all around him. By his leadership and example the convoy was saved from damage and was brought safely to its destination.

But there was more to the action than described in the citation. Taking over command from the wounded Sherbrooke, Lieutenant Commander Kinloch, commanding from *Obedient*, led a fifth foray against *Admiral Hipper*. It was successful and *Admiral Hipper* turned away, but not before hitting *Achates* and killing her captain. The bold actions of 17th Destroyer Flotilla had given time for the cruisers HMS *Sheffield* and *Jamaica* to come up and their shells to hit *Admiral Hipper*. An amazing incident then took place. The captain of the German destroyer *Friedrich Eckholdt* hurried towards her mother ship, *Admiral Hipper*, to see if he could assist her. But he had made a basic error in recognition: the ship he thought was *Admiral Hipper* turned out to be HMS *Sheffield*, which promptly sank the *Friedrich Eckholdt*.

But the German naval commanders had not been stupid, merely lacking in resolution. Admiral Kummetz's plan was sound – *Admiral Hipper* and her destroyers would attack from one side, forcing the convoy to move in the other direction and towards the powerful *Lutzow* and her destroyers. It was a classic pincer movement in which the convoy should have been crushed. But the plan did not work out in practice largely because Kummetz himself and Stange, the *Lutzow*'s captain, were so afraid of Hitler's anger should they make a mistake that they did nothing. The convoy escaped intact. Far from avoiding Hitler's wrath, the German officers incurred it. When he got to the bottom of the Barents Sea fiasco the Führer ordered that Germany's big ships be scrapped. Admiral Erich Raeder, Commander-in-Chief of the German Navy, resigned.

Sherbrooke remained permanently blind in one eye. However, he returned to duty in February 1944 and became a rear admiral in 1951. He died in Nottinghamshire in 1972.

CHAPTER THREE

Raider VCs

Robert Edward Dudley Ryder, Stephen Halden Beattie and William Alfred Savage

The only dock in western France capable of holding the great German battleship *Tirpitz* was the *Normandie* Dock at Saint-Nazaire. It measured 1,148 feet by 164 feet and it was reached from the great River Loire. The Admiralty already knew what damage a German battleship could do – the *Bismarck* had proved that. So too had the pocket battleship *Admiral Graf Spee*. The *Admiral Graf Spee*, hounded by British ships, was scuttled by her own captain in December 1939 and the *Bismarck* was sunk by the British in May 1941.

When the *Tirpitz* was known to be operational it made sense to try to prevent her from using Saint-Nazaire dock. The decision made, much planning followed, some of it influenced by the Navy's raid on Zeebrugge in 1918 to prevent German submarines from emerging into the North Sea.

The plan, code-named 'Chariot', was for a destroyer with three tons of explosives aboard to ram the outer caisson or gate of the lock which gave entrance to the *Normandie* Dock. The destroyer selected was HMS *Campbeltown*, one of the 50 aged destroyers sent to Britain under the American-British destroyers bases deal of 1940. *Campbeltown* was to be escorted by one motor gunboat, one motor torpedo boat and 16 motor launches carrying Army Commandos. They were to land and blow up the dock and other installations.

In command of the raid and its 18 vessels was Commander Robert Ryder while Lieutenant Commander Stephen Beattie would command HMS *Campbeltown*. Both were aged 34 and they were vigorous and dedicated 'destroyer men'. The flotilla sailed from Falmouth in the early hours of 27 March 1942, a date carefully calculated to take advantage of the spring tides, then at their height. From Falmouth to the mouth of the River Loire was a distance of 410 miles and beyond that lay 5 miles of estuary, one of the Germans' most heavily guarded positions in western Europe. According to intelligence estimates, some 10,000 troops were stationed around Saint-Nazaire. Screening the 'Chariot' craft on their way to the French coast were the destroyers HMS *Atherstone* and *Tynedale* and they would also collect those raiders who managed to withdraw after the attack.

Ryder and Beattie had with them 62 naval officers and 291 ratings. Lieutenant-Colonel Charles Newman of the Essex Regiment, attached to Army Commandos, led 44 officers and 224 other ranks. Nobody taking part in the raid could have been in any doubt about the risks they were running, for even if it turned out to be successful the German defences would be so thoroughly aroused that there was little chance of anybody getting back to England. However, Ryder and Beattie and the other planners believed that they could take the Germans by surprise, especially as *Campbeltown* had been remodelled to make her look like a German destroyer and was flying the Nazi naval flag.

Ryder himself chose to command the operation in Motor Gun Boat 314, commanded by Lieutenant Curtis, RNVR, and on which Able Seaman William Savage was the gun-layer.

A U-boat spotted part of Ryder's force and reported the sighting but the raiders were within 2 miles of their target before searchlights picked them up. Even then, Ryder calmly pressed on and by giving German identification signals he gained a precious three minutes. At this point, with much of the inner estuary as bright as day, the enemy could no longer be fooled and from both banks they began intensive fire with all kinds of weapons.

Beattie ordered full speed ahead – that was 20 knots – and at 1.34 a.m. on 28 March, just four minutes after the planned time, *Campbeltown* rammed the caisson with such force that her bow stuck, having penetrated to a depth of 36 feet. The great explosive charge was timed to go off 150 minutes later. Ryder landed under fire and, pleased to find that *Campbeltown* was exactly in the desired position, ordered MTB 74 to fire her torpedoes into the lock gates. They too were designed to go off later.

The Commandos on *Campbeltown*, carrying explosives satchels, ran at once to their assigned targets – the pumping house, a fuel tank and anti-aircraft gun positions. Soldiers from the launches landed at the Old Mole and the Old Entrance, partly to cause more damage but mainly to distract the defenders from what was happening at the lock gates. Another objective was to secure Île de Saint-Nazaire, the small island from which the withdrawal would be made.

Gunners on *Campbeltown* and on the launches were firing at enemy targets but the Germans had the advantage in that the raiding party was illuminated by searchlights. The boats were being shot to pieces and many Commandos did not reach the shore. When Ryder ordered a withdrawal only seven boats were functioning. Laden with wounded they set off downriver where they were intercepted by enemy torpedo boats. Although the crews fought back bravely one MTB was sunk and three were badly damaged. The destroyers *Atherstone* and *Tynedale* plucked the sailors and soldiers from the stricken boats and headed for Falmouth. Three other launches returned there under their own power.

At the time the Navy was said to have lost 85 officers and men killed or missing and the Army 59. The final proven number of dead was 144, 23 per cent of the raiding force. The Germans captured 215 while 271 got back to

England. Operation Chariot had been costly but not as much as some planners had feared.

The timer for *Campbeltown's* massive explosives charge was faulty and did not work when it should have done. However, the charge was not discovered and many German officers and men found reasons to go on board. Senior officers even took their wives or mistresses to sightsee. Then, at about noon on 29 May the *Campbeltown* blew up, killing 60 German officers and 320 men. Next day the torpedoes lying at the bottom of the lock gates went up and more Germans died. French dockyard workers, unwisely emboldened by the local defeat of a hated enemy, tried to take over the lock. Simultaneously the guncrews on duty panicked and opened fire indiscriminately, killing hundreds of their own men. Sadly they also killed 80 French dockyard workers.

Ryder reached England but Beattie and many other raiders were captured. Taken together the VCs awarded to three naval raiders, gazetted on 21 May 1942, reveal not only much about Operation Chariot and the dangers faced by the raiders but also about the award of the Victoria Cross itself in such circumstances. Those decorated with the supreme award were Commander Ryder, Lieutenant Commander Beattie and Able Seaman William Savage. Two Army men, Colonel Newman, who led the troops, and Sergeant T.F. Durrant of the Commandos, were also awarded the VC, Durrant posthumously. Their awards are dealt with under Army VC citations.

Commander Robert Edward Dudley Ryder, RN

For great gallantry in the attack on St. Nazaire. He commanded a force of small unprotected ships in an attack on a heavily defended port and led HMS *Campbeltown* in under intense fire from short range weapons at point blank range. Though the main object of the expedition had been accomplished in the beaching of *Campeltown*, he remained on the spot conducting operations, evacuating men from *Campbeltown* and dealing with strong points and close range weapons while exposed to heavy fire for one hour and sixteen minutes, and did not withdraw till it was certain that his ship could be of no use in rescuing any of the Commando Troops who were still ashore. That his motor gun boat, now full of dead and wounded, should have survived and should have been able to withdraw through an intense barrage of close range fire was almost a miracle.

Lieutenant-Commander Stephen Halden Beattie, RN, HMS *Campbeltown*

For great gallantry and determination in the attack on St. Nazaire in command of HMS *Campbeltown*. Under intense fire directed at the bridge from point blank range of about 100 yards, and in the face of the blinding glare of many searchlights, he steamed her into the lock gates and beached and scuttled her in the correct position.

This Victoria Cross is awarded to Lieutenant-Commander Beattie in recognition not only of his own valour but also of that of the unnamed officers and men of a very gallant ship's company, many of whom have not returned.

Able Seaman William Alfred Savage, RN

For great gallantry, skill and devotion to duty as gunlayer of the pom-pom in a motor gunboat in the St. Nazaire raid. Completely exposed, and under heavy fire he engaged positions ashore with cool and steady accuracy. On the way out of the harbour he kept up the same vigorous and accurate fire against the attacking ships, until he was killed at his gun.

This Victoria Cross is awarded in recognition not only of the gallantry and devotion to duty of Able Seaman Savage, but also of the valour shown by many others, unnamed, in Motor Launches, Motor Gun Boats and Motor Torpedo Boats, who gallantly carried out their duty in entirely exposed positions against enemy fire at very close range.

The raid had been a success, the gallantry prodigal and leadership exemplary. As a result, many other decorations were awarded: the DSO (4); DSC (17); MC (11); CGM (4); DCM (5); DSM (24); and MM (15). Another 51 men were Mentioned in Despatches, 22 of them posthumously. For the number of men involved, the Saint-Nazaire raid probably produced more decorations than any other British operation of the Second World War, amounting to about one man in eight being decorated, apart from the MIDs.

The citations for Beattie and Savage drew attention to the fact that their awards were also in recognition of other men's bravery. While there was no ballot – Beattie and Savage earned the VC in their own right – the authorities felt bound to draw attention to the general high level of valour. Some men who took part in the raid believed that additional VCs should have been awarded. Indeed, this was contemplated and some of the other awards could be considered as 'failed VCs'. Since there had to be a limit in order to maintain the decoration's standing as 'supreme', those officers responsible for making the final decisions had to make some hard choices. I have been told of one serviceman of warrant rank who 'came within an ace' of being awarded the VC.

Seamen-Gunners Who Died at Their Post

Jack Foreman Mantle and Alfred Edward Sephton

The tradition in the Royal Navy of keeping a ship's gun in action as long as one man remained alive to serve it has a long history. It was highlighted at the Battle of Jutland in 1916 when Boy 1st Class John ('Jack') Travers Cornwell won the VC. Cornwell, aged 16, was sight-setter for a forward gun on the cruiser HMS *Chester*. In front of him on the gunshield was a brass disc which he operated to raise or lower the gun, according to orders he received from gunnery control.

When the action started HMS *Chester*'s forward gun turret received the full force of the enemy's fire, with tons of metal travelling at 3,000 feet a second exploding around the gun. Jack Cornwell stood by the gun, his hand on the disc. A crash almost knocked him down and a man at his side was cut to pieces. Another staggered maimed across the deck, then another and another. Shell fragments ripped across Jack's body.

In a few minutes only three of the crew of ten were left. Then a shell burst overhead and only two were left, wounded but under cover. Jack Cornwell was standing alone, seriously wounded, and with nothing to shelter him. From his training he remembered that a gun must be kept firing as long as there was one man able to crawl. His duty was to stand by the gun until relieved or until ordered elsewhere, to stand until he dropped. He gritted his teeth, clenched one hand, kept the other on the disc and stood there for the entire 20 minutes the fight lasted. He was put ashore at Grimsby and taken to a local hospital where the matron asked him about the battle. 'Oh, we carried on all right,' he said. And then he died.

A picture of Jack, standing by his gun, soon occupied a prominent place in nearly every school in Britain. Every man and boy joining the Navy in the 1920s and '30s was told about Jack Cornwell and urged to emulate him.

During the sea war which began in 1939 and continued into 1945 seamen had many opportunities to show the Cornwell spirit, especially as the war at sea was even more dangerous than its counterpart during the First World War due to attacks from the air, which had never been a serious hazard during the earlier conflict. Warships now bristled with anti-aircraft weapons, through whose barrage, it was hoped, no aircraft could fly and survive. But many did and went on to cause havoc to British shipping in the early years of the war.

British harbours were dangerous places for they were attractive targets for enemy squadrons based in nearby France. The capitulation of France in mid-1940 had left Britain exposed. Dive bombers singled out one British harbour after another and on 4 July 1940 it was the turn of Portland, where some convoys were assembled. Part of the protecting force was the armed merchant cruiser HMS *Foylebank* and one of its 20 mm rapid-fire pom-pom guns was manned by 23-year-old Leading Seaman Jack Mantle of Wandsworth, London.

Mantle already had a reputation, being at that time one of the few naval gunners on convoy protection duty to have shot down a German raider. He had done this with an old-fashioned Lewis light machine gun while serving on a French ship and for this feat he had been Mentioned in Despatches. On 4 July 1940 he reclined in his gunner's swivel chair and faced the fearful sight of more than 20 Stukas diving at him, firing their machine guns and dropping bombs. His exemplary gallantry under fire was witnessed by *Foylebank*'s captain, P.J. Wilson. *Foylebank* was sunk and Jack Mantle lost his life. His VC citation on 3 September 1940 was brief and poignant.

Acting Leading Seaman Jack Foreman Mantle, P/JX 139070, HMS *Foylebank*

Leading Seaman Jack Mantle was in charge of the starboard pom-pom when *Foylebank* was attacked by enemy aircraft on 4th of July, 1940. Early in the action his left leg was shattered by a bomb, but he stood fast at his gun and went on firing with hand-gear only, for the ship's electric power had failed. Almost at once he was wounded again in many places. Between his bursts of fire he had time to reflect on the grievous injuries of which he was soon to die, but his great courage bore him up till the end of the fight, when he fell by the gun he had so valiantly served.

Jack Mantle's VC was the only one awarded to the Navy for an act of valour on mainland Britain. He had joined the Navy at the age of 16 and, fittingly, he was buried in the Royal Navy cemetery at Portland. His MID was gazetted on 11 July 1940.

Petty Officer Alfred Sephton also won the VC posthumously, in circumstances similar to Jack Mantle's, while serving on the cruiser HMS *Coventry*. In the Mediterranean during 1941 British vessels, both warships and freighters, were coming under relentless attack from German and Italian aircraft based in Italy; between the enemy planes and submarines the British losses were horrendous. Admiral Sir Andrew Cunningham, commanding in the Eastern Mediterranean, was determined that although the Italian fleet was much stronger than his own he would never allow the Italians to go on the offensive. Two major British victories in rapid succession put the Italian Navy further on the defensive – the Fleet Air Arm attack on the Italian battleships at Taranto and the night action off Cape Matapan. Cunningham's determination never wavered, even when substantial German forces arrived to bolster Italian morale. However, losses of British ships around Crete and Malta and off Greece were severe. Despite her aircover, the great new carrier HMS *Formidable* was attacked and badly damaged.

One response by the Royal Navy to the heavy air attacks was to turn some older fighting vessels into anti-aircraft ships. HMS *Coventry* was one such ship, fitted with 10 4-inch rapid-fire guns, and 80 guns of small calibre. Its immense firepower was controlled from two director-towers, where specialist teams passed information to the gun crews. Nobody on the ship was more exposed to danger than the director crews but the survival of the ship itself and of those vessels sheltering under its firepower, depended on them. Cold-blooded courage was needed by those crews to maintain the flow of information about the attacking aircrafts' altitude, speed, range and bearing.

It was German strategy to attack any and every ship, even hospital ships. On 18 May 1941 Stuka squadrons attacked the hospital ship *Aba*, south of Crete and heading for Alexandria. Her captain called for protection and HMS *Coventry*, under Lieutenant-Commander Dalrymple-Hay, was sent to provide it. Pairs of German Stukas broke off their attack on *Aba* and swept in on *Coventry*. On a director platform Petty Officer Sephton was director-layer, one of an experienced team of four led by Lieutenant James Robb. Despite Dalrymple-Hay's high-speed evasive tactics and the tremendous fire put up by his guns one Stuka dived through and machine-gunned the bridge, director-towers and the deck.

One bullet passed through Sephton's body and wounded the man behind him. His VC citation, gazetted on 2 December 1941, succinctly described the petty officer's subsequent courage.

Petty Officer Alfred Edward Sephton, HMS *Coventry*

For valour and fortitude in action against the Enemy on 18th May, 1941 Petty Officer Alfred Edward Sephton was Director Layer when HMS *Coventry* was attacked by aircraft, whose fire grievously wounded him. In mortal pain and faint from loss of blood he stood fast doing his duty without fault until the Enemy was driven off. Thereafter until his death his valiant and cheerful spirit gave heart to the wounded. His high example inspired his shipmates and will live in their memory.

As was so often the case during the Second World War the citation would have benefited from further details or comment. For instance, Admiral Cunningham himself wrote that Sephton's action in remaining at his key post 'may well have saved the *Coventry* and the *Aba*'.

With both its director-towers operational, *Coventry* was able to give *Aba* the protection she so desperately needed and the Stukas did not press their attack further. *Coventry* herself was not hit by a bomb.

Sephton's valour continued after the action. He insisted that his crewmate, Able Seaman Fisher, wounded by the same bullet, be rescued from the director-tower first. Sephton himself died of his wounds that night and was buried at sea next day. He was 30 and like so many seamen of his time he had joined the Navy as a boy. As a boy, he must certainly have learnt about Jack Cornwell VC.

Navy Flier

Eugene Esmonde

In the winter of 1941–2 the German battleships *Scharnhorst* and *Gneisenau*, together with the heavy cruiser *Prinz Eugen* were defensively in harbour at Brest, western France. *Scharnhorst* and *Gneisenau* were massively powerful, each with a displacement of 26,000 tons and a main armament of nine 11-inch guns. Both had taken part in the invasion of Norway in 1940, after which they became commerce raiders. Relentlessly harried by the Royal Navy, the three ships found refuge at Brest, where they were encircled by hundreds of anti-aircraft guns. Hitler and his naval Commander-in-Chief, Admiral Erich Raeder, were fearful of losing any of these valuable ships. While they remained operational it was not even necessary to use them at sea – the threat that they posed was enough to dictate naval strategy, at least in the Atlantic and northern waters.

After RAF raids damaged *Scharnhorst* the German High Command decided to move all three ships to home waters at Wilhelmshaven. Vice Admiral Otto Ciliax was given the necessary orders. It would be a desperately hazardous venture for the ships would have to pass through the narrow Straits of Dover, where they would be vulnerable to British attack. The date of 12 February was fixed for what became known as the 'Channel Dash'.

British Intelligence knew from reports by agents in France and Germany that the enemy ships would make a break from Brest and that they would take the Channel route; any other passage would take much longer. Staff officers at the Admiralty were fairly certain of the date – 11, 12 or 13 February. There could be no strategic surprise in the German plan but they could still achieve tactical surprise – by sending the ships out of Brest in broad daylight. All the British contingency plans assumed that the ships would dash out on a moonless night; apparently nobody had considered that they might leave in daylight.

One contingency plan, code-named Operation Fuller, involved 825 Squadron of the Fleet Air Arm, then standing by at Manston Airfield, Kent. Its commander was Lieutenant-Commander Eugene Esmonde, who had led the air attack on the *Bismarck*. His leadership, courage and ability had won him the DSO on that occasion.

All three qualities would be essential in any attack on the great German ships and their protective screen. No 825 Squadron Fleet Air Arm was equipped with the Fairey Swordfish torpedo attack plane, which had been much maligned as being nothing more than a target because its top speed when carrying a torpedo and bombs was a mere 100 mph. However, this was an ideal speed at which to launch a torpedo and for scouting. Also, the slower speed allowed for more deliberate bombing. What the Swordfish could not do well was engage in a dogfight with enemy fighters.

The 33-year-old Esmonde had been flying since 1928 and was immensely experienced. He had formed his plan for an attack on the German ships on the basis of the intelligence briefings – that they would make their break under cover of darkness. Indeed, it was on this information that Esmonde had volunteered his squadron. On the morning of 12 February he was called to the telephone operations room to be told that the ships were already at sea. Since he had volunteered on the basis of incorrect information it was open to Esmonde to say, 'Sorry, my six aircraft would be shot out of the sky in a daylight attack.' But he didn't. At noon Esmonde had another call: No 11 Group Fighter Command offered him an escort of five fighter squadrons, but they had not turned up when 825 Squadron took off. He well understood the urgency – the German ships had to be attacked before they reached the broader waters of the North Sea north of Calais; there they would have more room to manoeuvre. Esmonde's plan was for his six aircraft, in two sections, to launch their torpedoes at an altitude of 50 feet. Obviously flak fire would be heavy but the Navy planes might be relatively safe from the German fighters, Messerschmitts and Focke-Wulfs. The Fairey Swordfish had just one Lewis machine gun, fired from the rear cockpit, for its defence in air combat.

On his way to the target area Esmonde linked up with ten Spitfires, numerically well short of the promised five squadrons. Anybody seeing the German ships in the Channel that day would have been impressed by the lengths to which the Kriegsmarine and Luftwaffe had gone to ensure the safe passage of the capital ships. They were screened by at least 30 destroyers as well as smaller boats and submarines. Overhead was a canopy of hundreds of fighter planes.

No 825 Squadron was making a suicide attack. The citation for the VC awarded to Eugene Esmonde and gazetted on 3 March 1942 makes clear the hopelessness of his mission.

The late Lieutenant-Commander (a) Eugene Esmonde DSO, RN

For valour and resolution in action against the Enemy. On the morning of Thursday, 12th February, 1942, Lieutenant-Commander Esmonde, in command of a Squadron of the Fleet Air Arm, was told that the German Battle-Cruisers *Scharnhorst* and *Gneisenau* and the Cruiser *Prinz Eugen*, strongly escorted by some thirty surface craft, were entering the Straits of Dover, and that his Squadron must attack before they reached the sand-banks North East of Calais.

Lieutenant-Commander Esmonde knew well that his enterprise was desperate. Soon after noon he and his squadron of six Swordfish set course for the Enemy, and after ten minutes flight were attacked by a strong force of Enemy fighters. Touch was lost with his fighter escort, and in the action which followed all his aircraft were damaged. He flew on, cool and resolute, serenely challenging hopeless odds, to encounter the deadly fire of the Battle-Cruisers and their Escort, which shattered the port wing of his aircraft. Undismayed, he led his Squadron on, straight through this inferno of fire, in steady flight towards their target. Almost at once he was shot down; but his Squadron went on to launch a gallant attack, in which at least one torpedo is believed to have struck the German Battle-Cruisers, and from which not one of the six aircraft returned.

His high courage and splendid resolution will live in the traditions of the Royal Navy, and remain for many generations a fine and stirring memory.

All six Fairey Swordfish aircraft were shot down. Five survivors were fished out of the icy Channel waters and only one of these men was unwounded. Four of them were awarded the DSO, the other the CGM. About seven weeks later Eugene Esmonde's body, in his lifejacket, was washed ashore in the Thames Estuary near the River Medway. The air combat historian Chaz Bowyer suggests that perhaps Esmonde's finest epitaph is contained in the German War Diary entry for 12 February 1942: ' . . . the mothball attack of a handful of ancient planes, piloted by men whose bravery surpasses any other action by either side that day'. Bowyer also quotes the RAF commander of Manston Airfield, Wing Commander Tom Gleave: 'Those Swordfish crews were courage personified.'

It was stated in Esmonde's citation that one torpedo was believed to have struck a German ship. This was later confirmed but the ships reached safety. In Britain their escape was seen as a scandal. *The Times* was outraged: 'Nothing more mortifying to the pride of seapower has happened in home waters since the seventeenth century.' This was strong language in wartime when newspapers often pulled their punches for the sake of national morale.

The *Gneisenau* was damaged in RAF raids on Kiel, decommissioned in July 1942 and scuttled in Gdynia at the end of the war. *Scharnhorst* was damaged by mines during the Channel Dash and was immobilized until early 1943. She later operated from northern Norway against the Allied convoy routes until 26 December 1943 when, unaided, she engaged a British force which included the battleship HMS *Duke of York* in the Battle of North Cape. *Scharnhorst* was sunk with the loss of 1,864 men. *Prinz Eugen* survived the war and was turned over to the Allies.

It must be asked why the British military leaders persisted in making the attack with Fairey Swordfish aircraft since it was obvious that they had virtually no chance of doing any serious damage to the German warships. The answer must be that they were so desperate to maintain British political and military credibility that they were prepared to take a chance in a million. Since intelligence and decision-making at the most senior levels had failed, and the enemy ships were getting away, it was necessary to do something – anything – to repair the damage. A cynic might argue that 'Higher Authority', having sent Esmonde and his crews to certain death, sought to distract attention from this unpalatable fact by awarding Esmonde a VC and the survivors a superior decoration. Indeed, cynics have said this to me, always with the comment, 'Of course, Esmonde deserved his VC but I question the motives of his superiors in recommending it.' According to Chaz Bowyer, the original recommendation was made by Wing Commander Gleave. Esmonde is buried in Woodlands Cemetery, Gillingham, Kent.

Royal Marines

Thomas Peck Hunter

After landing in Italy in September 1943 the Allies fought their way north sustaining considerable losses but, nevertheless overcoming one German line after another. Major landings took place at Salerno and Anzio and one of history's great battles was fought out at Monte Cassino between February and July 1944. Rome was recaptured from the Germans in June but still the Germans held out strongly along the River Arno, 168 miles north of Rome. The Arno River Line was forced but ahead lay yet another German defensive system, the Gothic Line.

Many units were in action in this stop-and-go warfare and one of them was No 43 Royal Marine Commando, part of the British 5th Army. The unit had disembarked at Castellano on 9 January 1944 and in its ranks was Temporary Corporal Thomas Hunter, aged 22, from Stenhouse, Edinburgh.

During the Battle of Lake Comacchio the Marine Commandos were moved into the Argenta Gap, near Ravenna Ferrara, where they were heavily engaged. It was here on 3 April 1945 that Corporal Hunter won the VC. This is his citation, gazetted on 12 June 1945.

The late Corporal (Temporary) Thomas Peck Hunter, RM (attached Special Service Troops) (43rd Royal Marine Commando)

In Italy during the advance by the Commando to its final objective, Corporal Hunter of 'C' Troop was in charge of a Bren group of the leading sub-section of the Commando. Having advanced to within 400 yards of the canal, he observed the enemy were holding a group of houses South of the canal. Realizing that his Troop behind him were in the open, as the country there was completely devoid of cover, and that the enemy would cause heavy casualties as soon as they opened fire, Corporal Hunter seized the Bren gun and charged alone across two hundred yards of open ground. Three Spandaus from the houses, and at least six from the North bank of the canal opened fire and at the same time the enemy mortars started to fire at the Troop.

Corporal Hunter attracted most of the fire, and so determined was his charge and his firing from the hip that the enemy in the houses became demoralized. Showing complete disregard for the intense enemy fire, he ran through the houses, changing magazines as he ran, and alone cleared the houses. Six Germans surrendered to him and the remainder fled across a footbridge onto the North bank of the canal.

The Troop, dashing up behind Corporal Hunter, now became the target for all the Spandaus on the North of the canal. Again, offering himself as a target, he lay in full view of the enemy on a heap of rubble and fired at the concrete pillboxes on the other side. He again drew most of the fire, but by now the greater part of the Troop had made for the safety of the houses. During the period he shouted encouragement to the remainder, and called only for more Bren magazines with which he could engage the Spandaus. Firing with great accuracy up to the last, Corporal Hunter was finally hit in the head by a burst of Spandau fire and killed instantly. There can be no doubt that Corporal Hunter offered himself as a target in order to save his Troop, and only the speed of his movement prevented him being hit earlier. The skill and accuracy with which he used his Bren gun is proved by the way he demoralized the enemy, and later did definitely silence many of the Spandaus firing on his Troop as they crossed open ground, so much so that under his covering fire elements of the Troop made their final objective before he was killed.

Throughout the operation his magnificent courage, leadership and cheerfulness had been an inspiration to his comrades.

In effect, the Royal Marines are 'sea soldiers' but they have often fought as infantry; this applies especially to Royal Marine Commandos. Corporal Hunter's exploit was a classic action by an infantry junior leader. He had been well trained on the Isle of Wight, where he learnt about amphibious operations, and later at Achnacarry in Scotland. Late in 1943 his unit trained at Ramsgate and Dover for raids on the coast of Europe which never materialized. Hunter was becoming impatient for 'real action' and he found it in Italy.

Hunter's charge is interesting in that it was a calculated attack, not a do-or-die rush inspired by hot-headedness. Having seen that there was almost a quarter of a mile of dangerous open country between his small party and the occupied village, his tactical decision was to occupy the enemy's entire attention in order to give his men time to capture the village. As he ran he zig-zagged. His second charge was even more dangerous because the Germans were now under cover of two concrete pill-boxes. The Marines were advancing to help Hunter but still the Germans concentrated their fire on the one man who had driven them from what should have been an unassailable position against a mere troop of Marines. The enemy succeeded in killing him only when he ran out of ammunition. Moments later the surviving Germans were surrendering.

Corporal Hunter was buried in Argenta Gap War Cemetery and his parents were presented with his VC by King George VI at a private investiture in the palace of Holyrood House, Edinburgh. A ship's memorial bell and plaque were unveiled at Depot RM Lympstone in 1946 and in March 1954 eight houses built at Stenhouse Street West were completed and dedicated to his memory.

CHAPTER FOUR

Submarine VCs

At the onset of the First World War, the submarine was a comparatively new weapon, although Britain had 56 of this underwater fighting ship to Germany's 28. The British superiority in numbers did not at first help and on 5 September 1914 the U21 drew first blood, sinking HMS *Pathfinder* off the east Scottish coast. Later that month another U-boat sank an entire cruiser force of three ships off the Dutch coast. After U-boats sank a passenger ship fear gripped the British government and people. The U-boat menace was mastered by a combination of counter-measures, including the Q ships, armed vessels with almost the firepower of a frigate but which looked like battered trawlers. Q ships destroyed 13 U-boats, while submarine nets and depth charges accounted for more. However, the Royal Navy lost 54 submarines of its own and U-boats sank more than 5,000 merchant ships.

As a nation Britain did not learn much from her experiences in the First World War, but one lesson that it did take to heart was that should another war break out the Royal Navy would need a strong submarine force, if only to intercept enemy transports carrying troops, armaments and raw materials.

The German long-range heavily armed U-boats of 1917–18 greatly influenced the design of submarines by all the maritime nations in the years after the war. This was strange because the German Navy itself decided that these 'great' submarines were clumsy and less efficient than their standard 'Mittel-U' and UB–111 models. Yet many a navy built submarines armed with 6-inch and 8-inch deck guns, as if expecting them to perform as surface fighting vessels, when the 3-inch gun was inadequate. The most bizarre idea was to build a hangar on a submarine to house its own reconnaissance aircraft, which would be fired off by catapult.

The British built a giant submarine, known as a cruiser-submarine and called it the X.1. The Royal Navy experimented also with its M.2 by giving it a float-plane, but these ventures were short-lived. The L Class boats were found to be efficient and from them came the S Class, which proved to be an excellent boat that could dive in almost 24 seconds. It was now the mid-1930s and the naval planners were assuming that their submarines would be operating in restricted waters off hostile coasts. Then came the T boat, a larger patrol boat.

Unlike most other naval planners, those of the Royal Navy wanted their submarines to be able to fire a salvo of torpedoes from the bow – that is, with the sub pointing finger-like at its target. The S Class provided six torpedo tubes, the T Class eight. The basic idea was that at maximum range one of a spread of six or eight torpedoes would surely hit the target.

British subs may have had the most reliable torpedo of the war – the Mark 8, a 'tin fish' of 21-inch diameter operated by a Brotherhood Cycle engine. Throughout the war the sub crews swore by the Mark 8.

Under the London Naval Treaty of 1930 Britain, as well as the US and Japan, was permitted a submarine capacity of 52,700 tons and the Royal Navy built subs up to this maximum. Germany, Britain's likely enemy, was forbidden by the Treaty of Versailles to possess U-boats so its leaders, even before Hitler appeared on the political scene, sent its design teams to work in Holland, where they designed and helped to build subs for other nations' navies.

The new German U-boats authorized by Hitler after he had repudiated the Treaty of Versailles were immensely successful from the beginning. In the first months of the Second World War a U-boat torpedoed HMS *Courageous* and then penetrated the defences of Scapa Flow to sink the battleship *Royal Oak* in October. However, in the spring of 1940 British subs also had great success, damaging the battleship *Gneisenau* and the light cruiser *Leipzig* and sinking the light cruiser *Karlsruhe* and the torpedo boat *Luchs* between April and July 1940.

The U-boats were supreme following the fall of France because they at once had the benefit of bases on the French coast from which they could attack British shipping in the Atlantic. British subs had far fewer targets to attack but in the Mediterranean they came into their own. The Germans and Italians had substantial forces in North Africa and the only way they could be adequately supplied and reinforced was by sea. Axis transports and troopers crossing the Mediterranean faced as much danger as did the trans-Atlantic British convoys contending with U-boat packs.

Based in Gibraltar and in the Grand Harbour of Malta, the British subs wreaked havoc among the enemy. The 10th Submarine Flotilla stationed at Malta had success after success, even when Axis bombing of Malta made the Grand Harbour untenable as a British base for some months. The pressure put on Italian shipping by the British submarines forced Hitler to send 12 of his U-boats into the Mediterranean when he would have preferred to keep them in the Atlantic. All of these U-boats were sunk but not before they had torpedoed the aircraft carriers *Eagle* and *Ark Royal* and the battleship *Barham*. Italian submarines, which had many technical problems, achieved comparatively little.

The people of Gibraltar and Malta always knew when a British submarine had been successful; they only had to 'read' the sub's Jolly Roger flying from its masthead. The following insignia were used: white bars for enemy transports sunk; a white U for a U-boat killed; red bars for warships sunk; eight stars around crossed guns represented each successful gun action against enemy shipping; a dagger showed clandestine operations, such as landing or picking up agents and Commandos; while a drawing of a locomotive truck or rail van indicated successful attacks on enemy transport. *Turbulent*'s Jolly Roger indicated an electric train shot up with a streak of lightning across it.

British submariners were paid more than other seamen but no amount of money could adequately compensate them for the risks they took and for the tension and discomfort they endured. Comforts did not exist in an inevitably crowded submarine.

Right foward were the torpedoes and the 'torpedo tackle'. The control room was directly beneath the conning tower and periscope and it was always crowded with officers and men on duty. A long narrow passage provided a thoroughfare of kinds and at intervals were even narrower openings where a bulkhead door could be slammed and locked to prevent water from flooding the entire boat in the case of damage from a depth charge. Down one side of the passageway were the bunks, each of which provided a minimum of space for a crew member. On the other side were three messes, one for seamen, one for petty officers and a third for the officers. The latter was the wardroom, which on a conventional warship could be spacious; in a submarine it contained only a table with cramped seats on two sides and curtains on the other two. To the rear – abaft – of the control room was the radio room, galley, engine room, motor room, the steering gear and heads (lavatories). The captain was the only officer with anything like a cabin but it was still cramped.

The entire crew lived in fetid and at times debilitating air, a mixture of fumes, cooking smells and just stale air. It was not unusual for a submarine to spend two-thirds of its time on patrol underwater. Even when it surfaced to charge its batteries – this could only be done on the surface – only a few of the crew had any duty on the conning tower or on deck.

Men needed a special kind of temperament to live in such close proximity under such conditions for long periods and officers and senior petty officers required superior qualities of leadership and man-management to maintain morale. Distractions, such as card-playing, were few and most men found it difficult to concentrate on reading.

In action and especially under attack the atmosphere in a submarine was one of disciplined tension. To sit on the bottom or at great depth under a sustained depth-charge attack by enemy warships was one of the greatest strains imposed on any serviceman. Sometimes hundreds of depth charges were dropped, producing damage that resulted in cracks in the casing through which water leaked and sometimes poured. The electrical or steering system could be damaged and there was always the fear that a depth charge could explode the sub's torpedoes or blow the boat apart. While they sat and waited for the hunting ships to move away, the crew had to maintain strict silence as any noise could be picked up by the enemy ships' listening devices.

Alastair Mars DSO, DSC and Bar, a great submarine commander, described the tension in his boat after firing a torpedo at a target:

> The scene in the control-room might have been transplanted from a militant Madame Tussaud's – the tense, still figures, some standing, some sitting, others crouching, all rigidly silent, unblinking and tight-lipped, straining to catch the sound of a torpedo striking home. For two minutes and fifteen seconds we were like that, until a great clattering explosion brought a back-slapping roar of triumph to shatter the illusion.

> In *Unbroken – The True Story of a Submarine*,
> Frederick Muller, 1953.

A submariner's life was entirely devoid of 'glamour'. Because the boats were so desperately needed their crews were granted only short periods of leave and when they were at home they could say little of their exploits. The Axis intelligence network was particularly interested in movements of submarine flotillas. For this reason, public announcements about awards of the VC and other decorations were often delayed by months – as was news about the loss of a submarine. The families of submarine crews lived with a terrible sense of fatalism for they understood the risks which their men were constantly enduring.

All submarine captains lived with a secret fear – that they might torpedo the wrong target. This happened to the skipper of HMS *Sahib*, operating in the Mediterranean and doing good work against Italian shipping. In September 1942, *Sahib* had surfaced one night in the Gulf of Sirte, North Africa, to charge batteries. The 2,000-ton Italian freighter *Saillin* was sighted in the moonlight and *Sahib*'s 3-inch gun opened fire. A single torpedo followed and *Saillin* went down, leaving men struggling in the water. As *Sahib* moved in to pick up survivors the crew were horrified to find that the enemy freighter had been carrying British prisoners of war on their way to Italy. *Sahib* saved 26 but another 760 drowned, together with about 170 Italians. Among *Sahib*'s crew was Sub-Lieutenant Ian Fraser, a future VC winner.

Malcolm David Wanklyn

The Submarine Service won nine VCs; five of them went to the crew members of conventional large submarines, the other four to members of the crew of midget submarines. By consensus among military historians – and in the Submarine Service itself – the greatest submariner of them all was Lieutenant-Commander David Wanklyn, whom some writers consider to be the most outstanding submarine captain in international naval history. Certainly, Wanklyn was dramatically successful.

He had joined the first submarine, HMS *Oberon*, in September 1933. As first lieutenant he served on five submarines between 1936 and 1939 and in January 1940, with the new war against Germany four months old, he was given his first command, H.31. The *Upholder* was under construction and Wanklyn went home on leave to watch it being built, assuming command in August 1940.

Experienced, calm, thoughtful and humane, Wanklyn gave his crew much confidence when *Upholder* passed into the dangerous Mediterranean. Wanklyn knew that the Med would become a cockpit of conflict, with both the Germans and Italians committed to campaigns in North Africa.

Life in *Upholder*, as in any submarine of the time, was arduous and stressful. During daylight the sub was submerged, surfacing well after dark to recharge batteries. The crew – most of whom did not see daylight for days or even weeks – were organized into three watches, two hours on and four off. Two hours was considered the maximum period that a man could hold his concentration.

Upholder under Wanklyn made one patrol after another from Malta. Towards the end of his seventh patrol Wanklyn had sunk five vessels – supply ships from 5,000 to 8,000 tons – and had probably sunk two others. His first victim, the 8,000-tonner, Wanklyn attacked at night on the surface to conserve torpedoes. *Upholder* was itself close pressed by Italian warships; in one short period after a successful torpedo attack the Italians dropped 26 depth charges.

The heavily bearded Wanklyn may at first have seemed like a silent and merciless killer to some of his crew but he slept badly after sinking a merchant ship. He understood very well the chaos, death and suffering his torpedoes caused, but unlike some of his fellow sub captains he could not put these things out of his mind. Even so, he had a sense of humour, as he showed after a boarding party brought back sub-machine guns, German helmets and Nazi flags. When *Upholder* returned to Malta its guard of honour to meet the flotilla commander were dressed in these helmets and carried the German weapons.

On the evening of 24 May 1941, off the coast of Sicily, *Upholder*'s officer of the watch spotted four Italian destroyers escorting a convoy of obvious troopships. The sub's listening gear was inoperable at the time and *Upholder* narrowly missed being rammed by a destroyer which had not seen the sub. With inspired navigation, Wanklyn lined up the largest troopship in his periscope sights and fired his torpedoes, sinking the target. *Upholder* then endured a furious hour of depth-charging before heading for Valletta harbour. Here *Upholder* wore her Jolly Roger, with a fresh white bar for another ship destroyed. It marked the end of Wanklyn's seventh patrol.

Wanklyn had already been awarded the DSO. Now came the VC, gazetted on 26 December 1941. The citation read:

Lieutenant-Commander Malcolm David Wanklyn DSO, RN

On 24 May 1941 in the Mediterranean, south of Sicily, Lieutenant-Commander M.D. Wanklyn, commander HM Submarine *Upholder*, torpedoed a troopship which was with a strongly protected convoy. The troopship sank and *Upholder* endured a strong counter-attack in which 37 depth-charges were dropped. By the end of 1941 Lieutenant-Commander Wanklyn had sunk nearly 140,000 tons of enemy shipping, including a destroyer and troopships, tankers, supply and store ships.

Wanklyn's was the first submarine VC of the war and his wife, Elspeth, heard about it while staying with her parents in Scotland. But there was to be no leave for the crew of *Upholder* to celebrate their commander's great decoration. The Germans and Italians were active in trying to reinforce and resupply their armies in North Africa, while the British and Empire forces were themselves mounting a campaign for 1942. Wanklyn maintained his aggressiveness with a concentration and dedication that amazed his crew. As if to show that he really had deserved his VC, in the two weeks after its award he sank his first U-boat, two 10,000-ton transports, another tanker, his fifth supply ship and two destroyers. One day he took *Upholder* stealthily into an enemy harbour to examine a barge and two schooners moored to a jetty. Again to conserve torpedoes, he calculated that just two 'tin fish' blowing up between the schooners would sink all three vessels. The resulting explosion was so enormous that it made *Upholder* heel under water. The three ships had been packed with explosives and chemicals and there was nothing much left of the harbour as *Upholder* headed back to the open sea.

Upholder was now ordered into the Aegean Sea, where, in the space of four days, its crew sank five ships, including a trooper. One of Wanklyn's most dramatic exploits occurred during the last night of this hectic period while his sub was on the surface for a battery recharge.

A small armed escort of about 300 tons shepherding three troop-carrying vessels approached *Upholder* without sighting the submarine. *Upholder*'s deck gunners fired a shell into the escort, setting it ablaze. A trooper was also set afire and simultaneously *Upholder* drew alongside the third ship. By now more of the sub's crew were on deck and shot dead a German about to drop a grenade and an officer with a revolver. While a young officer vaulted on to the enemy ship to capture a Nazi naval swastika flag Wanklyn ordered the placement of a high explosive charge, which destroyed the ship.

Ordering the conning tower closed, Wanklyn then dived. He was ready to return to base but with one torpedo remaining he was reluctant to do so. While the crew was at breakfast the duty officer reported an Italian tanker in sight. *Upholder*'s last torpedo sent it to the bottom and Wanklyn took his crew back to base for a rest.

Towards the end of 1941 the Italians sent three of their fastest and largest troopships, *Neptunia, Oceania* and *Vulcania*, on a run to Libya with troop reinforcements. This precious convoy was protected by six destroyers but the screen was penetrated by *Upholder* and *Unbeaten* (under Lieutenant-

Commander Woodward). In a night attack, *Upholder* sank *Neptunia* and damaged *Oceania*, finishing this ship off with a second attack in daylight. In the meantime, *Unbeaten* dealt with *Vulcania*.

Wanklyn's direct superior, Captain 'Shrimp' Simpson, twice tried to return Wanklyn to Britain for the rest he so badly needed but he resisted, almost to the point of defiance. He would return to Britain, he said, when the entire crew and *Upholder* herself qualified for home leave. That meant at the end of 25 patrols. In the meantime, *Upholder* continued to enhance its already formidable reputation, with 150,000 tons of enemy shipping destroyed, not to mention their priceless cargoes of troops, munitions and supplies.

On 6 April 1942, *Upholder* sailed from Malta on her 25th patrol to operate in the Gulf of Tripoli and kept a rendezvous with *Unbeaten*. On 14 April two other British subs operating near *Upholder*'s area heard sustained depth-charging and on 18 April the Italian Navy claimed that a torpedo boat had sunk a submarine. Precise details were never established but it seems likely that this was how *Upholder* and her crew met their end. The Admiralty did not reveal the loss for several months.

An Admiralty press release was generally terse but in the case of Wanklyn and *Upholder* it was detailed and generous, though no more than was deserved.

The history of British submarines is full of great exploits and great names. Under the command of Lieut-Commander Malcolm David Wanklyn VC, DSO, RN, HM Submarine *Upholder* earned the distinction achieved not by luck nor by opportunist exploitation but by careful planning and brilliant handling, cool courage and the highest efficiency over a long period. When the *Upholder* sailed on patrol it was a foregone conclusion that she would report the greater discomfiture of the enemy; and when she returned from patrol the accounts of her attacks were an inspiration and an example to the other submarines of her flotilla. It was a flotilla operating continually in the most dangerous waters close to the enemy's bases in the central Mediterranean, where it has inflicted very serious loss upon the enemy. It was from her twenty-fifth patrol in the Mediterranean that HM Submarine *Upholder* did not return. In the 24 successful patrols which this submarine had carried out in these waters she had built up a long record of success against the enemy and of 36 attacks no less than twenty-three had been successful. The *Upholder* sank three U-boats, a destroyer and an armed trawler, probably sank a cruiser and another destroyer and possibly a second cruiser. Against the enemy's reinforcements and supplies the *Upholder*'s successes were even more notable. She sank 15 enemy transports and supply ships, totalling over 122,000 tons and probably sank two others. Among the ships she is known to have sunk were the large transport *Conte Roddo* of 17,800 tons and the *Neptunia* and *Oceania*, each of 19,500 tons.

Sir Max Horton, Admiral Submarines, wrote to Mrs Wanklyn: 'Everybody in submarines feels David's loss deeply, but his name, qualities and record will remain always in the front of our memories as an example of a splendid man, of whom the Royal Navy and the Submarine Service are most justly proud.'

Captain Simpson, who knew Wanklyn well, wrote: 'His record of brilliant leadership will never be equalled. He was by his very qualities of modesty, ability, determination, courage and character a giant among us.' According to Simpson, the people of the beleaguered island of Malta worshipped him.

The official Admiralty communiqué was no less glowing:

It is seldom proper for Their Lordships [of the Admiralty] to draw distinction between different services rendered in the course of naval duty but they take this opportunity of singling out those of HMS *Upholder*, under command of Lieutenant-Commander Wanklyn, for special mention. She was long employed against enemy communications in the central Mediterranean and she became noted for the uniformly high quality of her services in that arduous and dangerous duty. Such was the standard of skill and daring set by Lieutenant-Commander Wanklyn and the officers and men under him that they and their ship became an inspiration not only to their own flotilla but to the Fleet of which it was part and to Malta, where for so long HMS *Upholder* was based. The ship and her company are gone but the example and the inspiration remain.

On 3 March 1943, Wanklyn's widow, mother and son Ian, aged three, attended an investiture at Buckingham Palace to receive his VC and three DSOs. Few people have had the distinction of receiving four such high honours at one time. Wanklyn's portrait, painted for the Admiralty after his death, hangs permanently in HMS *Dolphin*, home base for submariners.

Anthony Miers

Commander Anthony Miers had been specializing in submarines since 1929 so by the time war broke out in 1939 he was immensely experienced and as a lieutenant-commander he commanded HM Submarine *Torbay*. He was an early winner of the DSO and then came a second DSO for his part in sinking 11 enemy ships in the Mediterranean. On 31 December 1941 he was promoted to commander.

He was a firm believer in follow-up attacks whenever possible, if a torpedo did not finish off a target. On one Mediterranean night he closed with a wounded ship that was reluctant to sink and sent a boarding party to scuttle it. His crew were well trained and as the sub's engineer and his helpers placed the explosive charges, the cooks of the sub's three messes hurriedly replenished their food stores from the stricken ship's supplies. The whole job had to be done in minutes – a submarine could not afford to be surprised on the surface.

In fact, this happened just once to *Torbay*, when batteries were being recharged and Miers himself was on deck with some members of his crew. Then a lookout shouted, 'Destroyer astern, Sir, heading straight for us!'

'Crash dive!' Miers ordered. Many times drilled for such an emergency, the topside men slithered through the conning-tower hatch and down the steps. Miers, bringing up the rear, could not close the outer hatch and only just managed to slam the lower hatch as the waters closed over the sub. Water filled the conning tower as depth charges' shock waves hammered the boat. After the emergency was over Miers found that a cushion he had been using while on deck had prevented the hatch from closing.

In March 1942 *Torbay* followed three Italian destroyers and a convoy of ships into a Corfu harbour. This was a dangerous, delicate and slow manoeuvre and as night fell Miers knew he could not attack until the morning. There was a further problem: the batteries had to be recharged or *Torbay* would not get out of the harbour next day. Miers' VC citation on 7 July 1942 succinctly sets out much of what happened next.

Commander Anthony Cecil Capel Miers DSO, RN

For valour in command of HM Submarine *Torbay* in a daring and successful raid on shipping in a defended enemy harbour, planned with full knowledge of the great hazards to be expected during seventeen hours in waters closely patrolled by the enemy. On arriving in the harbour he had to charge his batteries lying on the surface in full moonlight, under the guns of the enemy. As he could not see his target he waited several hours and attacked in full daylight under a glassy calm. When he had fired his torpedoes he was heavily counter-attacked and had to withdraw through a long channel with anti-submarine craft all around and continuous air patrols overhead.

In fact, the Italians well knew that the enemy sub had only one way out, along that narrow channel, and they had ships of all kinds watching it. *Torbay* survived probably 50 depth charges before reaching the open and deeper waters of the Aegean Sea.

Numerous decorations were proposed for the crew of *Torbay* and apparently the four officers were to have been invested at one ceremony and the ratings at another. It is said that Commander Miers stated that he would refuse his VC if all his men could not be invested together. On 28 July 1942 in a single ceremony, Miers did receive his VC, three officers were awarded either a DSO or DSC and 24 ratings received DSMs or Bars to a DSM already held. He died in Scotland in 1985.

John Wallace 'Tubby' Linton

Like Wanklyn and Miers, Lieutenant-Commander John Wallace ('Tubby') Linton was a career submariner in the 1920s and 1930s and so was immensely experienced when he came to command HM Submarine *Turbulent*, in January 1942. His area of operations was in the eastern Mediterranean and he sank his first victim in late February 1942. March was a good month and *Turbulent*'s pickings were rich. On just one night Linton sank three Italian destroyers before diving deep to evade the depth charge pattern laid by escorting destroyers. His haul that night was one of the best during a single attack throughout the war.

In another attack he sank a German U-boat, a difficult feat since it required a special kind of skill for one sub to kill another. Before spring 1943 Linton and *Turbulent* deprived the enemy forces in North Africa of desperately needed men, ammunition and supplies. He had been awarded both the DSO and the DSC.

But Linton had targets other than enemy ships. On at least three occasions Linton took *Turbulent* to the surface to attack shore targets in Italy. These operations were carefully calculated by periscope observation before *Turbulent* was positioned for the strike. Linton shot up a road convoy and trains and on other occasions he landed special agents on dangerous enemy shores. Although such daring enterprises courted danger, all this was stimulating for his crew. Since they had to spend most of their time under water, it was a relief to be on the surface for some action even if only a few men could take part. When they went below they had enthralling stories to tell.

Like Wanklyn, Linton was reluctant to return to Britain, but there came a time when he was told that he must obey orders and take a rest at home. In March 1943 *Turbulent* set out on her final patrol before home leave. On the 26th, the Admiralty sent a top secret signal to the Commander-in-Chief, Mediterranean and Commander-in-Chief, Levant:

It is with the deepest regret that their Lordships have learnt of the loss of *Turbulent* with the presumption of the death of Commander J.W. Linton. In view of the very special and distinguished services of this officer, who has been in command of submarines throughout the whole period of this war and whose outstanding characteristics and achievements were so well known through the Mediterranean commands, they wish to express their sympathy to you and to the Mediterranean submarine flotillas. Their Lordships do so with assurance that Commander Linton's inspiring leadership will long be remembered by all those who are so worthily upholding the traditions of the Royal Navy and the submarine service in the Mediterranean at the present time.

The public announcement that *Turbulent* had been lost with all hands was made on 4 May. The boat may have been caught in a minefield between Corsica and Sardinia. On 25 May Linton's VC was gazetted.

Commander John Wallace Linton DSO, DSC, RN

The King has been graciously pleased to approve the award of the Victoria Cross for valour in command of HM Submarines to Commander John Wallace Linton DSO, DSC. From the outbreak of war until HMS *Turbulent*'s last patrol Commander Linton was constantly in command of submarines and during that time inflicted great damage on the enemy. He sank one cruiser, one destroyer, one U-boat, 28 supply ships, some 100,000 tons in all, and destroyed three trains by gunfire. In his last year he spent two hundred and fifty four days at sea, submerged for nearly half that time, and his ship was hunted thirteen times and had two hundred and fifty depth charges aimed at her.

His many and brilliant successes were due to his constant activity and skill and the daring which never failed him when there was an enemy to attack. On one occasion, for instance, in HMS *Turbulent*, he sighted a convoy of two merchantmen and two destroyers travelling in mist and moonlight. He worked his submarine around ahead of the convoy and dived to attack it as it passed through the moon's rays. On bringing his sights to bear he found himself right ahead of a destroyer. Yet he held his course till the destroyer was almost on top of him and, when his sights came on the convoy, he fired. His great courage and determination were rewarded. He sank one merchantman and one destroyer outright and set the other merchantman on fire so that she blew up. John Linton met his end when his submarine was sunk in Maddelina Harbour, Italy, on 23 March 1943.

Ian Edward Fraser and James Joseph Magennis

The fourth submarine commander to be awarded the VC was Ian Fraser, who joined HMS *Royal Oak* as a midshipman a few months before war broke out. He volunteered to serve in submarines and after some non-combatant trips on outmoded L Class boats to learn the controls, he spent a period on H.43, which was helping to form a screen around Brest intended to contain the enemy ships *Scharnhorst*, *Gneisenau* and *Prinz Eugen*. However, the ships managed to slip away in broad daylight. Fraser's next posting was to the submarine *Sahib* and for a year he and the sub operated successfully in the Mediterranean (see p. 44), before being sent to Algiers. Here Fraser was awarded the DSC. In a wardroom accident he broke a foot, which kept him in hospital when *Sahib* next sailed. The sub was sunk and all but one of the crew were taken prisoner.

In March 1944, while first lieutenant aboard a training submarine Fraser was handed a 'secret' message: 'Two Lieutenants and two Sub-Lieutenants RN or RNR are requested for special and hazardous service in submarines. Name of volunteers should be signalled to Flag Officer Submarines immediately.' Fraser, ever ready to volunteer, soon found himself appointed as captain of the midget submarine XE–3. Six XEs were built and with their crews were sent to bases in Australia for possible use against the Japanese Navy.

In May 1945 Captain W.R. Fell commanding 14th Submarine Flotilla was asked if his subs could cut underwater cables used by the Japs. An additional operation was 'Operation Struggle', to be an attack on two enemy cruisers, *Takao* and *Mikyo*, anchored in Johore Straits, Singapore. The task was given to Fraser in XE–3 and to Lieutenant J.E. Smart in XE–1.

An XE had an overall length of 50 feet and carried a crew of four as well as two detachable explosive charges of two tons of Amatol and some limpet mines. To reach their targets the subs had to steer past minefields, listening posts, a buoyed boom and surface patrols for a distance of 40 miles. As Fraser was to discover, his target, the *Takao*, was moored only 75 feet from the shore with a mere 15 feet of water under her – yet Fraser had to place his sub in the best attacking position under *Takao*'s keel. The attack was successful and Fraser and his diver, Temporary Acting Leading Seaman James Magennis were each awarded the VC. Their citations show why they deserved the decoration and need to be read together to comprehend the appalling difficulties Fraser and his crew surmounted.

Temporary Acting Leading Seaman James Joseph Magennis, RN

Leading Seaman Magennis served as Diver in his Majesty's Midget Submarine XE–3 for her attack on 31st July, 1945, on a Japanese cruiser of the Atago class. Owing to the fact that XE–3 was tightly jammed under the target the driver's hatch could not be fully opened, and Magennis had to squeeze himself through the narrow space available.

He experienced great difficulty in placing his limpets on the bottom of the cruiser owing both to the foul state of the bottom and to the pronounced slope upon which the limpets would not hold. Before a limpet could be placed therefore Magennis had thoroughly to scrape the area clear of barnacles, and in order to secure the limpets he had to tie them in pairs by a line passing under the cruiser keel. This was very tiring work for a diver, and he was moreover handicapped by a steady leakage of oxygen which was ascending in bubbles to the surface. A lesser man would have been content to place a few limpets and then to return to the craft. Magennis, however, persisted until he had placed his full outfit before returning to the craft in an exhausted condition. Shortly after withdrawing Lieutenant Fraser endeavoured to jettison his limpet carriers, but one of these would not release itself and fall clear of the craft.

Despite his exhaustion, his oxygen leak and the fact that there was every probability of his being sighted, Magennis at once volunteered to leave the craft and free the carrier rather than allow a less experienced diver to undertake the job. After seven minutes of nerve-racking work he succeeded in releasing the carrier. Magennis displayed very great courage and devotion to duty and complete disregard for his own safety.

The other two members of Fraser's crew were also decorated as were Lieutenant Smart and his crew of XE–1.

Fraser's VC and his ten other medals were sold at a Sotheby's auction on 10 November 1988 for £33,000. For the fate of Magennis's award, see p. xix.

Lieutenant Ian Edward Fraser DSC, RNR

Lieutenant Fraser commanded His Majesty's Midget Submarine XE–3 in a successful attack on a Japanese heavy cruiser of the Atago class at her moorings in Johore Strait, Singapore, on 31st July 1945. During the long approach up the Singapore Straits XE–3 deliberately left the believed safe channel and entered mined waters to avoid suspected hydrophone posts.

The target was aground, or nearly aground, both fore and aft, and only under the midship portion was there just sufficient water for XE–3 to place herself under the cruiser. For forty minutes XE–3 pushed her way along the seabed until finally Lieutenant Fraser managed to force her right under the centre of the cruiser. Here he placed the limpets and dropped his main side charge.

Great difficulty was experienced in extricating the craft after the attack had been completed, but finally XE–3 was clear, and commenced her long return journey out to sea. The courage and determination of Lieutenant Fraser are beyond all praise. Any man not possessed of his relentless determination to achieve his object in full, regardless of all consequences, would have dropped his side charge alongside the target instead of persisting until he had forced his submarine right under the cruiser.

The approach and withdrawal entailed a passage of 80 miles through water which had been mined by both the enemy and ourselves, past hydrophone positions, over loops and controlled minefields, and through an anti-submarine boom.

Basil Charles Godfrey Place and Donald Cameron

The German battleship *Tirpitz*, completed in 1941 and sister ship to the more famous *Bismarck*, was one of the world's most powerful battleships. With a displacement of 32,000 tons, she had a main armament of eight 15-inch guns and had spent her war career in Norwegian waters operating against the Allied convoys destined for Russia. Her very presence obliged first Britain and then Britain's ally, the US, to maintain a large fleet in northern waters to guard against *Tirpitz*, when ships were desperately needed in the Atlantic. She was moored in the protected waters of Kaafiord in northern Norway and repeated fruitless attempts were made to sink the giant ship by aerial bombing.

In September 1942 an attempt was made to get through to the *Tirpitz* by 'Chariots', more popularly known as human torpedoes since two men sat astride the outside of a Chariot. Ten miles from their target the Chariots broke loose from their towing vessel in rough seas and sank.

In September 1943 six X-type midget submarines set out on a mission to sink the *Tirpitz* and some of her escorts. It turned out to be one of the great adventures of the war. X9 broke her tow and was lost on the voyage; X8 was damaged and consequently scuttled. X7, commanded by Lieutenant Basil Place, snagged a mine hawser and Place crawled along the sub casing where he used his feet to untangle it and its mine. Several times he had to push the mine away with his foot before the sub was freed. Place with X7 and Lieutenant Donald Cameron with X6 were bound for the *Tirpitz*, which they reached on the morning of 22 September as the large crew of the battleship was about to have breakfast. X6 ran aground, broke free, then hit a rock and broke surface. She dived again but the gyro was out of action and the periscope nearly unusable. Entangled in a net hanging from the battleship, X6 worked free but broke surface again. This time the alarmed crew of *Tirpitz* dropped grenades and fired machine guns at the submarine. Cameron went astern until X6's hydroplane guard touched *Tirpitz*'s hull and released his 2-ton Amatol charges. Then he scuttled X6 and ordered his crew to bail out. A picket boat from *Tirpitz* picked them up and took them aboard, where the crew was now at action stations as the ship began the slow process of moving. Cameron and his crew, all too aware of the charges under the ship, kept their cool as they waited for interrogation.

Place's X7 stuck in the *Tirpitz*'s net at 75 feet. He blew the air tanks, went full astern – and then several things happened quickly. X7 broke loose, turned side-on to the net and popped to the surface. Place dived so quickly that now X7 stuck at 95 feet, but after much manoeuvring the sub rose – and Place found that he was inside the net with *Tirpitz* only 30 yards away. He dived again and placed his charges but then became entangled in one net after another as he tried to reach deep water.

At 8.12 a.m., three minutes before the set time, the charges exploded – eight tons of Amatol straight into *Tirpitz*'s hull. The shock threw Cameron and his crew off their feet. It also sent the *Tirpitz*'s crew into a frenzy of panic. The guncrews shot up their own tankers and small boats and wiped out a shore position, killing 120 of their own men.

The shock helped the stuck X7 by shaking her free of the steel net. But she was uncontrollable and each time she surfaced *Tirpitz*'s guns fired at her. Place, from on the sub's casing, ordered abandon ship but he was the only one able to get away at once. Only one of the other three brave men survived.

The damage to *Tirpitz* was immense and she was crippled. She limped to Tromso, where she was finally sunk by the 'Dam Busters' squadron of the RAF in April 1944. Cameron and Place were awarded the VC, their awards being gazetted on 22 February 1944. The other four surviving members of their crews were also decorated for their part in 'a magnificent feat of arms', as Admiral Submarines, Sir Max Horton, described the crippling of the *Tirpitz*.

Unusually, but not uniquely, Lieutenants Place and Cameron were given a joint citation while still prisoners of war. Some people connected with the administration and award of decorations felt that the announcements of their VC citations might lead the Germans to treat them harshly – after all, the *Tirpitz* and *Bismarck*, also sunk by the Royal Navy, were close to Hitler's heart. However, the young submarine captains were not badly treated. Their VCs might even have given them additional security while they were held captive.

Lieutenant Basil Charles Godfrey Place DSC, RN
Lieutenant Donald Cameron, RNR

Lieutenants Place and Cameron were the Commanding Officers of two of His Majesty's Midget Submarines X7 and X6 which on 22nd September 1943 carried out a most daring and successful attack on the German Battleship *Tirpitz*, moored in the protected anchorage of Kaafiord, North Norway.

To reach the anchorage necessitated the penetration of an enemy minefield and a passage of fifty miles up the fiord, known to be guarded by nets, gun defences and listening posts, this after a passage of at least a thousand miles from base.

Having successfully eluded all these hazards and entered the fleet anchorage, Lieutenants Place and Cameron, with a complete disregard for danger, worked their small craft past the close anti-submarine and torpedo nets surrounding the *Tirpitz*, and from a position inside these nets, carried out a cool and determined attack.

Whilst they were still inside the nets a fierce enemy counter attack by guns and depth charges developed which made their withdrawal impossible. Lieutenants Place and Cameron therefore scuttled their craft to prevent them falling into the hands of the enemy. Before doing so they took every measure to ensure the safety of their crews, the majority of whom, together with themselves, were subsequently taken prisoner.

In the course of the operation these very small craft pressed home their attack to the full, in doing so accepting all the dangers inherent in such vessels and facing every possible hazard which ingenuity could devise for the protection in harbour of vitally important Capital Ships.

The courage and endurance and utter contempt for danger in the immediate face of the enemy shown by Lieutenants Place and Cameron during this determined and successful attack were supreme.

Lieutenant Cameron died in Scotland in 1961.

Peter Scawen Watkinson Roberts and Thomas William Gould

A joint citation accompanied the VCs awarded to two other submariners, Lieutenant Peter Roberts and Petty Officer Thomas Gould, gazetted on 9 June 1942. The award was unusual in that Roberts and Gould were not 'in the presence of the enemy', if that condition were to be strictly applied. But they had been in the enemy's presence only a short time before they performed the act of bravery which brought them the VC. Their citation adequately describes it.

Lieutenant Peter Scawen Watkinson Roberts, RN
Petty Officer Thomas William Gould, RN

On February 16th, in daylight, HM Submarine *Thrasher* attacked and sank a heavily escorted supply ship. She was at once attacked by depth charges and was bombed by aircraft.

The presence of two unexploded bombs in the gun-casing was discovered when after dark the submarine surfaced and began to roll.

Lieutenant Roberts and Petty Officer Gould volunteered to remove the bombs, which were of a type unknown to them. The danger in dealing with the second bomb was very great. To reach it they had to go through the casing which was so low that they had to lie at full length to move in it. Through this narrow space, in complete darkness, they pushed and dragged the bomb for a distance of some 20 feet until it could be lowered over the side. Every time the bomb was moved there was a loud twanging noise as of a broken spring, which added nothing to their peace of mind.

This deed was the more gallant as HMS *Thrasher*'s presence was known to the enemy; she was close to the enemy coast, and in waters where his patrols were known to be active day and night. There was a very great chance, and they knew it, that the submarine might have to crash-dive while they were in the casing. Had this happened they must have been drowned.

Roberts died in Devon in 1979.

The British Army VCs

Background to Bravery

Military courage shows itself in response to a cause and a particular set of circumstances and is demonstrated most dramatically in a crisis. Valour is one reaction to a crisis. Exploits worthy of the award of the Victoria Cross had a recognized value at the time of the particular act of valour because they were widely publicized, firstly when they were announced and secondly when the recipient attended a royal investiture. Two generations after the event there is little recognition of the valour that played such a large part in public consciousness in the years 1940–6. This is why it is necessary to give a brief account of the circumstances of the period.

I have grouped Army VC awards according to the theatres of war and the years in which they were won.

- France 1940 – the Dunkirk period; the Dieppe and Saint-Nazaire raids of 1942;
- Malaya;
- North Africa, including Somaliland, 1940–3;
- Italy 1943–4;
- North-West Europe: D-Day and after, to the end of the war;
- Burma and Assam.

CHAPTER FIVE

France 1940–2

The Fall of France 1940

In the early hours of 1 September 1939 fleets of German bombers attacked Polish cities and at dawn 60 divisions of troops – more than 1,250,000 men – invaded Poland. Nine of the divisions were armoured, each with 150 tanks, and there was great artillery strength.

The hardy Poles fought bravely but except for the air force their equipment was greatly inferior to that of the Germans. Their planes were destroyed in surprise attacks. In four days the attacking German armies smashed through the Polish defences and by 8 September their tanks were on the edge of Warsaw. The capital fell on 27 September; the fortress of Modlin was overrun on 28 September; the main naval base surrendered on 1 October and by 5 October resistance had ceased. In those five weeks the Poles had lost 66,000 men killed and 200,000 wounded and the rest of the forces were captive. The Germans had lost 10,000 men killed and 30,000 wounded.

The German generals rightly compared their fighting methods to the speed and power of lightning – they called it *Blitzkrieg*, lightning war.

In the west, however, there was only '*Sitzkrieg*' – what amounted to little more than sitting around. Britain and France had fulfilled their promise to Poland and declared war on 3 September – but after this very little happened. The French troops stayed passively in their trenches and in the Maginot Line while the Germans continued to develop their own defensive system in response, the Siegfried Line, which Hitler had begun a few years earlier. Hitler had fewer than 400,000 men holding the incomplete Siegfried Line and he was still weak in the west, but France and Britain were reluctant to invade Germany.

Hitler invaded Norway but all the time he was preparing to attack the French and British armies in France. As always, the German preparations were thorough and on a vast scale, built around 104 infantry divisions, 8 motorized divisions and 10 armoured divisions – 2,500,000 men in all. The main striking force was massed next to the frontiers of Belgium and Luxembourg.

The French had almost as many tanks as the Germans but only three armoured divisions. They had dispersed all their other tanks throughout the army, which in any case lacked the confidence of the German forces. The British Expeditionary Force (BEF) had 10 divisions under General Lord Gort, who was himself under the French General Maurice Gamelin. On paper the Belgian Army had 22 divisions and the Dutch Army 14 divisions but all were poorly trained and equipped.

Between the Allied French and British and the Allied Belgians and Dutch no coordinated plans existed. Convinced that Hitler's generals would advance through Holland and Belgium to avoid having to attack the much vaunted Maginot Line, Gort and Gamelin prepared 'Plan D': in essence, when the Germans attacked the Belgians and Dutch, the stronger part of the British and French forces would advance to the River Dyle, in Belgium.

On 10 May the Luftwaffe attacked Belgium and Holland, while paratroopers were dropped near Rotterdam and The Hague to seize key bridges over the Rhine and Meuse. The Dutch and Belgian Armies were routed, the Belgians falling back to the River Dyle to join the French and British. The German generals had also outsmarted the French by pushing through the supposedly impassable Ardennes hills and forests to reach the River Meuse, where a thin line of French defenders gave way. By the evening of 15 May the Germans had smashed a gap 50 miles wide in the French line and they were in the Allies' rear. The French and British hurried back but they were too late to plug the great gap and German spearheads were racing virtually unopposed along the Somme river valley towards the English Channel.

The Germans faced serious opposition only twice. On 17 May General Charles de Gaulle led an armoured counter-attack but without infantry support he had to withdraw. On 19 May de Gaulle tried again but this time he lost so many tanks his 'campaign' was finished.

By 21 May German armour and infantry had cut the Allies in two: one part in Flanders, that is the northern tip of France and southwest Belgium, the other part south of the German corridor. At Boulogne, the main British supply base, some units put up spirited resistance. In Flanders the German pressure was relentless, though the best of the British and French units fought so well that for a time they stopped the enemy advance. But the Belgian Army was helpless and useless and rather than see his men massacred King Leopold surrendered the entire Belgian Army on 27 May. With Flanders gone, the British troops were being pressed back to the sea and were forced to rely on the Navy to rescue them.

A rearguard of British and French troops bravely held off German attempts to annihilate or capture the entire BEF and those French troops still fighting or joining the evacuation. In any case, the enemy pressure eased because Hitler and his Luftwaffe chief, Goering, wanted the Luftwaffe to play a major part in the defeat of the British as they tried to board the motley fleet sent to evacuate them. At this point the RAF joined the fight, keeping the Luftwaffe so busy that relatively few air attacks were made on the British evacuation. By 2 June the last of 225,000 British and 112,000

French soldiers had been taken off the Dunkirk beaches and brought to England. It was against this background that five British soldiers won the VC between 15 May and 1 June.

Richard Wallace Annand

Second-Lieutenant Richard Wallace Annand, the Durham Light Infantry (Supplementary Reserve)

(London Gazette, 23 August 1940)

For most conspicuous gallantry on the 15th–16th May 1940 when the platoon under his command was on the south side of the River Dyle, astride a blown bridge.

During the night a strong attack was beaten off, but about 11 a.m. the enemy again launched a violent attack and pushed forward a bridging party into the sunken bottom of the river. Second-Lieutenant Annand attacked this party, but when ammunition ran out he went forward himself over open ground, with total disregard for enemy mortar and machine gun fire. Reaching the top of the bridge, he drove out the party below, inflicting over twenty casualties with hand grenades. Having been wounded he rejoined his platoon, had his wound dressed, and then carried on in command. During the evening another attack was launched and again Second-Lieutenant Annand went forward with hand grenades and inflicted heavy casualties on the enemy.

When the order to withdraw was received, he withdrew his platoon, but learning on the way back that his batman was wounded and had been left behind, he returned at once to the former position and brought him back in a wheelbarrow, before losing consciousness as the result of wounds.

George Gristock

Warrant Officer Class II George Gristock, the Royal Norfolk Regiment

(London Gazette, 23 August 1940)

For most conspicuous gallantry on the 21st May 1940, when his company was holding a position on the line of the River Escaut, south of Tournai. After a prolonged attack, the enemy succeeded in breaking through beyond the company's right flank which was consequently threatened. Company Sergeant-Major Gristock, having organised a party of eight riflemen from company headquarters, went forward to cover the right flank.

Realising that an enemy machine-gun had moved forward to a position from which it was inflicting heavy casualties on his company, Company

Sergeant-Major Gristock went on, with one man as connecting file, to try to put it out of action. Whilst advancing, he came under heavy machine gun fire from the opposite bank and was severely wounded in both legs, his right knee being badly smashed. He nevertheless gained his fire position, some twenty yards from the enemy machine gun post undetected, and by well aimed rapid fire killed the machine-gun crew of four and put their gun out of action. He then dragged himself back to the right flank position from which he refused to be evacuated until contact with the battalion on the right had been established and the line once more made good.

By his gallant action, the position of the company was secured, and many casualties prevented. Company Sergeant-Major has since died of his wounds.

The award to the 26-year-old Lieutenant Annand from South Shields, County Durham, was the first Army VC of the war and it set the standard by which potential VC exploits would be judged. Annand survived the war and became a captain. George Gristock, regarded by his men with great affection, was the archetypal company sergeant major and he was 39 when he performed his 'act of signal valour' at the River Escaut (the River Scheldt). He was brought back to a hospital in Brighton and died there from his wounds on 16 June 1940. He is buried in Bear Road Cemetery, Brighton.

That two of the first five men to be awarded the VC during the Second World War were killed in action or died of their wounds is indicative of the odds against surviving a VC action. In fact, 50 per cent of the awards were posthumous.

Harold Marcus Ervine-Andrews

Lieutenant (acting Captain) (now Captain) Harold Marcus Ervine-Andrews, the East Lancashire Regiment

(*London Gazette*, 30 July 1940)

For most conspicuous gallantry on active service on the night of the 31st May/1st June, 1940. Captain Ervine-Andrews took over about a thousand yards of the defences in front of Dunkirk, his line extending along the Canal de Bergues, and the enemy attacked at dawn. For over ten hours, notwithstanding intense artillery, mortar, and machine gun fire, and in the face of vastly superior enemy forces, Captain Ervine-Andrews and his company held their position.

The enemy, however, succeeded in crossing the canal on both flanks; And owing to superior enemy forces, a company of Captain Ervine-Andrews' own battalion which was despatched to protect his flanks, was unable to gain contact with him. There being danger of one of his platoons being driven in, he called for volunteers to fill the gap, and then, going forward, climbed on to the top of a straw-roofed barn from which he engaged the enemy with rifle and light automatic fire, though at the time the enemy were sending mortar-bombs and armour-piercing bullets through the roof.

Captain Ervine-Andrews personally accounted for seventeen of the enemy with his rifle, and for many more with a Bren gun. Later, when the house which he held had been shattered by enemy fire and set alight, and all his ammunition had been expended, he sent back his wounded in the remaining carrier. Captain Ervine-Andrews then collected the remaining eight men of his company from this forward position and when almost completely surrounded, led them back to the cover afforded by the company in the rear, swimming or wading up to the chin in water for over a mile. Having brought all that remained of his company safely back, he once again took up position.

Throughout this action, Captain Ervine-Andrews displayed courage, tenacity, and devotion to duty worthy of the highest traditions of the British Army and his magnificent example imbued his own troops with the dauntless fighting spirit which he himself displayed.

The exploit by the 29-year-old Ervine-Andrews was one of the most decisive actions during the evacuation from Dunkirk. Sir John Smyth VC, MC, who was at Dunkirk, wrote, 'For over ten hours, under intense artillery, mortar and machine-gun fire Ervine-Andrews and his company held their position. Had he and his company not been so steadfast in repelling the fierce German attacks at this critical time it might have been even more difficult than it was to embark the last divisions of the BEF.'*

Harry Nicholls

Lance-Corporal Harry Nicholls, Grenadier Guards
(London Gazette, 30 July 1940)

On the 21st May, 1940, Lance-Corporal Nicholls was commanding a section in the right forward platoon of his company when the company was ordered to counter-attack. At the very start of the advance he was wounded in the arm by shrapnel but continued to lead his section forward, as the company came over a small ridge, the enemy opened heavy machine-gun fire at close range.

Lance-Corporal Nicholls, realizing the danger to his company, immediately seized a Bren Gun and dashed forward towards the machine

---

* *The Story of the Victoria Cross, 1856–1963.*

guns, firing from the hip. He succeeded in silencing first one machine gun then two other machine guns, in spite of being again severely wounded.

Lance-Corporal Nicholls then went up to a higher piece of ground and engaged the German infantry massed behind, causing many casualties and continued to fire until he had no more ammunition left. He was wounded at least four times in all but absolutely refused to give in. There is no doubt that his gallant action was instrumental in enabling the company to reach its objective and in causing the enemy to fall back across the River Scheldt.

Lance-Corporal Nicholls has since been reported to have been killed in action.

While Lieutenant Annand's exploit was the first action of the war to be distinguished by a VC, that of Lance-Corporal Nicholls was the first to be gazetted, on 30 July 1940. He was officially posted as 'Missing Believed Killed' and his citation affirms that he had been reported dead. In fact, though severely wounded, he had fallen into German hands and was taken to hospital. The news that he was alive reached London in September 1940 and Nicholls survived the war. Rarely has a single British soldier forced an entire enemy unit, probably half a battalion, to retreat across a river, but this is what Nicholls did. The citation's reference to Nicholls having been wounded by shrapnel was incorrect; Nicholls was wounded by a shell splinter. He was never again fit enough to rejoin his regiment. Nottingham born, Nicholls died in Leeds on 11 September 1975.

Christopher Furness

During the desperate days of May 1940 many gallant actions went unreported or under-reported. Communications were in confusion and records were lost as the BEF, though fighting stubbornly, was driven back towards the French coast. Some stands made by sub-units in the face of overwhelming odds could only end in defeat, but officers and men performed as if they fully expected to be victorious. One of these officers was 28-year-old Lieutenant Christopher Furness of the Welsh Guards whose citation for a posthumous VC could not be gazetted until 7 February 1946, when records could be studied and survivors back from POW camps could be interviewed. Furness's exploit took place near Arras, an important road and rail centre in northern France, which was held by a hastily formed British garrison. On 21 May the British launched an attack on the flank of the German armoured advance but the only British armour consisted of two tank battalions and they lacked the strength to be effective.

Lieutenant Furness's citation, covering a period of a week, concentrates on 23/24 May and indicates a standard of valour rarely equalled during the five years of war to come.

Lieutenant The Honourable Christopher Furness, Welsh Guards

Lieutenant the Honourable C. Furness was in command of the Carrier Platoon, Welsh Guards, during the period 17th–24th May, 1940, when his Battalion formed part of the garrison of Arras. During this time his Platoon was constantly patrolling in advance of or between the widely dispersed parts of the perimeter, and fought many local actions with the enemy. Lieutenant Furness displayed the highest qualities of leadership and dash on all these occasions and imbued his command with a magnificent offensive spirit.

During the evening of 23rd May, Lieutenant Furness was wounded when on patrol but he refused to be evacuated. By this time the enemy, considerably reinforced, had encircled the town on three sides and withdrawal to Douai was ordered during the night of 23–24th May. Lieutenant Furness's Platoon, together with a small force of light tanks, were ordered to cover the withdrawal of the transport consisting of over 40 vehicles.

About 02.30 hours, 24th May, the enemy attacked on both sides of the town. At one point the enemy advanced to the road along which the transport columns were withdrawing, bringing them under very heavy small arms and anti-tank gun fire. Thus the whole column was blocked and placed in serious jeopardy. Immediately Lieutenant Furness, appreciating the seriousness of the situation, and in spite of his wounds, decided to attack the enemy who were located in a strongly entrenched position behind wire.

Lieutenant Furness advanced with three Carriers,* supported by the light tanks. At once the enemy opened up with very heavy fire from small arms and anti-tank guns. The light tanks were put out of action but Lieutenant Furness continued to advance. He reached the enemy position and circled it several times at close range, inflicting heavy losses. All three Carriers were hit and most of their crews killed or wounded. His own Carrier was disabled and the driver and Bren gunner killed. He then engaged the enemy in personal hand-to-hand combat until he was killed. His magnificent act of self sacrifice against hopeless odds, and when already wounded, made the enemy withdraw for the time being and enabled the large column of vehicles to get clear unmolested and covered the evacuation of some of the wounded of his own Carrier Platoon and the light tanks.

---

* Bren carriers, also known as 'carriers universal', were armoured and tracked vehicles but they were completely open. Armed with Bren light machine guns, they were used to get men, ammunition and other essential supplies to forward units speedily and in some safety. However, they were vulnerable to enemy grenade attack and the driver was without protection from the waist up.

Lieutenant Furness's body was never recovered. He is commemorated on the Dunkirk Memorial, France, and in the Guards Chapel, Wellington Barracks, London.

The Saint-Nazaire Raid, 1942

Augustus Charles Newman

Operation Chariot, the spectacular raid on the great *Normandie* Dock at Saint-Nazaire, has been described in relation to the VCs awarded to three Royal Navy men, Commander R.E.D. Ryder, Lieutenant-Commander S.H. Beattie and Able Seaman W.A. Savage. On board the ships were 44 officers and 224 other ranks of the Commandos, led by Lieutenant-Colonel Augustus Newman. The 38-year-old Newman, born at Chigwell, Essex, was a career soldier of great experience and in effect he was joint commander of the raiding party. He had been told that all decisions about the role and use of the Commandos were his; he was even authorized to call off the landing once the block ship, the *Campbeltown*, had been rammed into position. The old destroyer was carrying most of the Commandos.

The Germans had spotted the flotilla, which came under such heavy fire that many Commandos were wounded on board while others could not land. The phrase 'all hell broke loose' is a greatly overused cliché in war writing but it was an apt description of the noise, flame and general mêlée at Saint-Nazaire. The citation for Colonel Newman's VC graphically and adequately describes his dominant role in the ensuing fighting.

Lieutenant-Colonel Augustus Charles Newman, the Essex Regiment (attached Commandos)

On the night of 27th/29th March, 1942, Lieutenant-Colonel Newman was in command of the military force detailed to land on enemy occupied territory and destroy the dock installations of the German controlled naval base at St. Nazaire.

This important base was known to be heavily defended and bomber support had to be abandoned owing to bad weather. The operation was therefore bound to be exceedingly hazardous, but Lieutenant-Colonel Newman, although empowered to call off the assault at any stage, was determined to carry to a successful conclusion the important task which had been assigned to him.

Coolly and calmly he stood on the bridge of the leading craft as the small force steamed up the estuary of the River Loire, although the ships had been caught in the enemy searchlights and a murderous crossfire opened from both banks, causing heavy casualties.

Although Lieutenant-Colonel Newman need not have landed himself, he was one of the first ashore and during the next five hours of bitter fighting, he personally entered several houses and shot up the occupants and supervised the operations in the town, utterly regardless of his own safety, and he never wavered in his resolution to carry through the operation upon which so much depended.

An enemy gun position on the roof of a U-boat pen had been causing heavy casualties to the landing craft and Lieutenant-Colonel Newman directed the fire of a mortar against this position to such effect that the gun was silenced. Still fully exposed, he then brought machine gun fire to bear on an armed trawler in the harbour, compelling it to withdraw and thus preventing many casualties in the main demolition area.

Under the brilliant leadership of this officer the troops fought magnificently and held vastly superior enemy forces at bay, until the demolition parties had successfully completed their work of destruction.

By this time, however, most of the landing craft had been sunk or set on fire and evacuation by sea was no longer possible. Although the main objective had been achieved, Lieutenant-Colonel Newman nevertheless was now determined to try and fight his way out into open country and so give all survivors a chance to escape.

The only way out of the harbour area lay across a narrow iron bridge covered by enemy machine guns and although severely shaken by a German hand grenade, which had burst at his feet, Lieutenant-Colonel Newman personally led the charge which stormed the position and under his inspiring leadership the small force fought its way through the streets to a point near the open country, when, all ammunition expended, he and his men were finally overpowered by the enemy.

The outstanding gallantry and devotion to duty of this fearless officer, his brilliant leadership and initiative, were largely responsible for the success of this perilous operation which resulted in heavy damages to the important naval base at St. Nazaire.

Few commanding officers have so thoroughly deserved the VC as Lieutenant-Colonel Newman. Many a citation refers to 'outstanding gallantry and devotion to duty', to 'brilliant leadership and initiative', to 'resolution and determination'. Newman displayed all these qualities in abundance and he sustained them for more than five hours. Leading only a small force, he created havoc among the Germans. At no time did he consider saving himself by trying to get on to a boat and head downriver. His charge to attempt to break through to open country was in itself an amazing exploit. Throughout the action, many German troops saw that the British effort centred on the rather large colonel who was obviously giving orders, and although they repeatedly fired at him he remained unwounded. He spent the rest of the war as a POW and his VC was not gazetted until 19 June 1945, after the war in Europe had ended. Back in Britain his heroism at Saint-Nazaire had been assumed but details were required. They were amply provided by the officers and men who had survived.

Newman came from Buckhurst Hill, Chigwell, Essex. After the war he was made an OBE, while the French conferred upon him the Legion d'Honneur and Croix de Guerre. He died in 1972 and is buried at Barham, Kent.

Thomas Frank Durrant

Much of the action during the Saint-Nazaire raid took place on the River Loire once the German defenders realized that the attack had the serious intent of blocking the entrance to the lock and dock. Saint-Nazaire was an important German naval base and all destroyers and patrol boats quickly put out to attack the British flotilla. Virtually every British boat was picked out by searchlights so that fire came from several directions.

Sergeant Frank Durrant, Royal Engineers attached Commandos, was the Lewis gunner on HM Motor Launch 306. Durrant, born at Green Street Green, Farnborough, Hampshire, had joined the Royal Engineers, Regular Army, in February 1937 and in March 1940 had taken part in the expedition to Norway. He was posted to an Independent Commando company later that year and he found it was service he liked. He had always been considered a 'born soldier' and this he proved himself to be on the dangerous night of 28 March 1942, as his VC citation shows.

Sergeant Thomas Frank Durrant, Corps of Royal Engineers, attached Commandos (Green Street Green, Farnborough, Kent)

For great gallantry, skill and devotion to duty when in charge of a Lewis gun in HM Motor Launch 306 in the St. Nazaire raid on the 28th March, 1942.

Motor Launch 306 came under heavy fire while proceeding up the River Loire towards the port. Sergeant Durrant, in his position abaft the bridge, where he had no cover or protection, engaged enemy gun positions and searchlights on shore. During this engagement he was severely wounded in the arm but refused to leave his gun.

The Motor Launch subsequently went down the river and was attacked by a German destroyer at 50–60 yards range and often closer. In this action Sergeant Durrant continued to fire at the destroyer's bridge with the greatest coolness and with complete disregard of the enemy's fire. The Motor Launch was illuminated by the enemy searchlight and Sergeant Durrant drew on himself the individual attention of the enemy guns and was again wounded in many places. Despite these further wounds he stayed in his exposed position, still firing his gun, although after a time only able to support himself by holding on to the gun mounting.

1. Captain Bernard Warburton-Lee, RN, 10 April 1940 (pp. 17–19)

2. Lt-Commander Gerard Roope, RN, 6 April 1940 (pp. 19–20)

3. HMS *Glowworm* rams the the great German cruiser *Admiral Hipper* in a final valiant effort to cripple her

4. Lieutenant Richard Stannard, RN,
28 April–2 May 1940 (pp. 20–1)

5. Captain Edward Fegen, RN,
5 November 1940 (pp. 21–3)
(© Royal Naval Museum)

6. Lieutenant Thomas Wilkinson, RNR,
14 February 1942 (pp. 23–5)

7. Captain Frederick Peters, RN,
8 November 1942 (pp. 25–6)

8. Captain Robert Sherbrooke, RN, 31 December 1942 (pp. 27–8)

9. The shell-torn destroyer HMS *Onslow* on her return to port after the action in which her commander Captain Sherbrooke won the VC

10. The Saint-Nazaire raid, 27–8 March 1942

11. Commander Robert Ryder, RN,
28 March 1942 (pp. 29–31)

12. Lt-Commander Stephen Beattie, RN,
27 March 1942 (pp. 29–32)

13. Able Seaman William Savage, RN,
28 March 1942 (pp. 29–32)

14. The investiture at Buckingham Palace
on 22 June 1945 of five VCs – Lt B. Place,
Lt-Cdr S. Beattie, L/Cpl H. Nicholls,
Lt D. Cameron and (seated) Maj. F. Tilston
of the Canadian Infantry

15. Leading Seaman Jack Mantle, RN,
4 July 1940 (pp. 32–4)

16. Petty Officer Alfred Sephton, RN,
18 May 1941 (pp. 32–5)

17. Lt-Commander Eugene Esmonde, RN,
12 February 1942 (pp. 35–8)

18. Corporal Thomas Hunter, RN,
3 April 1945 (pp. 39–40)

19. Lt-Commander Malcolm Wanklyn, RN,
24 May 1941 (pp. 44–7)

20. Commander Anthony Miers, RN,
4 March 1942 (pp. 48–9)

21. Commander John Linton, RN,
23 March 1943 (pp. 50–1)

22. Lt-Commander Ian Fraser, RN,
31 July 1945 (pp. 51–3)

23. Leading Seaman James Magennis, RN,
31 July 1945 (pp. 51–3)

24. A contemporary artist shows how
Magennis fixed limpet mines to a Japanese
cruiser in Johore Straits

25. Lieutenant Basil Place, RN,
22 September 1943 (pp. 53–6)

26. Lieutenant Donald Cameron, RN,
22 September 1943 (pp. 53–6)

27. Lieutenant Peter Roberts, RN,
16 February 1942 (p. 56)

28. Petty Officer Thomas Gould, RN,
16 February 1942 (p. 56)

ARMY VCs

29. Captain Philip Gardner, Royal Armoured
Corps, 23 November 1941 (pp. 4–5)

30. Gardner's exploit illustrated by a
contemporary artist

31. Captain Philip Gardner (left), with fellow officers and a member of his tank crew in the turret, shortly before the action in which he won the VC

32. Captain Richard Annand, Durham Light Infantry, 15–16 May 1940 (p. 63)

33. CSM George Gristock, Royal Norfolk Regiment, 21 May 1940 (pp. 63–4)

34. Captain Marcus Ervine-Andrews, East Lancashire Regiment, 31 May–1 June 1940 (pp. 64–5)

35. Lance-Corporal Harry Nicholls, 3rd Battalion Grenadier Guards, 21 May 1940 (pp. 65–6)

36. Lieutenant Christopher Furness, 1st Battalion Welsh Guards, 23–4 May 1940 (pp. 66–8)

37. Lieutenant-Colonel Augustus Newman, Essex Regiment attached No 2 Commando, 27 March 1942 (pp. 68–70)

38. Sergeant Thomas Durrant, Royal Engineers, 28 March 1942 (pp. 70–1)

39. Captain Patrick Porteous, Royal Regiment of Artillery, 19 August 1942 (pp. 71–2)

40. Captain Eric Wilson, East Surrey Regiment attached Camel Corps, 11–15 August 1940 (pp. 73–4)

41. Lieutenant George Gunn, 3rd Regiment Royal Horse Artillery, 21 November 1941 (pp. 77–8)

42. Lieutenant-Colonel Geoffrey Keyes, Royal Scots Greys attached 11th Scottish Commando, 17–18 November 1941 (pp. 75–7)

43. He is buried between two private soldiers in Benghazi War Cemetery

44. Rifleman John Beeley, King's Royal Rifle Corps, 21 November 1941 (pp. 78–9)

45. Captain James Jackman, Royal Northumberland Fusiliers, 25 November 1941 (pp. 79–81)

46. Brigadier John Campbell, Royal Horse Artillery commanding 7th Armoured Division, 21–2 November 1941 (pp. 81–3)

47. Lieutenant-Colonel Henry Foote, 7th Royal Tank Regiment, 27 May–15 June 1942 (pp. 83–5)

48. A contemporary artist's impression of Lt-Col. Foote's heroic acts in Libya

49. Private Adam Wakenshaw, Durham Light Infantry, 27 June 1942 (pp. 85-6)

50. Lieutenant-Colonel Victor Turner, Royal Green Jackets, 27 October 1942 (pp. 86–8)

51. Major Herbert Le Patourel, Hampshire Regiment, 3 December 1942 (pp. 88–9)

52. Lieutenant-Colonel Derek Seagrim, 7th Battalion Green Howards, 20–1 March 1943 (pp. 89–91)

53. Lieutenant-Colonel Lorne Campbell, Argyll and Sutherland Highlanders, 6 April 1943 (pp. 91–3)

54. Private Eric Anderson, East Yorkshire Regiment, 6 April 1943 (pp. 93–4)

55. Lieutenant John Anderson, Argyll and Sutherland Highlanders, 23 April 1943 (pp. 94–6)

56. Lieutenant Wilwood Clarke, Loyal North Lancashire Regiment, 23 April 1943 (p. 97)

57. Captain Charles Lyell, 1st Battalion Scots Guards, 22–7 April 1943 (pp. 98–9)

58. Capt. Lyell's grave marker at Bou Arada, Tunisia

59. Lance Corporal John Kenneally, Irish Guards, 28–30 April 1943 (pp. 99–100)

After a running fight, the Commander of the German destroyer called on the Motor Launch to surrender. Sergeant Durrant's answer was a further burst of fire at the destroyer's bridge. Although now very weak he went on firing, using drums of ammunition as fast as they could be replaced. A renewed attack by the enemy vessel eventually silenced the fire of the Motor Launch but Sergeant Durrant refused to give up until the destroyer came alongside, grappled the Motor Launch and took prisoner those who remained alive.

Sergeant Durrant's gallant fight was commended by the German officers on boarding the Motor Launch.

This very gallant Non-Commissioned Officer later died of the many wounds received in action.

The German naval officers who boarded HM Motor Launch 306 did their best for Durrant and sent him to hospital but he had so many serious wounds that there was no hope for him. He is buried in the Commonwealth War Graves Cemetery at Escoublac-la-Baule near Saint-Nazaire. The award of Durrant's VC was not gazetted until 19 June 1945, after the officers and men taken prisoner at Saint-Nazaire had returned home to speak of his heroism and his refusal to surrender. His gallantry was very similar to that of Able Seaman Bill Savage, who also died on the River Loire during the Saint-Nazaire raid.

Dieppe 1942

Patrick Anthony Porteous

On the morning of 19 August 1942 the Allies made an amphibious assault on the port of Dieppe, partly to test the German defences along the 'Atlantic Wall', partly to try out their own tactics. In effect, it was a large raid rather than a serious attack because the entire force consisted of only 5,100 Canadians and 1,000 British Commandos and American Rangers. It was supported by 252 ships, none larger than a destroyer, and 69 squadrons of aircraft.

En route to France, German coastal patrols ran into the raiding force and fought an engagement with some British ships, thus robbing the assault of any element of surprise. Without the support of heavy gunfire from the sea and with only sporadic help from their aircraft, the Canadians suffered terribly. Within six hours three-quarters of them had been killed, wounded or taken prisoner. Dieppe was a débâcle relieved only by the courage of the men involved, though Allied High Command presumably gained invaluable experience of air and naval support, intelligence, communications and tactical operations.

A more cynical view is that the Dieppe raid, Operation Jubilee, was intended to deceive the Germans into thinking that the Allies were planning an invasion. Because it failed – as, according to this theory, it was intending to do – the Germans were deceived about how the Second Front would be created. Thus, the outcome of the Dieppe raid was the one anticipated by the Allied leaders.

Probably more VCs were earned than awarded but few witnesses to the actions survived. However, the exploit of Major Patrick Porteous was witnessed by many. His VC was gazetted on 2 October 1942.

Captain (temporary Major) Patrick Anthony Porteous, Royal Regiment of Artillery (Fleet, Hants)

At Dieppe on the 19th August, 1942, Major Porteous was detailed to act as Liaison Officer between the two detachments whose task was to assault the heavy coast defence guns.

In the initial assault Major Porteous, working with the smaller of the two detachments, was shot at close range through the hand, the bullet passing through his palm and entering his upper arm. Undaunted, Major Porteous closed with his assailant, succeeded in disarming him and killed him with his own bayonet thereby saving the life of a British Sergeant on whom the German had turned his aim.

In the meantime the larger detachment was held up, and the officer leading this detachment killed and the Troop Sergeant-Major fell seriously wounded. Almost immediately afterwards the only other officer of the detachment was also killed.

Major Porteous, without hesitation and in the face of a withering fire, dashed across the open ground to take over the command of this detachment. Rallying them, he led them in a charge which carried the German position at the point of the bayonet, and was severely wounded for the second time. Though shot through the thigh he continued to the final objective where he eventually collapsed from loss of blood after the last of the guns had been destroyed.

Major Porteous's most gallant conduct, his brilliant leadership and tenacious devotion to a duty which was supplementary to the role originally assigned to him, was an inspiration to the whole detachment.

The 26-year-old Porteous, from Fleet, Hampshire, later became a colonel in the Royal Artillery. His VC was one of three awarded for the Dieppe raid; the others went to a Canadian battalion commander and a Canadian chaplain.

CHAPTER SIX

North Africa

When the Italian dictator, Benito Mussolini, declared war on France and Britain on 10 June 1940 he did not expect to have to fight the British in North Africa. Germany had just beaten France and Britain in Europe and Mussolini expected that both countries would surrender. He was only half right. Churchill made it clear that Britain would fight on. Even so, Mussolini did not anticipate much trouble in controlling the Mediterranean and North Africa.

Italy had several colonies in North and north-west Africa and Mussolini built up his military strength there. In August 1940 Churchill sent to North Africa Britain's only armoured brigade. That same month Italian troops from Ethiopia invaded British Somaliland and overran its small garrison. A great Italian army prepared to move from Libya across northern Egypt to seize the Suez Canal and cut Britain's lifeline to Australia, New Zealand and India and the Far East.

This Italian invasion was commanded by Field Marshal Rodolfo Graziani who had 200,000 men and a strong air force. The vanguard of this immense army reached Sidi Barrani and here came to a halt because Graziani was worried about supplying his troops over the Western Desert. Much of the fighting in the next three years took place in this vast and trackless rocky desert with its many wadis that made military manoeuvring so difficult. Control of the Mediterranean coast road was vital. From the British side it began in Alexandria and passed through El Alamein, Mersa Matruh, Sidi Berrani, Bardia, Tobruk, Derna and finally Benghazi.

The Italians built up their strength to about half a million men in Ethiopia and Libya. Field Marshal Wavell could not bring his British forces up to 100,000, yet he had to keep some troops in Sudan, Kenya, Palestine and Iraq.

Somaliland

Eric Charles Twelves Wilson

The first VC of the many North African campaigns went to Captain Eric Wilson, fighting a hopeless and little known war in Somaliland. It was gazetted on 11 October 1940.

Lieutenant (acting Captain) Eric Charles Twelves Wilson, the East Surrey Regiment (attached Somaliland Camel Corps)

For most conspicuous gallantry on active service in Somaliland. Captain Wilson was in command of machine-gun posts manned by Somali soldiers in the key position of Observation Hill, a defended post in the defensive organisation of the Tug Argan Gap in British Somaliland. The enemy attacked Observation Hill on August 11, 1940. Captain Wilson and Somali gunners under his command beat off the attack and opened fire on the enemy troops attacking Mill Hill, another post within his range. He inflicted such heavy casualties that the enemy, determined to put his guns out of action, brought up a pack battery to within seven hundred yards and scored two direct hits through the loopholes of his defences, which, bursting within the post, wounded Captain Wilson severely in the right shoulder and in the left eye, several of his team being also wounded. His guns were blown off their stands but he repaired and replaced them and, regardless of his wounds, carried on, whilst his Somali sergeant was killed beside him.

On August 12th and 14th the enemy again concentrated field artillery fire on Captain Wilson's guns, but he continued, with his wounds untended, to man them.

On August 15th two of his machine-gun posts were blown to pieces, yet Captain Wilson, now suffering from malaria in addition to wounds, still kept his own post in action.

The enemy finally over-ran the post at 5 pm on the 15th August when Captain Wilson, fighting to the last, was killed.

The citation killed off the 28-year-old Wilson prematurely. He survived not only his wounds but the acute malaria from which he was suffering at the time. The Italians took him prisoner but he was freed later when British forces captured Eritrea from them. It was understandable, in the confused conditions of 1940, that he was thought to have been killed in action.

On his release from the Italians, Wilson served for a year in North Africa with the Long Range Desert Group as the unit's adjutant. After a period in Britain, he served as second in command in the 11th King's African Rifles in the advance down the Kabaw Valley to the River Chindwin. Down-graded for medical reasons, he commanded as a lieutenant-colonel at the Infantry Training Centre at Jinja, Uganda. The war ended while he was there.

On to the Western Desert

In December 1940 General O'Connor masterminded a series of bold movements to strike the Italians at their weakest and most isolated posts. With speed that emulated the attacks of the Germans in Europe he captured Sidi Barrani and Bardia and, in January 1941, Tobruk. The British took prisoner

90,000 Italians and at Beda Fomm took another 113,000 prisoners. At Tobruk Corporal John Edmondson (see pp. 8–9) won a posthumously awarded VC.

The Germans had not yet entered the war in North Africa and when Mussolini's campaign in Greece stalled Hitler moved to help his weaker ally. Strong German forces swept through Yugoslavia, Greece and Crete between 6 April and 27 May. No British VCs were won here, but a New Zealander won a VC in Greece and two other New Zealanders were awarded the decoration for exploits in Crete.

Hitler sent two Panzer divisions to Libya under General Erwin Rommel. Hitler's plan for Africa was to back the Italians just enough to keep them in the war, and Rommel, at that time under the Italian High Command, was ordered not to undertake offensive action. Rommel, however, was not a defensive general and he saw great opportunities to engage offensively in a war of armoured movement. Intuition told him that the British forces were weak because Wavell had been forced, under political pressure, to send troops to Greece, Crete and East Africa and, if Churchill had his way, he would soon be sending them to Syria as well. Rommel planned a pincers movement to link up with the German forces pouring into the Russian Caucasus.

At El Agheila, on 31 March 1941, Rommel struck. The Germans captured General O'Connor, a great loss to the British effort, and knocked out most of the British armour. The Australian 9th Division held Tobruk, making it a thorn and irritant for Rommel. Meanwhile, both sides engaged in much planning and in building up supplies. The VCs won from this time on were earned against a desert background, where it was difficult to find concealment from view and cover from fire. However, 'desert' is a misleading term since it seems to imply vast areas of shifting sand and little else. In fact, much of the battlefield of North Africa consisted of rocky and uneven ground, from which grew millions of small and spiky thorn bushes. The coastal beaches were wide and sandy but from Tobruk westwards lay a steep escarpment which was itself the edge of a wide plateau. In general, the terrain lent itself to open warfare but the climate was hot, steamy and enervating by day and cold by night, even in mid-summer. Without cloud cover, the ground quickly lost its heat.

Egypt–Libya VCs

Geoffrey Charles Tasker Keyes

The British High Command, both political and military, recognized that Rommel, the most brilliant of German generals, posed a great threat and the decision was taken to send Commandos to snatch him from his house at Beda Littoria, Libya, or to kill him if that became essential. Three other Commando assaults, all far behind enemy lines, were planned to coincide with the attempt to capture Rommel. The targets were Italian HQ at Cyrene, the Italian intelligence centre at Apollonia, and telephone communications.

Six officers and 53 other ranks of Scottish Commando were to reach their operational area in two submarines, HMS *Torbay* and HMS *Talisman*, and make their raids from the beach. In overall command was Colonel J.R. Laycock, while Lieutenant-Colonel Geoffrey Keyes, with a captain and 17 other ranks, would raid Rommel's house. On the night of 17 November 1941, in heavy rain, Keyes and his men were ready for zero hour, which was to be 11.59 p.m. What happened after this is described in the citation for his posthumously awarded VC, gazetted on 19 June 1942.

Major (temporary Lieutenant-Colonel) Geoffrey Charles Tasker Keyes MC, the Royal Scots Grays (2nd Dragoons), Royal Armoured Corps

Lieutenant-Colonel Keyes commanded a detachment of a force which landed some 250 miles behind the enemy lines to attack Headquarters, Base Installations and Communications.

From the outset Lieutenant-Colonel Keyes deliberately selected for himself the command of the detachment detailed to attack what was undoubtedly the most hazardous of these objectives – the residence and Headquarters of the General Officer Commanding the German forces in North Africa. This attack, even if initially successful, meant almost certain death for those who took part in it.

He led his detachment without guides, in dangerous and precipitous country and in pitch darkness, and maintained by his stolid determination and powers of leadership the morale of the detachment. He then found himself forced to modify his original plans in the light of fresh information elicited from neighbouring Arabs, and was left with only one officer and an NCO with whom to break into General Rommel's residence and deal with the guards and Headquarters Staff.

At zero hour on the night of 17th–18th November, 1941, having despatched the covering party to block the approaches to the house, he himself with the two others crawled forward past the guards, through the surrounding fence and so up to the house itself. Without hesitation he boldly led his party up to the front door, beat on the door and demanded entrance.

Unfortunately, when the door was opened, it was found impossible to overcome the sentry silently, and it was necessary to shoot him. The noise of the shot naturally aroused the inmates of the house and Lieutenant-Colonel Keyes, appreciating that speed was now of utmost importance, posted the NCO at the foot of the stairs to prevent interference from the floor above.

Lieutenant-Colonel Keyes, who instinctively took the lead, emptied his revolver with great success into the first room and was followed by the other officer who threw a grenade.

Lieutenant-Colonel Keyes with great dash then entered the second room on the ground floor but was shot almost immediately on flinging open the door and fell back into the passage mortally wounded. On being carried outside by his companions he died within a few minutes.

By his fearless disregard of the great dangers which he ran and of which he was fully aware, and by his magnificent leadership and outstanding gallantry, Lieutenant-Colonel Keyes set an example of supreme self-sacrifice and devotion to duty.

Keyes's raid, one of the most outstanding adventures of the war, deserved a better result. He was not to know that Rommel was absent from the house at the time. The 24-year-old officer, from Buckinghamshire, is buried in the Commonwealth War Graves Commission Cemetery, Benghazi, Libya.

Three German lieutenant-colonels of Rommel's staff and a number of other Germans were killed and much damage was done to the building. Colonel Laycock and Sergeant Terry were the only members of the Commando raiding party to reach British lines safely, 41 days after they had set out on their adventure. Some of the others were taken prisoner and survived the war. For the record, it must be said that it was not Keyes who knocked at the door and demanded admission but the German-speaking Captain Campbell and it was Campbell who shot the enemy soldier who opened the door.

George Ward Gunn

On the very day that Lieutenant-Colonel Keyes made his raid on Rommel's house, General Sir Claude Auchinleck, who had replaced Wavell as commander of the Eighth Army, began his major campaign, Operation Crusader. A desperate armoured battle ensued and both sides incurred heavy losses. The Germans had a better anti-tank gun, the 88 mm, and their tanks were stronger. British tactics, too, were inferior. Auchinleck and his subordinate generals divided their forces and committed them piecemeal. This made each sub-formation more vulnerable and more certain to suffer losses.

A number of relatively small but fierce actions took place during this battle as British guns endeavoured to knock out German tanks. A pivotal point during these battles was Sidi Rezegh and its airfield, 20 miles south-east of Tobruk, and both armies strove for possession. Heavy casualties were always inevitable in such battles because towed guns and tank guns were firing at a range of only 800 yards and of even shorter distances should a squadron of tanks rush a British gun position. In such conditions a particular form of stubborn courage was needed to stand to a gun and serve it from behind its flimsy shield.

On 17 November 1941 Second-Lieutenant George Ward Gunn MC, aged 29, of Wirral, Cheshire, was engaged at Sidi Rezegh in a gun duel with an overwhelming force of enemy tanks. The citation for his posthumous VC, gazetted on 21 April 1942, has echoes of many another famous action in which gunner officers and their men have fought to the death.

Second-Lieutenant George Ward Gunn MC, Royal Horse Artillery

On the 21st November, 1941, at Sidi Rezegh, Second-Lieutenant Gunn was in command of a troop of four anti-tank guns which was part of a battery of twelve guns attached to the Rifle Brigade Column. At 10.00 hours a covering force of enemy tanks was engaged and driven off but an hour later the main attack developed by about sixty enemy tanks. Second-Lieutenant Gunn drove from gun to gun during this period in an unarmoured vehicle encouraging his men and reorganizing his dispositions as first one gun and then another was knocked out. Finally only two guns remained in action and were subjected to very heavy fire. Immediately afterwards one of these guns was destroyed and the portée [the ammunition container] of another was set on fire and all the crew killed or wounded except the Sergeant, though the gun itself remained undamaged. The Battery Commander then arrived and started to fight the flames. When he saw this, Second-Lieutenant Gunn ran to his aid through intense fire and immediately got the one remaining anti-tank gun into action on the burning portée, himself sighting it while the sergeant acted as loader. He continued to fight the gun, firing between forty and fifty rounds regardless alike of the enemy fire which was by then concentrated on this one vehicle, and of the flames which might at any moment have reached the ammunition with which the portée was loaded. In spite of this, Second-Lieutenant Gunn's shooting was so accurate at a range of about 800 yards that at least two enemy tanks were hit and set on fire and others were damaged before he fell dead, having been shot through the forehead.

Second-Lieutenant Gunn showed the most conspicuous courage in attacking this large number of enemy tanks with a single unarmoured gun, and his utter disregard for extreme danger was an example which inspired all who saw it. He remained undismayed by intense fire and overwhelming odds, and his gallant resistance only ceased with his death.

But for this very gallant action the enemy tanks would undoubtedly have over-run our position.

Lieutenant Gunn is buried in the Commonwealth War Graves Commission Cemetery, Acroma, Libya.

John Beeley

On the same day that Second-Lieutenant Gunn was engaged in a fight to the death against German tanks, a battalion of the King's Royal Rifle Corps was attempting to capture the Sidi Rezegh airfield. The capture of an airfield is always difficult because, of necessity, it is flat. On normal terrain a trained infantryman can find folds or shallow depressions in the ground, at least deep enough to provide cover for him to slither towards enemy posts. Sidi Rezegh had no such advantage, yet it was essential to capture the airfield so that ammunition, weapons and reinforcements could be flown in.

One company in particular was pinned down, from both flank and front by fire so heavy that all the officers but one and many of the sergeants and corporals had been killed or wounded. It was time for desperate action and the soldier who acted was Rifleman John Beeley, whose posthumous citation for the VC was gazetted on 21 April 1942.

Rifleman John Beeley, the King's Royal Rifle Corps

On the 21st November 1941, during the attack by a Battalion of The King's Royal Rifle Corps at Sidi Rezegh against a strong enemy position, the company to which Rifleman Beeley belonged was pinned down by heavy fire at point-blank range from the front and flank on the flat and open ground of the aerodrome. All the officers but one of the Company and many of the other ranks had been either killed or wounded. On his own initiative, and when there was no sort of cover, Rifleman Beeley got to his feet carrying a Bren Gun and ran forward towards a strong enemy post containing an anti-tank gun, a heavy machine gun and a light machine gun. He ran thirty yards and discharged a complete magazine at the post from a range of twenty yards, killing or wounding the entire crew of the anti-tank gun. The post was silenced and Rifleman Beeley's platoon was enabled to advance, but Rifleman Beeley fell dead across his gun, hit in at least four places.

Rifleman Beeley went to certain death in a gallant and successful attempt to carry the day. His courage and self-sacrifice were a glorious example to his comrades and inspired them to further efforts to reach their objective, which was eventually captured by them, together with 700 prisoners.

Between them Lieutenant Gunn and Rifleman Beeley captured Sidi Rezegh. Rifleman Beeley, a 23-year-old Mancunian, is buried in the Commonwealth War Graves Cemetery of Knightsbridge, Acroma, Libya. His one-man charge exemplified the type of exploit most frequently awarded the VC.

James Joseph Bernard Jackman

One of the British regiments which formed the garrison of Tobruk in 1941 was the 1st Battalion the Royal Northumberland Fusiliers. Under intense pressure from the Germans and Italians, the defenders were forced back into the port town, which was then besieged by the enemy. Earlier, when the Italians had held the place, they created a fortified perimeter 10 miles deep, a strong position with an anti-tank ditch and barbed wire. For the British, life within the perimeter was arduous and uncomfortable, with water strictly rationed. All troops lived in caves or dugouts, but even so they did not escape the frequent raids by Stuka dive bombers.

By autumn 1941 the British High Command had decided on a breakout from Tobruk to link with a general advance of British and Empire forces from the Egyptian frontier. A major objective of the units operating from the Tobruk perimeter was to capture strategic positions, notably the 'Tobruk Corridor' and the Ed Adem escarpment, an east–west feature 8 miles south of Tobruk itself. The difficulties were immense for the Corridor contained twelve enemy strongholds.

The breakout from Tobruk, code-named 'Crusader', began on the night of 19/20 November 1941. Z Company of the Royal Northumberland Fusiliers, under Captain James Jackman, was part of an infantry–tank–artillery force given the task of capturing Ed Duda Ridge. On that morning the initial British attack ran into strong opposition and was stopped dead. Jackman observed what happened and realized that decisive action was needed. He took command of a platoon, under a second-lieutenant, and making a wide circle he attacked the enemy's right flank under shell fire. Reaching and capturing the objective, Jackman routed the defenders. With only one platoon he had achieved what an entire battalion and a tank squadron had failed to do.

The advance on Ed Duda commenced on the afternoon of 26 November, not the 25th as stated in the citation for Captain Jackman's posthumous VC, which was gazetted on 31 March 1942.

Lieutenant (temporary Captain) James Joseph Bernard Jackman, the Royal Northumberland Fusiliers

On 25th November, 1941, at Ed Duda, South East of Tobruk, Captain Jackman showed outstanding gallantry and devotion to duty above all praise when he was in command of a Machine Gun Company of The Royal Northumberland Fusiliers in the Tank attack on the Ed Duda ridge. His magnificent bearing was contributory in a large measure to the success of a most difficult and hard fought action. As the tanks reached the crest of the rise they were met by extremely intense fire from a large number of guns of all descriptions: the fire was so heavy that it was doubtful for a moment whether the Brigade could maintain its hold on the position.

The tanks, having slowed to 'hull-down' positions, settled to beat down the enemy fire, during which time Captain Jackman rapidly pushed up the ridge leading his Machine Gun trucks and saw at once that Anti-Tank

Guns were firing at the flank of the tanks, as well as the rows of batteries which the tanks were engaging on their front.

He immediately started to get his guns into action as calmly as though he were on manoeuvres and so secured the right flank. Then, standing up in front of his truck, with calm determination he led his trucks across the front between the tanks and the guns – there was no other road – to get them into action on the left flank.

Most of the tank commanders saw him, and his exemplary devotion to duty regardless of danger not only inspired his own men but clinched the determination of the tank crews never to relinquish the position which they had gained.

Throughout he coolly directed the guns to their positions and indicated targets to them and at that time seemed to bear a charmed life but later he was killed while still inspiring everyone with the greatest confidence by his bearing.

Jackman had indeed been fortunate earlier in the action but the circumstances of his death were unlucky. He was killed by a splinter from the only enemy mortar bomb to hit his company's position while it was consolidating. It passed through his neck and cut his jugular vein. The importance of his work in capturing Ed Duda Ridge is evident not only from the award of his VC but from the other decorations given to his Z Company. The second in command, Captain Derek Lloyd, and Lieutenant Ward, officer of the platoon Jackman had used on 19/20 November, were each awarded the MC; CSM G. Hughes won the DCM.

Two other soldiers of the company received the DCM and another six the MM. Few infantry companies received so many decorations for a single operation during the Second World War. It seems that Captain Jackman was recommended for the VC for his exploits during the action of 19/20 November; some eyewitnesses stated that his bravery on that occasion had exceeded that which he displayed on 26 November.*

Captain Jackman, who was born in Dunloaghaire, Dublin, was aged 25 when he lost his life; he is buried in Tobruk Cemetery, Libya.

John Charles Campbell

Because the British in North Africa had a three-to-one superiority in the air, Rommel's reconnaissance aircraft were driven off and he was unable to find out exactly where the British troops were. This might seem extraordinary in such open country, but the areas were so vast that space itself 'concealed' entire formations. When General Auchinleck launched his powerful

---

* According to an assessment in *The Seven VCs of Stonyhurst College* (THCL Books, Blackburn, 1987), H.L. Kirby and R.R. Walsh.

Operation Crusader on 17 November 1941 the Germans and Italians were taken by surprise. However, they quickly recovered – particularly the Germans – and fought back. Now took place one of the most confused and hard-fought battles of history, across the enormous and desolate Western Desert, south of Tobruk and Sollum.

One of the most important strategic points of the entire battlefield was Sidi Rezegh, where Lieutenant Gunn and Rifleman Beeley – both to be awarded the VC – lost their lives on 21 November. The British officer commanding at Sidi Rezegh was Brigadier John Campbell DSO, MC of the Royal Horse Artillery, commanding the 7th Armoured Division. The 50-year-old Campbell, who had seen service as a young officer during the First World War, was a seasoned campaigner. No officer in the British Army could have been better qualified to command at Sidi Rezegh on that crucial day in 1941. Since his force was vastly outnumbered by the enemy inspiring leadership and superb tactical skills were needed. Campbell had both, as his citation, gazetted on 3 February 1942, shows.

John Charles Campbell DSO, MC, Royal Horse Artillery

In recognition of most conspicuous gallantry and devotion to duty at Sidi Rezegh on the 21st and 22nd November 1941.

On the 21st November Brigadier Campbell was commanding the troops, including one regiment of tanks, in the area of Sidi Rezegh ridge and the aerodrome. His small force holding this important ground was repeatedly attacked by large numbers of tanks and infantry. Wherever the situation was most difficult and the fighting hardest he was to be seen with his forward troops, either on his feet or in his open car. In this car he carried out several reconnaissances for counter-attacks by his tanks, whose senior officers had all become casualties early in the day. Standing in his car with a blue flag, this officer personally formed up tanks under close and intense fire from all natures of enemy weapons.

On the following day the enemy attacks were intensified and again Brigadier Campbell was always in the forefront of the heaviest fighting, encouraging his troops, staging counter-attacks with his remaining tanks and personally controlling the fire of his guns. On two occasions he himself manned a gun to replace casualties. During the final enemy attack on the 22nd November he was wounded but continued most actively in the foremost positions, controlling the fire of batteries which inflicted heavy losses on enemy tanks at point blank range, and finally acted as loader to one of the guns himself.

Throughout these two days his magnificent example and his utter disregard of personal danger were an inspiration to his men and to all who saw him. His brilliant leadership was the direct cause of the very heavy casualties inflicted on the enemy. In spite of his wound he refused to be evacuated and remained with his command, where his outstanding bravery and consistent determination had a marked effect in maintaining the splendid fighting spirit of those under him.

Brigadier Campbell, from Thurso, Caithness, had in fact been awarded two DSOs, not simply the one referred to in his citation. He was promoted to major general but sadly he died in Libya on 26 February 1942. At least he knew of his VC award. He is buried in the Commonwealth War Graves Commission Cemetery, Cairo, and in All Saints Cathedral, Cairo, there is a plaque to his memory.

Captain Philip Gardner MC, Royal Armoured Corps, was also awarded a VC for valour during the Tobruk–Sidi Rezegh–Ed Duda operations of November 1941 (see chapter 1, pp. 4–5).

Henry Robert Bowreman Foote

After the fighting in North Africa of late 1941 the German-Italian forces were pushed back nearly 300 miles to El Agheila, where Rommel established strong defences. On his right flank he was protected by the Libyan Sand Sea, impassable for the British tanks. In any case, Auchinleck's forces had moved so fast that he needed further large stocks of fuel and ammunition and truck transport before he could attack Rommel.

British Intelligence underestimated the speed and strength of Rommel's build-up. British submarines were sinking hundreds of supply ships in the Mediterranean but many others were getting through to Tripoli, Rommel's main base, under a Luftwaffe umbrella. Auchinleck was also frustrated by the slow progress being made in capturing the Italian fortresses of Bardia and Sollum, which did not surrender until 17 January 1942. However, Auchinleck had a third problem – his own convoys were not getting through to Alexandria and Suez in sufficient numbers to reinforce his army with men, armaments and supplies.

Rommel struck first, attacking on 21 January. His thrust was dynamic and well planned and his principal initial objective was to capture British dumps of fuel supplies. His tanks, which were still superior to their British equivalents, overran the dumps before the British troops could destroy them. Then, at the end of January, Rommel captured the important town of Benghazi. Meanwhile, the British, working desperately hard, had established a new defensive line at Gazala. The Afrika Korps stopped here, not because the Gazala Line was strong – it was thin and vulnerable – but because Rommel had to wait for supplies to catch up with his vanguard troops.

A stand-off developed, with both sides positioned behind ever stronger lines. In the air the RAF flew thousands of sorties against Axis supply lines and blew up dumps and fuel stores. Rommel became increasingly anxious because he knew from spies, air reconnaissance and interrogation of prisoners that British strength was outstripping his own. On the night of

27/28 May 1942 he began what soon became known as the Battle of Knightsbridge, the name of a road junction. More precisely, it was the battle of Knightsbridge–Gazala–Bir Hacheim. It was on this line, in the fierce fighting over what the British troops aptly called 'The Cauldron', that the British Army won its next North African VC.

The recipient was Lieutenant-Colonel Henry Foote DSO of the Royal Tank Regiment and, unusually, his citation, gazetted on 18 May 1944, specified valour over a period of nearly three weeks, between 27 May, the day when Rommel's offensive began and 15 June. This lengthy period reflects not only Foote's sustained effort but the intensity of the fighting.

Major (temporary Lieutenant-Colonel) Henry Robert Bowreman Foote DSO, Royal Tank Regiment, Royal Armoured Corps

For outstanding gallantry during the period 27th May to 15th June, 1942.

On the 6th June, Lieutenant-Colonel Foote led his Battalion, which had been subjected to very heavy artillery fire, in pursuit of a superior force of the enemy. While changing to another tank after his own had been knocked out, Lieutenant-Colonel Foote was wounded in the neck. In spite of this he continued to lead his Battalion from an exposed position on the outside of a tank.

The enemy, who were holding a strongly entrenched position with anti-tank guns, attacked his flank. As a further tank had been disabled he continued on foot under intense fire encouraging his men by his splendid example. By dusk, Lieutenant-Colonel Foote by his brilliant leadership had defeated the enemy's attempt to encircle two of our Divisions.

On 13th June, when ordered to delay the enemy tanks so that the Guards Brigade could be withdrawn from the Knightsbridge escarpment and when the first wave of our tanks had been destroyed, Lieutenant-Colonel Foote reorganized the remaining tanks, going on foot from one tank to another to encourage the crews under intense artillery and anti-tank fire.

As it was of vital importance that his Battalion should not give ground, Lieutenant-Colonel Foote placed his tank, which he had then entered, in front of the others so that he could be plainly visible in the turret as an encouragement to the other crews, in spite of the tank being badly damaged by shell fire and all its guns rendered useless. By his magnificent example the corridor was kept open and the Brigade was able to march through.

Lieutenant-Colonel Foote was always at the crucial point at the right moment, and over a period of several days gave an example of outstanding courage and leadership which it would have been difficult to surpass. His name was a by-word for bravery and leadership throughout the Brigade.

Despite the gallantry and skill of the 38-year-old Colonel Foote, from Edgbaston, Birmingham, most of the British actions within the greater Battle of Knightsbridge–Gazala–Bir Hacheim were failures. Rommel's powerful tanks, with their 88 mm guns, crushed brave resistance. When the Afrika Korps crushed the Free French at Bir Hacheim on 11 June the entire British left wing collapsed. On many occasions British tanks were lured into ambushes and smashed by the 88s, so that by 13 June only 65 tanks remained. Tobruk was captured from the South Africans and with it huge quantities of stores. The broken Eighth Army headed for Egypt.

Adam Herbert Wakenshaw

A rearguard garrison courageously held a line at and south of Mersa Matruh. The Afrika Korps and its Italian allies had inflicted 80,000 casualties, including prisoners, on the British and it was the rearguard's mission to give cover to those men still retreating and to slow down and perhaps stop Rommel's relentless advance. Every man in the rearguard understood the risks he ran from enemy tanks and mobile guns. The men took some comfort from knowing that their positions had been skilfully sited, while anti-tank guns forward of infantry were in slit trenches and behind barbed wire. Among the rearguard troops was Private Adam Wakenshaw, from Newcastle upon Tyne, a member of the Durham Light Infantry. His citation for the award of a posthumous VC, gazetted on 11 September 1942, provides a classic example of the risks run by a rearguard when giving battle to a pursuing army.

Private Adam Herbert Wakenshaw, the Durham Light Infantry

On the 27th June, 1942, South of Mersa Matruh, Private Wakenshaw was a member of the crew of a 2-pounder anti-tank gun that was sited on a forward slope in front of the infantry position.

Shortly after dawn the enemy attacked and an enemy tracked vehicle towing a light gun was brought to within short range of the position. The gun crew opened fire and succeeded in putting a round through the engine immobilising the enemy vehicle.

Another mobile gun then came into action. All members of the crew manning the 2-pounder including Private Wakenshaw were killed or seriously wounded and the 2-pounder was silenced. In this respite the enemy moved forward towards their damaged tractor in order to get the light gun into action against our infantry.

Realising the danger to his comrades, under intense mortar and artillery fire which swept the gun site, Private Wakenshaw crawled back to his gun. Although his left arm was blown off above the elbow, he loaded the gun with one arm and fired five more rounds. These succeeded in setting the tractor on fire and damaged the light gun. A near miss then killed the gun aimer and blew Private Wakenshaw away from the gun, giving him further severe wounds. Undeterred he slowly dragged himself back to the gun, placed a round in the breech, and was preparing to fire when a direct hit on the ammunition killed him and destroyed the gun.

In the evening after the action, the body of Private Wakenshaw was found stretched out at the back of the breach block beside the ammunition box.

This act of conspicuous gallantry prevented the enemy from using their light gun on the infantry Company which was only 200 yards away. It was through the self-sacrifice and courageous devotion to duty of this infantry anti-tank gunner that the Company was enabled to withdraw and to embus in safety.

Private Wakenshaw was not the only Second World War British serviceman to complete an exploit, later recognized with a VC, while bleeding to death with a limb torn off, but his fortitude was remarkable. To load five rounds in the gun breach despite such appalling wounds shows truly remarkable determination. Wakenshaw, who was 28 when he died, is buried in the Commonwealth War Graves Commission Cemetery at El Alamein.

Victor Buller Turner

Late in August 1942 General Sir Harold Alexander replaced Auchinleck while General Sir Bernard Montgomery assumed command of the Eighth Army. First he defeated Rommel's thrust at Alam Halfa in September and then he massed men, weapons and equipment for his next move. This was the second Battle of Alamein, which began on 23 October 1942. There followed a 13-day battle of attrition, in which the British and Empire troops, now strengthened by American Grant tanks, did not once lose the initiative. During this battle infantry battalions were able to manoeuvre across open though sometimes deeply fissured ground in a way that had not previously been possible.

The lieutenant-colonel commanding a battalion, with his HQ staff around him, was able to manage his companies on an almost totally visual basis. In such circumstances the success of a battalion largely depended on the vigour and enterprise of its CO. On 27 October, when the Battle of Alamein was at its height, a battalion of the Rifle Brigade was sent a considerable distance into the battlefield on a mission to capture and occupy a strategic objective, code-named 'Snipe'. It was commanded by Lieutenant-Colonel Victor Turner, a 42-year-old regular soldier from Thatcham, Berkshire.

Turner was already renowned in the Eighth Army. In what became famous as 'the Benghazi handicaps' – the changing fortunes of the British and Axis armies – he was later taken prisoner and was assumed to be lost for the rest of the war. But with support from other prisoners he turned on his captors, took them prisoner and arrived back in his own lines with several trucks full of enemy soldiers.

The citation for the award of his VC was gazetted on 20 November 1942.

Major (temporary Lieutenant-Colonel) Victor Buller Turner, the Rifle Brigade (Prince Consort's Own)

For most conspicuous gallantry and devotion to duty on the 27th October, 1942, in the Western Desert.

Lieutenant-Colonel Turner led a Battalion of the Rifle Brigade at night for 4,000 yards through difficult country to their objective, where 40 German prisoners were captured. He then organised the captured position for all-round defence; in this position he and his Battalion were continuously attacked from 5.30 am to 7 pm, unsupported and so isolated that replenishment of ammunition was impossible owing to the concentration and accuracy of the enemy fire.

During this time the Battalion was attacked by not less than 90 German tanks which advanced in successive waves. All of these were repulsed with a loss to the enemy of 35 tanks which were in flames, and not less than 20 more which had been immobilised.

Throughout the action Lieutenant-Colonel Turner never ceased to go to each part of the front as it was threatened. Wherever the fire was heaviest, there he was to be found. In one case finding a solitary six-pounder gun in action (the others being casualties) and manned only by another officer and a Sergeant, he acted as loader and with these two destroyed 5 enemy tanks. While doing this he was wounded in the head, but he refused all aid until the last tank was destroyed.

His personal gallantry and complete disregard of danger as he moved about encouraging his Battalion to resist to the last, resulted in the infliction of a severe defeat on the enemy tanks. He set an example of leadership and bravery which inspired his whole Battalion and which will remain an inspiration to the Brigade.

The citation gives some figures, for instance, that 90 German tanks attacked the Rifle Brigade's positions, but perhaps a more meaningful 'statistic' is that Turner and his men destroyed or disabled 58 enemy tanks and self-propelled guns, an average of three to each of the battalion's 19 6-pounder guns. During the fifth enemy attack Turner and his gunners at one defensive point had only four rounds left to fight off three tanks. Steeling their nerves, they fired at virtually point-blank range and knocked out all three. In the sixth assault 30 tanks attacked another arc of the Rifle Brigade's position but stopped when the anti-tank gunners set fire to nine of them. Finally, 15 tanks charged the defenders, who had only three guns still serviceable. They hit and stopped six tanks and the remainder withdrew, not to return. Turner's exploit during 'Snipe' had been remarkable by any standards.

Tunisia

Herbert Wallace Le Patourel

With the Western Desert battles of October and November behind them, the British Eighth Army pursued the Afrika Korps and the Italian Army west towards Tunisia. General Montgomery's pursuit was not as vigorous as his punch at Alamein had been and the Germans and Italians were able to extricate a considerable part of their force.* From Tripoli, their main base, they took with them immense quantities of stores and ammunition.

The town and fortifications of Tebourba, 12 miles west of Tunis, was essential for either the defence or attack of Tunis. It lay in river plains backed by hills and had a bridge over the River Medjerda. The British seized the position on 27 November 1942 and the Axis units then fought vigorously to recover it. The Hampshire Regiment was heavily engaged in this bitter fighting and it was here that Major Herbert Le Patourel so distinguished himself that he was awarded the VC. His 'posthumous' citation was gazetted on 9 March 1943.

Captain (temporary Major) Herbert Wallace Le Patourel, the Hampshire Regiment

For conspicuous gallantry in action in the Tebourba area on the 3rd December 1942.

On the afternoon of the 3rd December 1942, the enemy had occupied an important high feature on the left of the Company commanded by this officer. Counter-attacks by a Company of another Battalion and detachments of Major Le Patourel's Company had been unable to regain the position. This officer then personally led four volunteers under heavy fire to the top in a last attempt to dislodge several enemy machine guns. The party was heavily engaged by machine gun fire and Major Le Patourel rallied his men several times and engaged the enemy, silencing several machine gun posts.

Finally when the remainder of his party were all killed or wounded, he went forward alone with a pistol and some grenades to attack enemy

---

* In 1967 Montgomery admitted to me that he should have closely pursued the Afrika Korps and crushed it. That he did not do so, he said, was because he feared heavy casualties among his own troops. He still had shocking memories of the slaughter of the First World War.

machine guns at close quarters and from this action he did not return. From reports received from wounded men, this officer died of wounds.

Major Le Patourel's most gallant conduct and self-sacrifice, his brilliant leadership and tenacious devotion to duty in the face of a determined enemy were beyond praise.

The exploit of this 26-year-old officer, who had been born in Guernsey, was reminiscent of several VC exploits from the First World War involving a small party of determined men led by a dynamic officer. However, the wounded soldiers who reported that Le Patourel had died of his injuries were mistaken. Though seriously wounded he was picked up by the Germans who threw the British out of Tebourba the following day, 4 December 1942, and held it until 6 May 1943 when they evacuated it under the pressure of the final British offensive. Le Patourel recovered from his wounds as a prisoner of war and after the war became a brigadier.

Derek Anthony Seagrim

During his retreat from Alamein Rommel had brilliantly reorganized his broken army and had the satisfaction and the comfort of knowing that another German army, under General Von Arnim, by superior tactics, had beaten the Allies in the race for Tunis. Thus Rommel was falling back on the powerful buffer provided by Von Arnim so that his rear was to a large extent protected. He himself arrived near Mareth early in January 1943 and set his engineers to work to strengthen the Mareth Line. It was Rommel's great good fortune that the French had built the Mareth Line fortification system on the Libyan–Tunisian border before 1939. At the time the French were worried that Mussolini had plans to advance from Libya to capture Tunisia. And indeed he had.

The Mareth Line began at the sea near Mareth and ran for about 40 miles inland. Montgomery's advance troops, having travelled 1,500 miles from Alamein, found their way blocked by the Mareth Line on 15 February 1943. Montgomery would have to break through the strong fortifications or make great sweeps into the desert to get around them. Meanwhile, the wily Rommel, supplied with good intelligence reports, knew that the Americans and French, approaching from the west, and the British First Army under General Sir Kenneth Anderson, were in a state of great confusion, particularly with regard to command. Nominally, they came under the command of General Dwight Eisenhower but he had made them subordinate to Anderson.

Rommel at once suggested to Hitler that his Panzer and motorized divisions together with Von Arnim's Fifth Army should attack. Hitler would not put both armies under Rommel's command, a major operational blunder. On his own initiative Von Arnim was prepared to make a limited attack but this did not suit Rommel who launched an offensive on 14 February against the Americans. They, and supporting units of the British First Army, suffered a sharp setback.

Montgomery's Eighth Army was not directly involved in the Tunisian operations until 20 March when he attacked the Mareth Line, only to be thrown back. Montgomery now sent a strong force, spearheaded by the New Zealand Division, westwards into the desert to get around the right flank of the Mareth Line.

Between 20 March and the end of April five officers and two other ranks men of the British Army performed exploits which resulted in the award of the Victoria Cross. That seven VCs, four of them posthumous, were awarded in little more than five weeks indicates the ferocity of the fighting at the Mareth Line and between that position and the enemy's final stand around Tunis.

This was very much an infantry campaign though the foot soldiers were supported by tanks and artillery. For the tanks and all forms of transport the wadis were constant obstacles. These deep gorges or ravines, dry except in the rainy season, were used by the Axis troops as anti-tank obstacles or as gun emplacements. They could only be captured by infantry assault.

The first VC of the 1943 fighting went to Lieutenant-Colonel Derek Seagrim, who commanded the 7th Battalion the Green Howards. His citation, gazetted on 13 May 1943, indicates not only the difficulties he faced but gave warning of those to come as the campaign progressed.

Major (temporary Lieutenant-Colonel) Derek Anthony Seagrim, the Green Howards (Alexandra, Princess of Wales's Own Yorkshire Regiment)

On the night of the 20th/21st March, 1943, the task of a Battalion of the Green Howards was to attack and capture an important feature on the left flank of the main attack on the Mareth Line. The defence of this feature was very strong and it was protected by an anti-tank ditch twelve feet wide and eight feet deep with minefields on both sides. It formed a new part of the main defences of the Mareth Line and the successful capture of this feature was vital to the success of the main attack.

From the time the attack was launched the Battalion was subjected to the most intense fire from artillery, machine-guns and mortars and it appeared more than probable that the Battalion would be held up, entailing failure of the main attack.

Realizing the seriousness of the situation, Lieutenant-Colonel Seagrim placed himself at the head of his Battalion which was, at the time, suffering heavy casualties and led it through the hail of fire.

He personally helped the team which was placing the scaling ladder over the anti-tank ditch and was himself the first to cross it. He led the assault firing his pistol, throwing grenades, and personally assaulting two machine-gun posts which were holding up the advance of one of his Companies. It is estimated that in this phase he killed or captured twenty Germans.

This display of leadership and personal courage led directly to the capture of the objective.

When dawn broke the Battalion was firmly established on the position, which was of obvious importance to the enemy who immediately made every effort to regain it. Every post was mortared and machine-gunned unmercifully and movement became practically impossible, but Lieutenant-Colonel Seagrim was quite undeterred. He moved from post to post organizing and directing the fire until the attackers were wiped out to a man.

By his valour, disregard for personal safety and outstanding example he so inspired his men that the Battalion successfully took and held its objective thereby allowing the attack to proceed.

Lieutenant-Colonel Seagrim subsequently died of wounds received in action.

The 40-year-old colonel died in hospital on 6 April 1943. His brother, Major H.P. Seagrim, was posthumously awarded the GC for gallantry in Burma during the period February 1943 to February 1944. The brothers are the only instance of the VC and GC being awarded to the same family. Both awards were posthumous. Colonel Seagrim, who came from Bournemouth, is buried in the Commonwealth War Graves Commission Cemetery at Sfax, Tunisia. He is commemorated by a plaque in Whissonsett Church, Norfolk.

Lorne MacLaine Campbell

On the day that Colonel Seagrim died in an Army hospital, another battalion commander, Lieutenant-Colonel Lorne MacLaine Campbell, commanding the 7th Battalion the Argyll and Sutherland Highlanders, was given one of the most difficult tasks faced by any British battalion commander during the war. The gallant way in which he carried out his mission earned him the VC, gazetted on 8 June 1943. The citation is one of the longest of the war and is a model of composition. I am sure that many an exploit would have attracted a VC award had it been as convincingly and compellingly written as that for Colonel Campbell. It is no way overblown nor are incidents dramatized, but it provides a description of an event which more senior officers, not there to witness it for themselves, could appreciate and assess. Nobody could fail to be impressed by the 41-year-old colonel's superb leadership and personal valour.

Major (temporary Lieutenant-Colonel) Lorne MacLaine Campbell DSO, TD, the Argyll and Sutherland Highlanders (Princess Louise's Own)

On the 6th April, 1943, in the attack upon the Wadi Akarit position, the task of breaking through the enemy minefield and anti-tank ditch to the East of the Roumana feature and of forming the initial bridgehead for a Brigade of the 51st Highland Division was allotted to the Battalion of the Argyll and Sutherland Highlanders commanded by Lieutenant-Colonel Campbell.

The attack had to form up in complete darkness and had to traverse the main off-shoot of the Wadi Akarit at an angle to the line of advance. In spite of heavy machine-gun and shell fire in the early stages of the attack, Lieutenant-Colonel Campbell successfully accomplished this difficult operation, captured at least 600 prisoners and led his Battalion to its objective, having to cross an unswept portion of the enemy minefield in doing so.

Later, upon reaching his objective he found that a gap which had been blown by the Royal Engineers in the anti-tank ditch did not correspond with the vehicle lane which had been cleared in the minefield. Realizing the vital necessity of quickly establishing a gap for the passage of anti-tank guns, he took personal charge of this operation. It was now broad daylight and under very heavy machine-gun fire and shell fire he succeeded in making a personal reconnaissance and in conducting operations which led to the establishing of a vehicle gap.

Throughout the day Lieutenant-Colonel Campbell held his position with his Battalion in the face of extremely heavy and constant shell fire, which the enemy was able to bring to bear by direct observation.

About 1630 hours determined enemy counter-attacks began to develop, accompanied by tanks. In this phase of the fighting Lieutenant-Colonel Campbell's personality dominated the battlefield by a display of valour and utter disregard for personal safety which could not have been excelled. Realizing that it was imperative for the future success of the Army plan to hold the bridgehead his Battalion had captured, he inspired his men by his presence in the forefront of the battle, cheering them on and rallying them as he moved to those points where the fighting was heaviest.

When his left forward company was forced to give ground he went forward alone into a hail of fire and personally reorganized their position, remaining with the company until the attack at this point was held. As reinforcements arrived upon the scene he was seen standing in the open directing the fight under close range fire of enemy infantry and he continued to do so although already painfully wounded in the neck by shell fire. It was not until the battle died down that he allowed his wound to be dressed. Even then, although in great pain, he refused to be evacuated, remaining with his Battalion and continuing to inspire them by his presence on the field.

Darkness fell with the Argylls still holding their positions, though many of its officers and men had become casualties.

There is no doubt that but for Lieutenant-Colonel Campbell's determination, splendid example of courage and disregard of pain, the bridgehead would have been lost. This officer's gallantry and magnificent leadership when his now tired men were charging the enemy with the bayonet and fighting them at hand grenade range, are worthy of the highest honour, and can seldom have been surpassed in the long history of the Highland Brigade.

Campbell's high reputation in the 51st (Highland) Division was assured even before the Tunisian battle and his VC. Much of the division had been lost during the débâcle that followed the Battle of France in 1940. Campbell had led 200 of his men in a tightly disciplined unit, determined to get himself and them back to Britain. He reconnoitred alone, by night, then collected his men and penetrated the German lines to reach safety. For that enterprise he had been awarded the DSO. Later he was awarded another DSO as well as the American Legion of Merit. Colonel Campbell was born at The Airds, Argyllshire.

Eric Anderson

During the action at Wadi Akarit, in which Lieutenant-Colonel Campbell and his Scots had been so active, a battalion of the East Yorkshire Regiment was also involved. In its ranks was Private Eric Anderson, a stretcher-bearer (or medic) with A Company. Since medics carried long stretchers and wore Red Cross armbands they were obviously non-combatants but this rarely afforded them any protection. When enemy troops in defensive positions fired at attackers they did not try to avoid hitting medics. If one got in the way, that was his bad luck. Sometimes the enemy shot deliberately at a medic, particularly if he happened to be the only man still standing.

The valour which won a posthumous VC for Eric Anderson, a 27-year-old from Bradford, was calculated and cold-blooded. His job was to save lives. His citation, gazetted on 29 July 1943, shows with what courageous conscientiousness he did so.

Private Eric Anderson, the East Yorkshire Regiment (the Duke of York's Own)

On the 6th April, 1943, a Battalion of the East Yorkshire Regiment [the 5th Battalion] was making a dawn attack on a strong enemy locality on the Wadi Akarit with 'A' Company leading.

After some progress had been made and 'A' Company was advancing over an exposed forward slope, it suddenly came under most intense and accurate machine gun and mortar fire from well concealed enemy strong points not more than 200 yards away. Further advance in that direction was impossible and 'A' Company was able to withdraw behind the crest of a hill, with the exception of a few men who were wounded and pinned to the ground by strong and well directed small arms fire.

Private Anderson, a stretcher bearer attached to 'A' Company, seeing these men lying wounded in 'no man's land' quite regardless of his personal safety, went forward alone through intense fire and single-handed carried back a wounded soldier to a place of safety where medical attention could be given. Knowing that more men were lying wounded in the open he again went out to the bullet swept slope, located a second wounded man and carried him to safety.

Private Anderson went forward once again and safely evacuated a third casualty. Without any hesitation or consideration for himself he went out for a fourth time but by now he was the only target the enemy had to shoot at and when he reached the fourth wounded man and was administering such first aid as he could to prepare for the return journey, he was himself hit and mortally wounded.

Private Anderson, by his valour, complete disregard for his personal safety, and courage under fire, probably saved the lives of three of his comrades and his example was an inspiration to all who witnessed his gallant acts.

Eric Anderson is buried in the Commonwealth War Graves Commission Cemetery at Sfax, Tunisia. His immediate superior, Captain R.F. Clark, the Medical Officer of the 5th Yorkshires, wrote to Mrs Anderson to describe how her husband repeatedly went forward under fire to rescue wounded men:

It was on one of these occasions that Private Anderson was mortally wounded and was buried on the ridge, which saw so much of his fine work, beneath the sands of the desert we know so well. I have nothing but admiration for the way in which he conducted himself both in and out of battle. I came to know him well and I found him to be a man of outstanding character, with lofty ideals which he gave his life to uphold. Our small squad [the medical section] has lost a friend we could ill afford to lose, whose dauntless courage and untiring devotion to duty was out of the realms of men to fathom. His memory will always be hallowed in our ranks.

John Thompson McKellar Anderson

To break the German grip on Tunisia and advance to Tunis itself it was necessary for the British to capture Hill 290, known to the Army as

Longstop Hill, sometimes as Christmas Hill. Whoever held this hill controlled the Medjerda Valley. The Eighth Army had first assaulted it on 22–24 December 1942 – the reason it was called Christmas Hill – but had been repulsed.

A new attack, this time by the First Army, was made on 23 April 1943 and one of the main British units involved was 8th Battalion the Argyll and Sutherland Highlanders whose second in command was Major John Anderson. Anderson was a splendid soldier. He was one of the 200 men of the Highland Division brought out of France, at the time of Dunkirk, by Lieutenant-Colonel Lorne Campbell VC and in North Africa he had already been awarded the DSO for gallantly leading a company in action. He was still only 25 years of age at the time of his greatest military trial on 23 April 1943.

His VC citation, gazetted on 29 June 1943, and other reports of the Longstop action indicate that here was an operation whose success was due to just one man. The history of VC awards relates many astonishing occasions when one man captured a machine gun to win a small and local tactical victory but Major Anderson's feat was to capture an entire enemy position that was barring an army's progress.

Lieutenant (temporary Captain) (acting Major) John Thompson McKellar Anderson DSO, the Argyll and Sutherland Highlanders (Princess Louise's Own)

For conspicuous gallantry and outstanding devotion to duty during the attack on 'Longstop' Hill, Tunisia, on the 23rd April 1943.

Over a period of five hours Major Anderson led the attack through intense enemy machine-gun and mortar fire. As leading Company Commander he led the assault on the Battalion's first objective, in daylight, over a long expanse of open sloping hillside and most of the time without the effective cover of smoke. Enemy infantry opposition was most determined and very heavy casualties were sustained, including all other rifle Company Commanders, before even the first objective was reached.

On the first objective and still under continual enemy fire, Major Anderson reorganized the Battalion and rallied men whose Commanders, in most cases, had been either killed or wounded. The Commanding Officer having been killed, he took command of the Battalion and led the assault on the second objective. During this assault he received a leg wound, but in spite of this he carried on and finally captured 'Longstop' Hill with a total force of only four officers and less than forty other ranks. Fire had been so intense during this stage of the attack that the remainder of the Battalion were pinned down and unable to advance until Major Anderson had successfully occupied the hill.

During the assault, he personally led attacks on at least three enemy machine-gun positions and in every case was the first man into the enemy pits; he also led a successful attack on an enemy mortar position of four mortars defended by over thirty of the enemy.

Major Anderson's force on the hill captured about 200 prisoners and killed many more during the attack. It is largely due to this officer's bravery and daring that 'Longstop' Hill was captured, and it was the inspiration of his example which encouraged leaderless men to continue the advance.

Encouraging 'leaderless men to continue the advance' is the key element of leadership at a time of acute crisis, when casualties are heavy and defeat is imminent. At this moment the most dynamic boldness is required. At Longstop Hill, John ('Jack') Anderson provided it. From Bagshot, Surrey, Anderson went on to fight in Italy where, at Termoli, he was killed on 5 October 1943. He is buried in the Sangro River Commonwealth War Graves Commission Cemetery.

Since this book is an analysis of the courage and leadership required to be 'noticed' for the award of a VC, it is instructive to read the citation for John Anderson's DSO, also awarded for an exploit in Tunisia.

In command of 'Y' Company on the 3rd March, 1943, at Hunts Gap, this officer led his Company with great skill and determination and forced the Germans back to the reverse slope pressing them closely to the rocks and cliffs to within a hundred yards. The company was unable to dislodge the enemy who were above them but held them and prevented them from threatening the flank of 'X' Company on the lower feature. Captain Anderson led his men personally and appeared to them to bear a charmed life. He walked calmly along in enemy machine gun and mortar fire. One mortar bomb burst beside him and killed or wounded those immediately next to him. During the fighting he took command of a Section and personally led it to out-flank the enemy position. He took over the Bren gun of this section and effectively dealt with an enemy machine gun post in face of rifle and machine gun fire. He recovered a light machine gun dropped by the No 1 who was wounded and restored it to the Section Commander.

His Company Sergeant Major, Ian McIntosh, said that after the mortar bomb explosion 'Captain Anderson came walking out of the slope just scratching his leg and walked on. He was an inspiration to everyone.' The CSM also reported that Anderson crawled out 50 yards with a lieutenant to bring in a wounded man and that later he, with a corporal, scoured the hill in front of the Germans and brought in seven of his wounded men and their weapons. The DSO citation and other evidence of Anderson's outstanding behaviour in the same action strongly suggest that this should have been regarded as a VC rather than as a DSO exploit.

Wilwood Alexander Sandys Clarke

While Longstop Hill, where Major John Anderson had been prominent, was the main tactical feature on the British Tunisian front, there were several minor ones on either side of it. One of these was Guiriat El Atach, the name given to a tiny settlement, now in ruins, and to a low hill feature. From this position German machine gunners commanded a wide part of the front on which the British were attacking.

On 23 April 1943, the Loyal Regiment was on the flank of the Argyll and Sutherland Highlanders when, just after dawn, a critical situation developed. Once again a quick-thinking junior officer came to the fore to turn defeat into victory. He was 23-year-old Lieutenant Wilwood Clarke, whose citation for a posthumous VC was gazetted on 29 June 1943. (The citation incorrectly gives his first name as Willward.)

Lieutenant Willward Alexander Sandys Clarke, the Loyal Regiment (North Lancashire)

For most conspicuous gallantry in action at Guiriat El Atach on the 23rd April, 1943.

By dawn on that date, during the attack on the Guiriat El Atach feature, Lieutenant Clarke's Battalion had been fully committed. 'B' Company gained their objective but were counter-attacked and almost wiped out. The sole remaining officer was Lieutenant Clarke, who, already wounded in the head, gathered a composite platoon together and volunteered to attack the position again.

As the platoon closed on to the objective, it was met by heavy fire from a machine-gun post. Lieutenant Clarke manoeuvred his platoon into position to give covering fire and then tackled the post single-handed, killing or capturing the crew and knocking out the gun. Almost at once the platoon came under heavy fire from two more machine-gun posts. Lieutenant Clarke again manoeuvred his platoon into position and went forward alone, killed the crews or compelled them to surrender and put the guns out of action. This officer then led his platoon on to the objective and ordered it to consolidate. During consolidation, the platoon came under fire from two sniper posts. Without hesitating, Lieutenant Clarke advanced single-handed to clear the opposition but was killed outright within a few feet of the enemy.

This officer's quick grasp of the situation and his brilliant leadership undoubtedly restored the situation whilst his outstanding personal bravery and tenacious devotion to duty were an inspiration to his Company and were beyond praise.

Lieutenant Clarke had been born in Southport, Lancashire, and joined his regiment at Egerton, Lancashire. He is buried in the Commonwealth War Graves Commission Cemetery at Massicault, Tunisia.

The Lord Lyell

That the German and Italian armies continued to hold Tunisia in the face of great pressure from the Allies was testimony to Hitler's obstinacy, the dynamic command first of Rommel and after 23 February of Von Arnim, and to the skill and courage of the veteran troops they led. Even at the end of March 1943 the Germans and Italians still had more than 11 divisions, including surviving units of the old Panzer Army Africa.

Their supply situation was worrying. During January, 22 out of 51 transports had been sunk. Then the airlift organized to supplement the cargoes of sea convoys could bring in only 25,000 of the necessary 80,000 tons of supplies. The Germans used MC323 Gigant motorized gliders but on 22 April Allied fighters shot down 16 of 21 Gigants flying petrol to the Tunisian airfields.

Hitler ordered that quantities of the first Tiger tanks – formidable machines indeed – should be rushed to Tunisia, but some were lost in swampy ground and others were penetrated by rounds fired from Allied tank-attack weapons. About the end of the third week of April, Von Arnim had only 76 tanks still running and his engineers were so desperately short of fuel that they were distilling it from Tunisian wines and spirits.

For the British, New Zealand and American troops on the ground all this meant little because the enemy still had plenty of ammunition for their rifles and machine guns, artillery and mortars.

On the day that British fighters were shooting down the Gigant petrol-tankers, another British officer was beginning a six-day period of outstanding service that led both to the award of the VC and his death. He was Captain the Lord Lyell of the Scots Guards from Kirriemuir, Angus. His citation was gazetted on 12 August 1943.

Lieutenant (temporary Captain) The Lord Lyell, Scots Guards

From the 22nd April, 1943, to 27th April, 1943, Captain The Lord Lyell commanded his Company, which had been placed under the orders of a Battalion of the Grenadier Guards, with great gallantry, ability and cheerfulness. He led it down a slope under heavy mortar fire to repel a German counter-attack on 22nd April, led it again under heavy fire through the Battalion's first objective on 23rd April in order to capture and consolidate a high point, and held this point through a very trying period of shelling, heat and shortage of water. During this period, through his energy and cheerfulness he not only kept up the fighting spirit of his Company but also managed through Radio Telephony, which he worked himself from an exposed position, to bring most effective artillery fire to bear on enemy tanks, vehicles and infantry positions.

At about 18.00 hours on 27th April, 1943, this officer's Company was taking part in the Battalion's attack on Di Bou Arara. The Company was held up in the foothills by heavy fire from an enemy post on the left: this post consisted of an 88 millimetre gun and a heavy machine gun in separate pits. Realizing that until this post was destroyed the advance could not proceed, Lord Lyell collected the only available men not pinned down by fire – a sergeant, a lance-corporal and two guardsmen – and led them to attack it. He was a long way in advance of the others and lobbed a hand grenade into the machine gun pit, destroying the crew. At this point his sergeant was killed and both the guardsmen were wounded. The lance-corporal got down to give covering fire to Lord Lyell who had run straight on towards the 88 millimetre gun pit and was working his way round to the left of it. So quickly had this officer acted that he was in among the crew with the bayonet before they had time to fire more than one shot. He killed a number of them before being overwhelmed and killed himself. The few survivors of the gun crew then left the pit, some of them being killed while they were retiring, and both the heavy machine gun and 88 millimetre gun were silenced.

The Company was then able to advance and take its objective. There is no doubt that Lord Lyell's outstanding leadership, gallantry and self-sacrifice enabled his Company to carry out its task which had an important bearing on the success of the Battalion and of the Brigade.

The 30-year-old Lord Lyell, who had been born at Cadogan Gardens, London, is buried in Massicault Commonwealth War Graves Cemetery, Tunisia. His exploit was similar to that carried out by Major John Anderson on 23 April.

John Patrick Kenneally

By early March 1943 Hitler knew that he could no longer hold Tunisia. He is reported to have said to his staff generals, 'This is the end and Army Group Africa might just as well be brought back.' Two days later he recalled Rommel, who was seriously ill, but he ordered General Von Arnim to fight to the last. Von Arnim did not have the charisma of Rommel but the troops did their best for him and they still resisted the Allied advance, particularly along the lines of approach to Tunis.

The Irish Guards were in the forefront of the attack and at one particular point of tactical importance the actions of one man yet again had a great effect on the entire battle. He was Lance-Corporal John Kenneally, Birmingham-born and a mere 21 years of age. His VC citation was gazetted on 17 August 1943.

Lance-Corporal John Patrick Kenneally, Irish Guards

The Bou feature dominates all ground East and West between Medjez El Bab and Tebourba. It was essential to the final assault on Tunis that his feature should be captured and held.

A Guards Brigade assaulted and captured a portion of the Bou on the 27th April, 1943. The Irish Guards held on to points 212 and 214 on the Western end of the feature, which points the Germans frequently counter-attacked. While a further attack to capture the complete feature was being prepared it was essential for the Irish Guards to hold on. They did so.

On the 28th April, 1943, the positions held by one Company of the Irish Guards on the ridge between points 212 and 214 were about to be subjected to an attack by the enemy. Approximately one Company of the enemy were seen forming up preparatory to attack and Lance-Corporal Kenneally decided that this was the right moment to attack them himself. Single-handed he charged down the bare forward slope straight at the main enemy body, firing his Bren gun from the hip as he did so. This outstanding act of gallantry and the dash with which it was executed completely unbalanced the enemy Company which broke up in disorder. Lance-Corporal Kenneally then returned to the crest further to harass their retreat.

Lance-Corporal Kenneally repeated this remarkable exploit on the morning of the 30th April, 1943, when, accompanied by a Sergeant of the Reconnaissance Corps, he again charged the enemy forming up for an assault. This time he so harassed the enemy, inflicting many casualties, that this projected attack was frustrated: the enemy's strength was again about one Company. It was only when he was noticed hopping from one fire position to another further to the left, in order to support another Company, carrying his gun in one hand and supporting himself on a Guardsman with the other, that it was discovered he had been wounded. He refused to give up his Bren gun, claiming that he was the only one who understood that gun, and continued to fight all through that day with great courage, devotion to duty and disregard for his own safety.

The magnificent gallantry of this NCO on these two occasions, under heavy fire, his unfailing vigilance, and remarkable accuracy were responsible for saving many valuable lives during the days and nights in the forward positions. His actions also played a considerable part in holding these positions and this influenced the whole course of the battle. His rapid appreciation of the situation, his initiative and his extraordinary gallantry in attacking single-handed a massed body of the enemy and breaking up an attack on two occasions, was an achievement that can seldom have been equalled. His courage in fighting all day when wounded was an inspiration to all ranks.

Kenneally later became a company quarter master sergeant in the Irish Guards. His VC was the last awarded in North Africa, as the fighting slowly ended. An Allied combat air fleet of 4,500 machines was so overwhelming that the Luftwaffe abandoned Tunisia and left the German and Italian ground troops to save themselves. The British First Army broke the Axis Tunis–Bizerte front on 6 May and both cities fell next day. Remarkably,

German rearguards resisted for a further week and pulled back into Cape Bon. On 13 May even the most stubborn defenders, short of ammunition and with nothing much left to defend, surrendered. More than 275,000 Axis soldiers were taken prisoner, including the German and Italian commanders. For Mussolini the results of the North African campaigns were calamitous, for he had lost not only the greater part of the Italian Army but much of his empire as well.

For the British Army there had been many reverses and some great triumphs. The VC awards were like pearls strung along a long thread of conflict, each one marking a site of great courage, endurance, sacrifice and valour. There would now be new invasions, new campaigns, in Sicily and Italy.

CHAPTER SEVEN

Italy

Sicily was a stepping stone to Italy and it was used as such by the invading British and American Allies on 10 July 1943. The British Eighth Army went ashore on Sicily's south-east coast and the American Seventh Army on the south coast. General Alfred Guzzoni, the Axis commander, had a combined force of 200,000 men, consisting of about equal numbers of Germans and Italians, and 1,400 aircraft, so he should have been able to mount a spirited resistance. However, much Allied naval activity had deceived him into anticipating the main invasion on the west coast.

At first the Allies made rapid progress but strong German reinforcements poured in from Italy. The British were blocked but Patton's Americans made slow if steady progress, helped by small landings on the coast behind enemy lines. General Hans Hube saw that his entire German army could be cut off and he withdrew it in good order across the Straits of Messina, a manoeuvre completed by 17 August.

At the end of July the Italians turned against Mussolini, who found sanctuary with the Germans. Marshal Badoglio became prime minister and began peace negotiations with the Allies. This was supposed to be a secret but Hitler and his lieutenants found out and rushed ever more troops into Italy, both to prevent an Italian surrender and to strengthen the resistance against the Allied armies even then landing in Italy. Badoglio secretly agreed to surrender on 8 September.

The fighting in Sicily had been intense but no exploits were recognized as being worthy of a VC award. However, it was obvious to all observers – and even more to the Allied commanders – that the Germans intended to fight yard by yard to hold Italy. Once more British troops would be expected to show exemplary valour.

Peter Harold Wright

Early on 9 September 1943 British and American troops of General Mark Clark's Fifth Army waded ashore on the beaches along the coast of the Gulf of Salerno, about 30 miles south of Naples. While the landings were successful, the Allies were surprised to find that the Germans had a division near Salerno. The German commander in Italy, General Kesselring, had anticipated a landing at Salerno, just as he had anticipated one at Taranto, at the foot of Italy.

He was prepared to withdraw from Taranto but he intended to hold Salerno, if only to keep open the routes of escape for those retiring from the toe.

The Germans almost succeeded in pushing the British and Americans back to the shore line on 13 September. General Clark dropped an American parachute regiment behind the enemy lines, while many warships were brought up to pound the Germans' emplacements and their communications. Despite this assistance, supplies were slow to arrive and Salerno was at the maximum range of strategic bombers.

On 20 September 1943, with his divisions from the toe of Italy extricated, Kesselring eased his hold on Salerno. Even so, his troops contested every position that could be held. It was for an exploit at one of these positions, Pagliarolli Hill, near Salerno, that CSM Peter Wright, a splendid 27-year-old soldier from Wenhaston in Suffolk, was awarded the DCM that was later upgraded to the VC.

Warrant Officer Class II (Company Sergeant Major) Peter Harold Wright, Coldstream Guards

In Italy on the 25th September, 1943, the 3rd Battalion Coldstream Guards attacked the Pagliarolli feature, a steep wooded hill near Salerno. Before it reached the crest the right-hand company was held up by heavy spandau and mortar fire and all the officers had become casualties.

CSM Wright, seeing that his company was held up, went forward to see what could be done. Finding that there were no officers left he immediately took charge and crawled forward by himself to see what the opposition was. He returned with the information that three spandau posts were holding them up. He collected a section and put it into a position where it could give covering fire. Single-handed he then attacked each post in turn with hand grenades and bayonet and silenced each one. He then led the company on to the crest but realized that the enemy fire made this position untenable. CSM Wright therefore led them a short way down the hill and up on to the objective from a different direction.

Entirely regardless of enemy fire, which was very heavy, CSM Wright then reorganized what was left of the company and placed them into position to consolidate the objective.

Soon afterwards the enemy launched a counter-attack which was successfully beaten off. Later, with complete disregard of heavy enemy shell-fire on the area of company headquarters and the reverse slopes of the hill and of machine-gun fire from the commanding slopes on the left flank of the position, he brought up extra ammunition and distributed it to the company.

It is due to this Warrant Officer's superb disregard of the enemy's fire, his magnificent leadership and his outstanding heroism throughout the action that his battalion succeeded in capturing and maintaining its hold on this very important objective.

The King having been graciously pleased to approve the award of the Victoria Cross to CSM Wright, the award of the Distinguished Conduct Medal for the same acts of gallantry, announced in the *London Gazette* of the 27th January, 1944 is cancelled.

Only on rare occasions has a lesser award been upgraded to a VC and the case of CSM Peter Wright is the most notable in this respect. Although he had been recommended for the VC, on 27 January 1944 he was awarded the DCM, mainly because the British Commander-in-Chief in Italy, General Alexander, considered Wright's exploit 'not quite up to VC standard'. But other senior officers disagreed, believing that it did merit the supreme award, notably Lieutenant-General Loyd, General Officer Commanding Brigade of Guards. Tactfully, he took up the matter with the Military Secretary and pointed out that Wright's citation compared 'very favourably' with that of many VCs. The Military Secretary blocked this approach but Loyd received support from no less a personage than King George VI who at that time, July 1944, was visiting the Army in Italy. While it was impossible for the King to override General Alexander's decision, Alexander was tactfully told that provided he felt justified in reversing it, the procedure for granting a VC could be followed. With equal sensitivity Alexander wrote on 29 July 1944 to the War Office, 'I have had reason to reconsider this matter and I hereby submit the citation with a recommendation for the award of the Victoria Cross.' Even then, other formalities had to be completed, including cancellation of Wright's DCM. The *London Gazette* made medal history on 7 September 1944 when it published the notice of Wright's VC award and cancellation of his DCM. There can be no doubt that the higher award was merited.

CSM Wright, who came from Mettingham, Bungay, Suffolk, was 27 at the time of his exploit. He died in April 1990.

William Philip Sidney

The Allies made slow progress against German defences during the winter of 1943–4. The steep, mountainous country in that part of Italy was ideal for defence and Kesselring and his subordinates held it tenaciously. In January, on the line of the Rapido River the Americans lost thousands of men but the British breached the Gustav Line near the coast. Kesselring regarded this so seriously that he moved his reserves from around Rome to seal the breach. His action gave the Allies an opportunity on 22 January 1944 to make a landing in force – but against little opposition – at Anzio and Nettuno, 20 miles south of Rome. The landing threatened the rear of the German Gustav Line.

Hitler was furious but decisive. Ordering divisions from Germany, France, northern Italy and Yugoslavia towards the Anzio beachhead, he told his generals to remove 'the Anzio abscess' from the German positions. The British and Americans dug in as General Von Mackensen's Fourteenth Army fell upon them with a great weight of artillery and armour. The situation was desperate. The Germans held the high ground that ringed the beachhead but the Allies had to gain it in order that more men, armour, transport and equipment could be landed for the further campaigns already being planned. Anzio was developing into a cauldron of fire and one of the great battles of the war, with the opposing lines in places only yards apart. It was in this situation that Major William Sidney of the 5th Battalion Grenadier Guards found himself facing a series of crises in the hills and ridges around Anzio. The long citation describing his consequent exploits, for which he was awarded the VC, was gazetted on 30 March 1944.

Captain (temporary Major) William Philip Sidney, Grenadier Guards

For superb courage and utter disregard of danger in the action near Carroceto, in the Anzio Beach Head, in February 1944.

The period 6th–10th February, 1944, was one of critical importance to the whole state of the Anzio Beach Head. The Germans attacked a British Division with elements of six different divisions and a continuous series of fierce local hand-to-hand battles was fought, each one of which had its immediate reaction on the position of other troops in the neighbourhood and on the action as a whole. It was of supreme importance that every inch of ground should be doggedly, stubbornly and tenaciously fought for. The area Carroceto–Buonriposo Ridge was particularly vital.

During the night 7th–8th February Major Sidney was commanding the support company of a battalion of the Grenadier Guards, company headquarters being on the left of battalion headquarters in a gully South-West of Carroceto Bridge. Enemy infantry who had by-passed the forward rifle company North-West of Carroceto heavily attacked in the vicinity of Major Sidney's company headquarters and successfully penetrated into the wadi. Major Sidney collected the crew of a 3 inch mortar firing nearby and personally led an attack with Tommy guns and hand grenades, driving the enemy out of the gully. He then sent the detachment back to continue their mortar firing while he and a handful of men took up a position on the edge of the gully in order again to beat off the enemy, who were renewing their attack in some strength. Major Sidney and his party succeeded in keeping the majority of the Germans out but a number reached a ditch 20 yards in front, from which they could out-flank Major Sidney's position. This officer – in full view and completely exposed – dashed forward without hesitation to a point whence he could engage the enemy with his Tommy gun at point blank range. As a result the enemy withdrew, leaving a number of dead.

On returning to his former position on the edge of the gully, Major Sidney kept two guardsmen with him and sent the remainder back for more ammunition and grenades. While they were away the enemy vigoriously renewed his attack and a grenade struck Major Sidney in the face, bounced off and exploded, wounding him and one guardsman and killing the second man. Major Sidney single-handed and wounded in the thigh kept the enemy at bay until the ammunition party returned five minutes later, when once more they were ejected. Satisfied that no further attack would be made, he made his way to a nearby cave to have his wound dressed, but before this could be done the enemy attacked again. He at once returned to his post and continued to engage the enemy for another hour, by which time the left of the battalion position was consolidated and the enemy was finally driven off. Only then did Major Sidney, by that time weary from loss of blood and barely able to walk, allow his wound to be attended to.

Throughout the next day contact with the enemy was so close that it was impossible to evacuate this officer until after dark. During that time, as before, although extremely weak, he continued to act as a tonic and inspiration to all with whom he came in contact.

Throughout the engagement Major Sidney showed a degree of efficiency, coolness, gallantry and complete disregard for his personal safety of a most exceptional order and there is no doubt that as a result of his action, taken in the face of great odds, the battalion's position was re-established with vitally far reaching consequences on the battle as a whole.

The 35-year-old Major Sidney was son-in-law to Field Marshal Viscount Gort GC. Sidney later became the Viscount De L'Isle KG, GCMG, GCVO. His home was at Penhurst, Kent, except when he was Governor General of Australia, 1961–5. His death occurred in April 1991.

George Allan Mitchell

On 23 January 1944, the day after the Allied landings at and near Anzio, it was essential for the British units to gain a firm foothold on the hills to the rear of the town and beachhead. The ordinary soldier and very often the more junior officers thrown into a completely new area had no idea of the strategy of an operation and little comprehension of the tactics. They knew simply that they were required to attack a hill, a ridge line, a bridge, tunnel, building, village or wood. This was 'the objective', in Army parlance. Sometimes the action of a single man, section, platoon or company was responsible for gaining a great tactical advantage. Unfortunately, only the survivors had a chance of finding out the value of their efforts and courage. One soldier who, single-handed, achieved much but did not live to see the results was Private George Mitchell of the London Scottish, whose exploit took place on the wintry night of 23/24 January 1944. The citation for the award of his posthumous VC was gazetted on 10 August 1944.

Private George Allan Mitchell, the London Scottish (the Gordon Highlanders)

In Italy on the night of 23rd and 24th January, 1944, a Company of the London Scottish was ordered to carry out a local attack to restore the situation on a portion of the main Damiano ridge.

The Company attacked with two platoons forward and a composite platoon of London Scottish and Royal Berkshires in reserve. The Company Commander was wounded in the very early stages of the attack. The only other officer with the Company was wounded soon afterwards.

A section of this Company was ordered by the Platoon Commander to carry out a right flanking movement against some enemy machine guns which were holding up the advance. Almost as soon as he had issued the order he was killed. There was no Platoon Sergeant. The section itself consisted of a Lance-Corporal and three men, who were shortly joined by Private Mitchell, the 2-inch mortarmen from Platoon Headquarters and another private.

During the advance, the enemy opened heavy machine gun fire at point blank range. Without hesitation, Private Mitchell dropped the 2-inch mortar which he was carrying, and seizing a rifle and bayonet charged alone up the hill through intense spandau fire. He reached the enemy machine gun unscathed, jumped into the weapon pit, shot one and bayonetted the other member of the crew, thus silencing the gun. As a result, the advance of the platoon continued but shortly afterwards the leading section was again held up by the fire of approximately two German sections who were strongly entrenched. Private Mitchell, realising that prompt action was essential, rushed forward into the assault firing his rifle from his hip, completely oblivious of the bullets which were sweeping the area. The remainder of his section followed him and arrived in time to complete the capture of the position in which six Germans were killed and twelve made prisoner.

As the section was reorganizing, another enemy machine gun opened up on it at close range. Once more Private Mitchell rushed forward alone and with his rifle and bayonet killed the crew.

The section now found itself immediately below the crest of the hill from which heavy small arms fire was being directed and grenades were being thrown. Private Mitchell's ammunition was exhausted but in spite of this he called on the men for one further effort and again led the assault up the steep and rocky hillside. Dashing to the front, he was again the first man to reach the enemy position and was mainly instrumental in forcing the remainder of the enemy to surrender.

A few minutes later, a German who had surrendered, picked up a rifle and shot Private Mitchell through the head.

Throughout this operation, carried out on a very dark night, up a steep hillside covered with rocks and scrub, Private Mitchell displayed courage and devotion to duty of the very highest order. His complete disregard of the enemy fire, the fearless way in which he continually exposed himself, and his refusal to accept defeat, so inspired his comrades that together they succeeded in overcoming and defeating an enemy superior in numbers, and helped by all the advantages of the ground.

Private Mitchell's exploit can be told here in greater detail than was possible in his citation. The London Scottish, with other British regiments, had earlier made an assault crossing of the Garigliano River, south of Anzio, on the night of 17 January. Now, on the night of 23/24 January, A Company was ordered to make the attack 'to restore the situation' on the main Damiano Ridge. The company went in with two companies forward and a composite battalion of the London Scottish and the Royal Berkshires in reserve. In the early stages of the attack the company commander was wounded and the only other officer was wounded soon after.

The platoon commander of No 9 Platoon (Sergeant Hancock) ordered No 9 Section to make a right flanking movement against some enemy machine guns which were holding up the advance. Barely had he issued this order when he was killed, so the platoon had no designated leader. The section would normally have consisted of a corporal and 10 men, but was now down to a lance-corporal and three men. They were joined not only by Mitchell but by Private Miller, his mate on the 2-inch mortar. The action then continued as described in the citation.

The German who had so treacherously killed Mitchell after surrendering was himself shot by one of Mitchell's comrades. The wounded company commander realized that it would not be possible for the company to occupy the objective before daylight and sent an order to withdraw. Mitchell's section did not receive this order until after he had been killed. It needs to be understood that Mitchell's attack, carried out on a dark night, up the steep and rocky hillside, required outstanding courage.

Mitchell had been born in Highbury, London, but joined the London Scottish from Walthamstow. A regular soldier, he had served with his regiment in Persia (Iran), Iraq, Egypt and Sicily. He was 31 at the time of his death. After the Germans had been pushed back it was safe for War Graves Registration Units to operate and Mitchell's body was found. He is buried in the Commonwealth War Graves Commission New Military Cemetery at Sessa Arunca, overlooking the Garigliano River and the Damiano Mountains, which he had done so much to capture.

Richard Wakeford

Cassino, south-east of Rome and close to the Rapido river, was the scene of some of the most severe fighting in Italy. The Germans had made the town a major position of the Gustav Line, their winter defences. The Rapido always flooded in the spring and so was impassable to tanks and vehicles. Crowning Monte Cassino was an old and magnificent Benedictine monastery, where German troops were said to be stationed in force – though this has never been proved. Allied commanders were in dispute as to whether or not the abbey should be attacked. Some generals pointed out that even if the massive place were wrecked the Germans could still use it. Nevertheless on 15 February 1944 fleets of bombers reduced the abbey to rubble. The Germans at once made the ruins into a more effective strongpoint than respect for its religious use could ever have permitted beforehand. The stronghold and the positions around it would have to be captured by infantry and British, New Zealand, American, Polish and French units were involved in the campaign which was both difficult and bloody. Élite German units, including the Parachute Regiment, defended Cassino and they held to the last every defensive position. The terrain favoured defence and the assaulting troops depended greatly on skilled leadership from junior officers.

On 13 May the Hampshire Regiment was held up during an attack on high ground near Cassino and it was here that Captain Richard Wakeford of the 2nd/4th Battalion displayed the valorous leadership throughout a day's combat that led to his being awarded the VC. His citation was gazetted on 13 July 1944.

Lieutenant (temporary Captain) Richard Wakeford, the Hampshire Regiment

On 13th May, 1944, Captain Wakeford commanded the leading Company on the right flank of an attack on two hills near Cassino, and accompanied by his orderly and armed only with a revolver, he killed a number of the enemy and handed over 20 prisoners when the Company came forward.

On the final objective a German officer and 5 other ranks were holding a house. After being twice driven back by grenades, Captain Wakeford, with a final dash, reached the window and hurled in his grenades. Those of the enemy who were not killed or wounded surrendered.

Attacking another feature on the following day, a tank became bogged on the start line, surprise was lost and the leading infantry were caught in the enemy's fire, so that the resulting casualties endangered the whole operation. Captain Wakeford, keeping his Company under perfect control, crossed the start line and although wounded in the face and in both arms led his men up the hill. Half way up the hill his Company came under heavy spandau fire; in spite of his wounds, he organized and led a force to deal with this opposition so that his Company could get on.

By now the Company was being heavily mortared and Captain Wakeford was again wounded, in both legs, but he still went on and reaching his objective he organized and consolidated the remainder of his Company and reported to his Commanding Officer *before submitting to any personal attention.*

During the seven hour interval before stretcher-bearers could reach him his unwavering high spirits encouraged the wounded men around him. His selfless devotion to duty, leadership, determination, courage and disregard for his own serious injuries were beyond all praise.

Richard Wakeford came from Kensington, London, and was 22 at the time of his exploit. A barrister, he was appointed a Master of the Chancery Division of the Supreme Court in 1964 and he died at Leatherhead in 1972. His many wounds contributed to his relatively early death.

Francis Arthur Jefferson

Another British regiment which took part in the attack on the Gustav Line was the Lancashire Fusiliers. From an infantryman's point of view, the defences of the Gustav Line seemed virtually impregnable. Not only was it dominated by Monte Cassino, it lay behind the Garigliano and Rapido rivers and was linked to what the Germans called their Bernhard and Barbara Lines.

Hitler had ordered Field Marshal Kesselring to hold the Gustav Line 'for ever'. It was not to be seen merely as a way of delaying the Allied advance but of defeating it. Kesselring took the Führer's command seriously and his engineers and pioneers had fortified the line by building concrete gunpits, bunkers and machine-gun posts. Every possible avenue of enemy approach was protected by great spreads of barbed wire and minefields. At strategic points large shelters were built for the troops who would be used to make counter-attacks against the Allies.

The Lancashire Fusiliers were deployed in a significant attack made on 16 May 1944. In their ranks was 22-year-old Fusilier Francis Jefferson, whose exploit that day was considered worthy of the VC, which was gazetted on 13 July.

Fusilier Francis Arthur Jefferson, the Lancashire Fusiliers

On 16th May, 1944 during an attack on the Gustav Line, an anti-tank obstacle held up some of our tanks, leaving the leading Company of Fusilier Jefferson's Battalion to dig in on the hill without tanks or anti-tank guns. The enemy counter-attacked with infantry and two Mark IV tanks, which opened fire at short range causing a number of casualties and eliminating one PIAT group entirely.

As the tanks advanced towards the partially dug trenches, Fusilier Jefferson, entirely on his own initiative, seized a PIAT and running forward alone under heavy fire took up a position behind a hedge; as he could not see properly he came into the open and standing up under a hail of bullets fired at the leading tank which was now only twenty yards away. It burst into flames and all the crew were killed.

Fusilier Jefferson then reloaded the PIAT and proceeded towards the second tank, which withdrew before he could get within range. By this time our own tanks had arrived and the enemy counter-attack was smashed with heavy casualties.

Fusilier Jefferson's gallant act not merely saved the lives of his Company and caused many casualties to the Germans but also broke up the enemy counter-attack and had a decisive effect on the subsequent operation. His supreme gallantry and disregard of personal risk contributed very largely to the success of the action.

The Allies smashed through the Gustav Line the following day, 17 May. The breakthrough was not caused by Fusilier Jefferson's exploit but, as his citation records, it had 'a decisive effect on the subsequent operation'. Example matters a great deal on critical days, not only to a brave soldier's comrades but to his enemies. Obviously, the crew of the second German tank were terrified by what had happened to the one attacked by Jefferson. It was not surprising that its commander quickly withdrew when confronted by a determined man armed with a PIAT (Projectile Infantry Anti-Tank). The PIAT was a rocket-launcher which fired a hollow-charge 3½lb projectile up to 400 yards. It gave infantry a powerful, lightweight weapon for use against tanks and fortifications. The recoil from the PIAT used by Fusilier Jefferson knocked him over but he scrambled to his feet and continued his attack. Major Fred Majdalany, who wrote a book about Monte Cassino, said of Jefferson, 'Such men are nice to have around in battles. It was one of those deeds the full implications of which don't really strike you until some time later, then leave you stunned and humble.'

Captain Kevin Hill of the Lancashire Fusiliers' C Company and Major Stuart Derbyshire of D Company won the Military Cross for the way they handled their companies during the Gustav Line fighting, while Military Medals were awarded to Fusilier O.E. McCarthy, Lance-Corporal C. Ranson and Fusilier F. Witherington.

Fusilier Jefferson VC, who came from Ulverston, Lancashire, died in Bolton, Lancashire, on 4 September 1982.

Gerard Ross Norton

After the Allies broke through the Gothic Line, Kesselring's engineers built yet more deep belts of fortifications across Italy's narrow and mountainous waist. They had time to do this because the forward German units held the River Arno in western Italy and the River Metauro in the east. Actually, there were three main strands to the new defences and they were collectively known as the Gothic Line. They were just as strong as the Gustav or Winter Line which had caused the Allies so much trouble during the winter.

Now, however, the Allies were stronger and wiser. During July and August units of the Fifteenth Army group advanced steadily, if slowly, through the German defences. Frequently though, stubborn German defenders clung to their emplacements in the Gothic Line. One of the strongest points in the entire German Line was at Monte Gridolfo, which confronted the 1/4th Battalion the Hampshire Regiment on 31 August 1944. It was here that Lieutenant Gerard Norton MM performed an exploit worthy of the VC and very similar to that of Lieutenant Richard Wakeford VC of the same regiment. His citation was gazetted on 26 October 1944.

Lieutenant Gerard Ross Norton MM, South African Forces attached the Hampshire Regiment

In Italy, on the 31st August, 1944, Lieutenant Norton was commanding a platoon during the attack on the Monte Gridolfo feature, one of the strong points of the Gothic Line defences and one which contained well sited concrete gun emplacements. The leading platoon of his Company was pinned down by heavy enemy fire from a valley on the right flank of the advance.

On his own initiative and with complete disregard for his personal safety, Lieutenant Norton at once engaged a series of emplacements in this valley. Single handed, he attacked the first machine gun position with a grenade, killing the crew of three. Still alone, he then worked his way forward to a second position containing two machine guns and fifteen riflemen. After a fight lasting ten minutes he wiped out both machine gun nests with his Tommy-gun, and killed or took prisoner the remainder of the enemy.

Throughout these attacks Lieutenant Norton came under direct fire from an enemy self-propelled gun and whilst still under heavy fire from this gun he went on to clear the cellar and upper rooms of a house, taking several more prisoners, and putting many of the enemy to flight. Although by this time wounded and weak from loss of blood, he continued calmly and resolutely to lead his platoon up the valley to capture the remaining enemy positions.

Throughout the attack Lieutenant Norton displayed matchless courage, outstanding initiative and inspiring leadership. By his supreme gallantry, fearless example and determined aggression, he assured the successful breach of the Gothic Line at this point.

To breach the Gothic Line, the strongest defences the Germans ever built in Italy, was a considerable feat and it lifted Allied morale while damaging that of the Germans. The 29-year-old Norton, though born in Cape

Province, South Africa, and a member of the Kaffrarian Rifles, was nevertheless attached to the Hampshire Regiment, which claims him as their own. He was later promoted captain in the Hampshires.

Richard Henry Burton

During September and October 1944, long after the D-Day landings of 6 June in France, the Allied troops in Italy were still fighting a much less publicized war. Facing powerful defences and veteran defenders, the Fifteenth Army Group reached to within 15 miles of Bologna, at the southern edge of the Po Valley.

The mountains were high, an exceptionally cold winter set in and fighting became difficult. The troops were exhausted and the High Command decided that further assaults over the terrible and treacherous terrain in winter could only weaken the armies for the final push against Germany in the spring of 1945.

Various changes took place at senior level. General Alexander was promoted Field Marshal and given command of the entire Mediterranean theatre. The American Mark Clark became commander of the Fifteenth Army Group, General Lucian Truscott was appointed leader of the Fifth Army and British General Sir Richard McCreery took over the Eighth Army.

The Fifteenth Army Group was now polyglot in composition, with British, American, New Zealand, Canadian, Newfoundland, South African, Gurkha, Indian, Polish, Italian and Japanese-American units. This remarkably heterogeneous mixture reflects the necessity earlier in the year to send veteran divisions to France for the Allied invasion.

Capturing the higher German positions was extremely difficult and dangerous but they could not be by-passed because they dominated the routes along which the Allied troops were advancing. From these fortified enemy positions, some of them 2,000 feet up, the German observers could call down artillery fire or request that armour be deployed to block the Allied advance.

On 8 October 1944 the 1st Battalion the Duke of Wellington's Regiment (West Riding) was brought up to capture such an enemy position at Monte Ceco. Every man who saw this hill of over 2,200 feet knew that it would be difficult to take and that casualties were likely to be heavy. They were, but not as heavy as they might have been were it not for the courage of Private Richard Burton, whose VC citation was gazetted on 4 January 1945.

Private Richard Henry Burton, the Duke of Wellington's Regiment (West Riding)

In Italy on 8th October, 1944, two Companies of the Duke of Wellington's Regiment moved forward to take a strongly held feature

760 metres high. The capture of this feature was vital at this stage of the operation as it dominated all the ground on the main axis of advance.

The assaulting troops made good progress to within twenty yards of the crest when they came under withering fire from Spandaus on the crest. The leading platoon was held up and the Platoon Commander was wounded. The Company Commander took another platoon, of which Private Burton was runner, through to assault the crest from which four Spandaus at least were firing. Private Burton rushed forward and engaging the first Spandau position with his Tommy gun killed the crew of three. When the assault was again held up by murderous fire from two more machine guns Private Burton, again showing complete disregard for his own safety, dashed forward toward the first machine gun using his Tommy gun until his ammunition was exhausted. He then picked up a Bren gun and firing from the hip succeeded in killing or wounding the crews of the two machine guns. Thanks to his outstanding courage the Company was then able to consolidate on the forward slope of the feature.

The enemy immediately counter-attacked fiercely but Private Burton, in spite of most of his comrades being either dead or wounded, once again dashed forward on his own initiative and directed such accurate fire with his Bren gun on the enemy that they retired leaving the feature firmly in our hands.

The enemy later counter-attacked again on the adjoining platoon position and Private Burton, who had placed himself on the flank, brought such accurate fire to bear that this counter-attack also failed to dislodge the Company from its position.

Private Burton's magnificent gallantry and total disregard of his own safety during many hours of fierce fighting in mud and continuous rain were an inspiration to all his comrades.

It is so rare to find a reference in a citation to 'mud and continuous rain' that we must infer that the officers who drafted Private Burton's citation themselves had to contend with these dreadful conditions, which were made even worse by the onset of winter.

Private Richard Burton, who came from Melton Mowbray, Leicestershire, was 21 at the time of his exploit. He was later promoted corporal. His death occurred in July 1993.

John Henry Cound Brunt

During November 1944, rains turned the battlefield into a ghastly morass. Allied losses were high, the Eighth Army losing 14,000 killed and wounded on the Adriatic coastal plains. The Canadians, in the van, captured Ravenna on 5 December but they suffered more heavily than any other divisions. The

Fifth Army, responsible for the centre sector, reached to within 9 miles of Bologna but suffered 15,000 killed and wounded. General Vietinghoff, who had replaced Kesselring as German commander in Italy, saw that the Fifth Army had been weakened and launched a counter-offensive that regained some of the ground the Germans had lost in September. That December conditions could hardly have been worse for fighting men, which makes the exploit of Captain John Brunt of the Sherwood Foresters all the more remarkable. In my opinion, his citation, gazetted on 8 February 1945, should have included mention of the terrain and the weather. Unfortunately, these matters were not known to the people who wrote up citations at distant headquarters.

Lieutenant (temporary Captain) John Henry Cound Brunt MC, the Sherwood Foresters (Nottinghamshire and Derbyshire Regiment)

In Italy, on the 9th December, 1944, the Platoon commanded by Captain Brunt was holding a vital sector of the line.

At dawn the German 90 Panzer Grenadier Division counter-attacked the Battalion's forward positions in great strength with three Mark IV tanks and infantry. The house, around which the Platoon was dug in, was destroyed and the whole area was subjected to intense mortar fire. The situation then became critical as the anti-tank defences had been destroyed and two Sherman tanks knocked out. Captain Brunt, however, rallied his remaining men, and moving to an alternative position, continued to hold the enemy infantry, although outnumbered by at least three to one. Personally firing a Bren gun, Captain Brunt killed about fourteen of the enemy. His wireless set was destroyed by shell-fire but on receiving a message by runner to withdraw to a Company locality some 200 yards to his left and rear, he remained behind to give covering fire. When his Bren ammunition was exhausted, he fired a Piat and a 2-inch Mortar, left by casualties, before he himself dashed over the open ground to the new position. This aggressive defence caused the enemy to pause, so Captain Brunt took a party back to his previous position and although fiercely engaged by small arms fire they carried away the wounded who had been left there.

Later in the day, a further counter-attack was put in by the enemy on two axes. Captain Brunt immediately seized a spare Bren gun and going round his forward positions, rallied his men. Then, leaping on a Sherman tank supporting the Company, he ordered the tank commander to drive from one fire position to another, whilst he sat or stood on the turret, directing Besa fire at the advancing enemy, regardless of the hail of small arms fire. Then, seeing small parties of the enemy, armed with bazookas, trying to approach round the left flank, he jumped off the tank and taking a Bren gun, stalked these parties well in front of the Company positions, killing more and causing the enemy finally to withdraw in great haste leaving their dead behind them.

Whenever the fighting was heaviest, Captain Brunt was always to be found, moving from one post to another, encouraging the men and firing any weapon he found at any target he could see. The magnificent action fought by this Officer, his coolness, bravery, devotion to duty and complete disregard of his own personal safety under the most intense and concentrated fire was beyond praise. His personal example and individual action were responsible to a very great extent for the successful repulse of these fierce enemy counter-attacks.

The next day Captain Brunt was killed by mortar fire.

It should be said that the citation did not have Brunt's regimental affiliations quite correct. While he was, as stated, from the Sherwood Foresters (the Nottinghamshire and Derbyshire Regiment), he was attached to the 6th Battalion the Lincolnshire Regiment at the time of his exploit. The bespectacled Brunt, who had only recently turned 23, had been born at Paddock Wood, Kent and came from Priest Weston, Chirbury, Shropshire. He is buried in the Commonwealth War Graves Commission Cemetery at Faenza, Italy, and is commemorated in the Soldiers' Chapel of St George at Lincoln Cathedral.

The 1944 campaign came to an end soon after John Brunt's death. It says much for his heroism and that of all his comrades that they could soldier on with so much spirit and fortitude in the face of such terrible adversity. All of them knew that back in Britain the Italian operations against Germany were seen as a sideshow. To a limited extent they were, because the Allied High Command could not afford to allow Hitler to move his fine divisions in Italy to the Western Front.

Germans and Allies settled down to a watchful winter of discomfort punctuated only by occasional raids and sporadic artillery fire.

Anders Frederik Emil Victor Schau Lassen

The last VC of the Italian campaign was awarded to one of the most outstanding British soldiers of the war – and yet he was a Danish subject. His name was Major Anders Frederik Emil Victor Schau Lassen MC and two Bars, of the Special Boat Squadron. Born in South Zealand, Denmark, in September 1922, Lassen had been at sea when the war broke out and when the German Army overran his country it was his good fortune that his ship was in a British port. In January 1941 he and 14 volunteers swore allegiance to the Danish flag and King Christian of Denmark and before long he had joined the British Commandos in secret training.

With two motor torpedo boats, a Commando unit under Major Gus March-Phillipps carried out raids on German targets on the French coast. So many of the raids succeeded that the Germans strengthened their positions on the Channel coast. In September 1942 this unit raided a lighthouse on Jersey and snatched the German crew as well as code books. On a later occasion, Lassen, under another commander, raided the island of Sark.

A born adventurer, Lassen flew to Cairo in February 1943 to join Major (Earl) Jellicoe in a new unit, Special Boat Service (SBS). In the middle of June five officers including Lassen and 17 men under Major David Sutherland embarked from Mersa Matruh on a mission to destroy aircraft on Crete and thereby reduce the attacks on troop convoys sailing from Haifa and Alexandria to Sicily. The raid on Kastelli Pediada airfield was successful but the Germans shot 52 Cretan hostages in retaliation.

Next came the British invasion of the Aegean Islands, in which Lassen played a major part in the many small-scale raids. He sought permission to raid the enemy-held island of Simi, where he destroyed an Italian artillery position and killed an officer and two men. On Nisiros he destroyed the Italian radio station. While on Leros, making other raids, he heard that he had been promoted captain. He took part in the defence of the island when German paratroops were dropped to capture it.

Before long Lassen was referred to in the British Army as 'the triple MC', though he rarely wore his decorations.

In August 1944 SBS moved its headquarters to Bari, Italy, and that same month Lassen commanded a patrol sent to Yugoslavia to demolish an important railway bridge. In a dangerous and daring operation he accomplished this task.

Earl Jellicoe, now a lieutenant-colonel, was appointed leader of Operation Bucketforce, which was at first intended to do nothing more than raid a German airfield on the Peloponnese, southern Greece, but which developed into the liberation of much of Greece. Lassen's task was to reconnoitre the sea route to Athens, gather information on German, Italian and Greek minefields and find a suitable naval base near Athens. Having done all that was asked of him, Lassen was promoted to major, made commander of M Squadron SBS and ordered to sail on a reconnaissance expedition to the Sporades Islands. It was said that he 'liberated Salonika' and that local people treated him as a god.

After many more adventures, in March 1945 Lassen and his squadron were sent to northern Italy, a posting which took him to the extreme right flank of the British front, which ended at Lake Comacchio. Between the Adriatic Sea and the lake lay a narrow strip of sand dunes which the Germans had heavily mined and fortified. Brigadier Tod, who commanded on this front, hoped to make a landing from the lake to take the Germans in the rear, an imaginative and daring idea. The lake, though large, had an average depth of only 2 feet which was why Lassen took with him canoes, folboats and other shallow-draft craft. The enemy held the northern, western and eastern shores and were well aware of the lake's tactical importance.

First of all, beginning on 3 April 1945, Lassen 'occupied' some of the islands in the middle of the lake, from which he planned to make a final reconnaissance before his diversionary attack. Somehow the Germans discovered the British presence and shelled their positions.

On the afternoon of 8 April Lassen received a coded radio message: 'The attacks must repeat must take place tonight as planned whether reconnaissance has taken place or not. Every reasonable risk must repeat must be taken. These military operations are vital to the completion of present plans.'

That night Lassen set out on his mission, apparently with a premonition that he would not return. The citation for his VC, gazetted on 7 September 1945, describes the young Dane's last daring operation.

Major (temporary) Anders Frederik Emil Victor Schau Lassen MC, General List

In Italy, on the night of 8th/9th April, 1945, Major Lassen was ordered to take out a patrol of one officer and seventeen other ranks to raid the north shore of Lake Comacchio.

His tasks were to cause as many casualties and as much confusion as possible, to give the impression of a major landing, and to capture prisoners. No previous reconnaissance was possible and the party found itself on a narrow road flanked on both sides by water.

Preceded by two scouts, Major Lassen led his men along the road towards the town. They were challenged after approximately 500 yards from a position on the side of the road. An attempt to allay suspicion by answering that they were fishermen returning home failed, for when moving forward again to overpower the sentry, machine-gun fire started from the position and also from two other blockhouses to the rear.

Major Lassen himself then attacked with grenades, and annihilated the first position containing four Germans and two machine-guns. Ignoring the hail of bullets sweeping the road from three enemy positions, an additional one having come into action from 300 yards down the road, he raced forward to engage the second position under covering fire from the remainder of the force. Throwing in more grenades he silenced this position which was then overrun by his patrol. Two enemy were killed, two captured and two more machine-guns silenced.

By this time the force had suffered casualties and its fire power was very considerably reduced. Still under a heavy cone of fire Major Lassen rallied and reorganized his force and brought his fire to bear on the third position. Moving forward himself he flung in more grenades which produced a cry of 'Kamerad'. He then went forward to within three or four yards of the position to order the enemy outside and to take their surrender.

Whilst shouting to them to come out he was hit by a burst of spandau fire from the left of the position and he fell mortally wounded, but even whilst falling he flung a grenade, wounding some of the occupants and enabling his patrol to dash in and capture this final position.

Major Lassen refused to be evacuated as he said it would impede the withdrawal and endanger further lives and as ammunition was nearly exhausted the force had to withdraw. By his magnificent leadership and complete disregard for his personal safety, Major Lassen had, in the face of overwhelming superiority, achieved his objects. Three positions were wiped out, accounting for six machine guns, killing eight and wounding others of the enemy, and two prisoners were taken. The high sense of devotion to duty and the esteem in which he was held by the men he led, added to his own magnificent courage, enabled Major Lassen to carry out all the tasks he had been given with complete success.

The citation can be expanded from evidence given by Sergeant Major Leslie Stephenson DCM who was with Lassen on the raid. When hit by Spandau fire, Lassen threw three grenades into the post, killing or wounding all the defenders. 'I heard him shout and ran over to him,' Stephenson said, 'I found him lying two yards in front of the pill box. I lifted him a little by picking him up under his arm and supported him against my knee. He asked who it was and I said, "Steve." He said, "Good – I'm wounded, Steve, I'm going to die. Try to get the others out." I was the last one to speak to him and I can testify that he died as he had lived – a very brave man.'

The survivors of Lassen's raid got back to their island base in the early hours of 9 April. That morning, with the fighting over, Italian pro-Allied partisans found Lassen and other dead British SBS men and carried them into the town. They were buried near an old stone wall and girls placed flowers on their graves, possibly the very girls whom Lassen, on one of his clandestine visits to the town, had promised to meet.

His attack did what it was intended to do. The Germans withdrew men from their main front to stiffen the garrison at Comacchio. When the main attack was made, as planned, 24 hours later, British casualties were lighter than might have been expected. The German surrender in Italy became effective on 2 May 1945.

To Lassen's many admirers, comrades and friends it seemed almost inevitable that sooner or later he would win the VC and probably die in the exploit that earned it. He had taken countless risks and he had been fired at many times. On numerous missions he had evaded capture through sheer daring and bluff. He was the ultimate warrior and ideally suited to the Commando-type warfare in which the SBS and SAS excelled.

The tall, slender and handsome Dane, British by adoption and war service, was idolized by the Greek, Aegean and Italian partisans with whom he worked. But he was ruthless in action and it has been said that as 'the SBS's terrible Viking'* he killed more enemy soldiers in the eastern Mediterranean than any other British or Allied soldier of any rank. If this

---

* The description used by Richard Capell in his book *Simiomata*.

seems ruthless it must be understood that these were ruthless times. The Germans indiscriminately killed Greeks and Cretans.

Still only 24 when he died, Anders Lassen was reinterred at the Commonwealth War Graves Commission Cemetery at Argenta Gap, Italy. His three MC citations make interesting reading, if only because they indicate that his VC exploit was not the one truly outstanding act of his military career.

The Military Cross
Second-Lieutenant Anders Frederik Emil Victor Schau Lassen, General List

Second-Lieutenant Lassen has at all times shown himself to be a very gallant and determined officer who will carry out his job with a complete disregard for his own personal safety. As well as, by his fine example, being an inspiring leader of his men, he is a brilliant seaman possessed of sound judgment and quick decisions. He was coxswain of the landing craft on an operation and effected a landing and subsequent re-embarkation on a dangerous and rocky island with considerable skill and without mishap. He took part in a further operation on which he showed dash and reliability. He recently took part in another highly successful operation in which he was the leader of a boarding party. Regardless of the action going on around him, Second-Lieutenant Lassen did his job quickly and coolly and showed great resource and ingenuity. Second-Lieutenant Lassen also took part in another operation, as bowman on landing, and then made a preliminary reconnaissance for a reported machine-gun post.

Second MC for Lieutenant Lassen

This officer was in command of the patrol which attacked Kastelli Pediada aerodrome on the night of 4th July. Together with Gunner Jones, J. (RA) he entered the airfield from the West, passing through formidable perimeter defences. By pretending to be a German officer on rounds he bluffed his way past three sentries stationed 15 yards apart guarding Stukas. He was, however, compelled to shoot the fourth with his automatic and in so doing raised the alarm. Caught by flares and ground searchlights he was subjected to very heavy machine-gun and rifle fire from close range and forced to withdraw. Half an hour later this officer and another rank again entered the airfield in spite of the fact that all guards had been trebled and the area was being patrolled and swept by searchlights. Great difficulty was experienced in penetrating towards the target, in the process of which a second enemy sentry had to be shot. The enemy then rushed reinforcements from the Eastern side of the aerodrome and forming a semi-circle drove the two attackers into the middle of an anti-aircraft battery, where they were fired upon heavily from three sides. This danger was ignored and bombs were placed on a caterpillar tractor which was destroyed. The increasing numbers of enemy in that area finally forced the party to withdraw. It was entirely due to this officer's diversion that planes and petrol were successfully destroyed on the Eastern side of the airfield since he drew off all the guards from that area. Throughout this attack and during the very arduous approach march, the keenness, determination and personal disregard of danger of this officer was of the highest order.

Third MC for Lieutenant Lassen – Second Bar to MC

This officer, most of the time a sick man, displayed outstanding leadership and gallantry throughout the operations by X Det [X Detachment] in Dodecanese, 13 Sep. 43 to 18 Oct. 43. The heavy repulse of the Germans from Simi on 7 Oct. 43 was due in no small measure to his inspiration and leadership on the one hand and the highest personal example on the other. He himself, crippled with a badly burned leg and internal trouble, stalked and killed at least 3 Germans at the closest range. At that time the Italians were wavering and I* attribute their recovery as due to the personal example and initiative of this Officer. He continued to harass and destroy German patrols throughout the morning. In the afternoon he himself led the Italian counter-attack which finally drove the Germans back to their caiques with the loss of 16 killed, 35 wounded, and 7 prisoners, as against a loss on our side of one killed and one wounded.

---

*   Colonel D.J.T. Turnbull, commanding Raiding Forces countersigned by Lieutenant General Anderson, commanding 3 Corps and General H.M. Wilson, Commander-in-Chief, Middle East Forces.

CHAPTER EIGHT

The Far East

Malaya 1942

Arthur Edward Cumming

The Japanese effort to capture the supposedly impregnable British fortress of Singapore began on 8 December 1941 when the 25th Army landed troops on the east coast of Malaya at Kota Bharu and on the eastern shores of Thailand. About the same time the Japanese 11th Air Fleet bombed Singapore itself, the first of many such attacks to be suffered by the island before its fall. Lieutenant-General Sir Arthur Percival, GOC Malaya Command, was responsible for the overall defence of colonial Malaya while Percival's 3rd Indian Corps, commanded by Lieutenant-General Sir Lewis Heath, which was responsible for Malayan defences north of the state of Johore, took the brunt of the aggressive Japanese advance down the Malay Peninsula.

The 12th Frontier Force Regiment, Indian Army, was part of Heath's corps and it was commanded by Lieutenant-Colonel Arthur Cumming MC. In the midst of defeat after defeat for the British, Colonel Cumming's stand, counter-attack and later withdrawal stands out. Even though British evacuation from the mainland to Singapore was completed by 31 January 1942 and even though total British surrender was only two weeks off, somehow the recommendation that Colonel Cumming be awarded the VC got through to London, where it was gazetted on 20 February, just five days after Percival surrendered.

It was the only British VC awarded for the ill-fated Malaya–Singapore campaign. Other gallant exploits took place, particularly by some Australians – one of whom was awarded the VC, but the tide of war washed away the records and many brave men did not survive the terrible years of captivity under the Japanese. This is Colonel Cumming's citation:

Lieutenant-Colonel Arthur Edward Cumming MC, 12th Frontier Force Regiment, Indian Army

On the 3rd January, 1942, in Malaya, a strong force of the enemy penetrated the position while Brigade Headquarters and a Battalion were being withdrawn. Lieutenant-Colonel Cumming with a small party of men immediately counter-attacked the enemy and prevented any further penetration of the position until his whole party had become casualties, and he himself had received two bayonet wounds in the stomach. By this brave counter-attack Lieutenant-Colonel Cumming enabled the major portion of our men and vehicles to be withdrawn. Later, in spite of pain and weakness from his wounds, this officer drove in a carrier for more than an hour under very heavy fire collecting isolated detachments of our men. He then received two further wounds, after which and while attempting to collect a further isolated detachment he lost consciousness and the driver of the carrier attempted to evacuate him. Lieutenant-Colonel Cumming, however, recovered consciousness and insisted on remaining where he was until he discovered that he and his driver were the sole survivors in the locality. He then decided to retire.

By his outstanding gallantry, initiative and devotion to duty, he was largely instrumental in the safe withdrawal of the Brigade.

After the war, General Percival wrote an account of the Malayan campaign in which he describes the events during the period immediately before Cumming's exploit. He tells of the confused fighting around Kuantan and its aerodrome, with many patrol encounters north of the airfield, indicating that the enemy intended to attack from that direction. As the pressure increased, the British commander faced a stark choice – abandon the airfield or seriously risk the loss of the 22nd Indian Brigade Group, which was vital to the defence of the entire region.

To quote Percival:

By dusk [3 January 1942] the Kuantan force, except for the rearguard of the 2nd Frontier Force Regiment with some attached troops, was withdrawing. At 7.30 pm the enemy delivered a furious attack against the rearguard as it was about to leave the aerodrome. There was fierce and bloody fighting at close quarters in the darkness which, added to the noise of shots and bursting shells, caused great confusion. Attack after attack was repelled as the rearguard gradually withdrew. Throughout, Lieutenant-Colonel Cumming, commanding 2nd Frontier Force Regiment, was a tower of strength.

The wounded Cumming was fortunate to be evacuated from Malaya before the British surrender. He was later promoted to brigadier and made an OBE. Born in Karachi, he was 46 at the time of his exploit; he died in 1971.

Burma and India

The British troops in Italy might have felt neglected but those in India and Burma were sure they had been forgotten. These were the men of the

British Eastern Army, whose first commander was General Sir Archibald Wavell. The British, untrained in jungle warfare, stayed on the roads and in cultivated areas, where they were outflanked and defeated by the Japanese. In February 1942 they destroyed a large British-Indian force. After this defeat Lieutenant-General William Slim became corps commander but the retreat went on and by mid-1942 it was a rout. In late 1942 two brigades of British and Indian troops made a seaborne attack on the Japanese port base of Akyab but again they were disastrously defeated.

Brigadier Orde Wingate's 3,000 Chindit raiders, supplied from the air, operated behind Japanese lines early in 1943 but the dreadful conditions forced their retreat to India. Fewer than 1,500 men survived but the Chindits' raids caused the Japanese High Command to change some of their plans. Overall, the Chindits' value was psychological rather than military.*

The rank and file knew nothing of the political and military squabbles among the British–American–Chinese allies in 1943, but news of top-level appointments filtered down to them. General Wavell was made Viceroy of India, Admiral Lord Louis Mountbatten became Supreme Commander South-East Asia. The British Eastern Army, renamed Fourteenth Army, was given to Slim, now a full general.

Meanwhile the Japanese forces became ever stronger. Like the Allies, the enemy commanders wanted to begin an offensive early in 1944. During the 18 months from January 1944 eleven members of the British Army in the India–Burma theatre were awarded VCs. *All were posthumous awards.*

The conditions under which the British, Indian and Gurkha troops in Burma fought were very different from those in North Africa, Italy and north-west Europe, and they were infinitely worse. The Japanese, fanatical and cruel, were but one enemy; the jungle and terrain another; the climate a third. The war was fought along muddy tracks, threaded by many roots that could bring men crashing down, while vines caught in their equipment. Overhead was a canopy of matted vegetation from which, for much of the year, rain dripped incessantly. Illnesses such as malaria, cholera, scrub typhus, trench feet, river fever and dysentery were rife and men were generally wet and hungry. The logistical system was a nightmare and the only way supplies reached forward units was on the backs of mules or men, until air drops became better organized. For long periods the troops were inadequately supplied with food, clothing, medicine and ammunition. Wounded men were operated on within 100 yards of the enemy and getting them out to safety was an appallingly difficult problem and often totally impossible. Some men survived the trauma of an

---

* Wingate gave his raiders the name of Chindits after the Chinthay, the mythical griffin, half-lion, half-eagle guardian of the Burmese temples. In Army records the Chindits were referred to as 'Special Force', or more formally in the Order of Battle as 3rd Indian Division Long Range Penetration Groups. The title '3rd Indian Division' was a misnomer intended to deceive the enemy.

operation only to die of infection. Others disappeared while on patrol in the jungle, while others drowned in the swift-flowing rivers which abound in Burma.

The Japanese troops were hard to see, always difficult to attack and when they themselves attacked they did so with fanatical fury. Early in 1944 they trapped 8,000 administrative troops, pioneers, sappers, signallers, ordnance and medical units and mule companies. The entire regular force of the 'Admin Box' – as the fighting area was called – consisted of two battalions of infantry, the Royal West Yorkshires and the Gurkhas, and a small artillery force. Much of the fighting was hand to hand. On misty days visibility was about 15 yards.

The Box, about 1 mile square was set in an area of dried-up paddy fields and its only high ground was Ammunition Hill, a mound 300 feet high. The Japanese held much higher ground all around the Box. Supplied from the air, the exhausted garrison, steadily suffering casualties, held on. On many occasions Japanese guns targeted an ammunition dump or other supplies. Every part of the Box was vulnerable to enemy fire and bombs; grenades and shells fell without respite.

Three field ambulances set themselves up as a Main Dressing Station at a place they called MDS Hill and the staff worked until they dropped. Major B.G.A. Lilwall DSO operated 252 times during the siege. One night a party of about six Japanese officers and 60 soldiers tore into the hospital, hacking and shooting everybody in sight. The defenders could not mount a counter-attack in the dark and shelling and mortaring the hospital would have killed even more patients and staff.

Some British tanks moved in next morning so the Japanese forced their sick prisoners, their hands bound, to go forward as screens against the tanks' machine-gun fire. The Japanese themselves squatted in foxholes and laughed, while refusing dressings to the wounded and water to the dying. They killed those whose groans might reveal the Japanese position.

Later, the Japanese shot and bayoneted every man of the medical staff whom they could find. Six doctors were lined up and each shot with a bullet through the ear. Two nights later a large party of Japanese who had been in the hospital made their way along a shallow river bed defended by the Royal West Yorkshires, who drenched the river bed with grenades. When the sun came up the British soldiers counted 45 enemy corpses in an area 40 yards square. This gives a brief picture of the war in Burma and of the ferocity of the Japanese enemy.

Alec George Horwood

On 15 January 1944 Mountbatten ordered the American General Stilwell to attack from the north, the 4th Corps of Lieutenant-General Scoones to attack on the central front and the 15th Corps under Lieutenant-General

A.F. Christison to attack from the south. One of the units involved was the Northamptonshire Regiment and attached to it was Lieutenant George Horwood DCM of the Queen's Royal (West Surrey) Regiment. Some idea of the ferocity of the fighting against Japanese troops who were well dug in is shown by the citation for Horwood's posthumous VC, gazetted on 30 March 1944.

Lieutenant Alec George Horwood DCM, the Queen's Royal Regiment (West Surrey), attached the Northamptonshire Regiment

At Kyauchaw on 18th January, 1944, Lieutenant Horwood accompanied the forward company of the Northamptonshire Regiment into action against a Japanese defended locality with his forward mortar observation post. Throughout that day he lay in an exposed position, which had been completely bared of cover by concentrated air bombing, and effectively shot his own mortars and those of a half troop of another unit while the company was manoeuvring to locate the exact position of the enemy bunkers and machine-gun nests. During the whole of this time Lieutenant Horwood was under intense sniper, machine-gun and mortar fire, and at night he came back with most valuable information about the enemy.

On 19th January he moved forward with another company and established an observation post on a precipitous ridge. From here, while under continual fire from the enemy, he directed accurate mortar fire in support of two attacks which were put in during the day. He also carried out a personal reconnaissance along and about the bare ridge, deliberately drawing the enemy fire so that the fresh company which he had led to the position and which was to carry out an attack might see the enemy positions.

Lieutenant Horwood remained on the ridge during the night 19th–20th January and on the morning of 20th January shot the mortars again to support a fresh attack by another company put in from the rear of the enemy. He was convinced that the enemy would crack and volunteered to lead the attack planned for that afternoon. He led this attack with such calm, resolute bravery that the enemy were reached and while standing up in the wire, directing and leading the men with complete disregard to the enemy fire which was then at point blank range, he was mortally wounded.

By his fine example of leadership on the 18th, 19th and 20th January when continually under fire, by his personal example to others of reconnoitring, guiding and bringing up ammunition in addition to his duties at the mortar observation post, all of which were carried out under great physical difficulties and in exposed positions, this officer set the highest example of bravery and devotion to duty to which all ranks responded magnificently. The cool calculated actions of this officer, coupled with his magnificent bearing and bravery which culminated in his death on the enemy wire, very largely contributed to the ultimate success of the operation which resulted in the capture of the position on the 24th January.

Coolness is mentioned in the citation and it was this quality which stands out in Lieutenant Horwood's exploit. Deliberately drawing enemy fire was a brave and daringly calculated action and he reconnoitred in the same deliberate way. He certainly laid the groundwork for the ultimate defeat of the Japanese at this position. Born at Deptford, London, George Horwood was just 30 when he was killed. His body was never found but his name is recorded on the British memorial in Rangoon.

Charles Ferguson Hoey

The exploit of Major Charles Hoey MC of 1st Battalion, the Lincolnshire Regiment, was much more impetuous than that of Lieutenant Horwood and it must be asked whether he was *too* brave, too dynamic. His heroic action lasted only a few minutes and at the end of it he was dead. His is one of the briefest Army VC citations of the war, reflecting his singularly purposeful leadership.

Captain (temporary Major) Charles Ferguson Hoey MC, the Lincolnshire Regiment

In Burma, on the 16th February, 1944, Major Hoey's Company formed part of a force which was ordered to capture a position at all costs.

After a night march through enemy held territory the force was met at the foot of the position by heavy machine-gun fire.

Major Hoey personally led his Company under heavy machine-gun and rifle fire right up to the objective. Although wounded at least twice in the leg and head he seized a Bren gun from one of his men and firing from the hip, led his Company onto the objective. In spite of his wounds the Company had difficulty in keeping up with him, and Major Hoey reached the enemy strong point first where he killed all the occupants before being mortally wounded.

Major Hoey's outstanding gallantry and leadership, his total disregard of personal safety and his grim determination to reach the objective resulted in the capture of this vital position.

Hoey's exploit took place at Ngakkyedauk in the Mayu Range of the Arakan. He was commanding B Company which, like other parts of the battalion, came under fire from high ground. The CO, who quickly arrived at the most critical area, found Major Hoey and his company concentrated and ready for action and he ordered Hoey to take Point 315, the dominant Japanese position. The mortar platoon officer got his mortars into action and the CO told Hoey that he would follow with D Company as soon as they could be collected. The regimental history completes the story:

> Charles Hoey dashed off, followed by his company. The mortars shot well, the second bomb landing in a group of Japs who were seen no more, but they could not go on for long for fear of hitting B Company, who could now not be seen but only heard in the jungle, going up the hill and encouraged all the time by the voice of their company commander. D Company were now ready and we followed B Company with the adjutant using the Pioneer Platoon as a rear party, keeping things safe behind. The advance gradually slowed down and Charles Hoey's voice could no longer be heard. He had reached his objective and had fallen at the top of the hill.

On 23 February the Japanese were driven back from Ngakkyedauk Pass and the following day they called off their offensive on that part of the front.

On 18 March, Lieutenant-Colonel C.A.C. Sinker CO of the 1st Battalion the Lincolnshire Regiment issued a special order of the day which read, in part:

> We are one of the few units and the only British unit that has been sent back to fight a second campaign in the Arakan. We may well be proud of this. We can take it. We have all seen something of the Japanese lately and should all feel now that we are better men and better soldiers than they. Furthermore, we are better equipped and better armed.
>
> We have recently been set a very perfect example by Major Hoey. His grim determination, his supreme courage and his willing self-sacrifice for his cause and regiment, should be an inspiration to us all. If we all aim at this ideal, which is of the highest, nothing can go wrong, and we shall finish this campaign with great honour and distinction and the firm knowledge that we have all taken our share and done our duty.

Many an Army commander, corps, division and battalion commander issued similar messages and orders of the day.

Born at Duncan, Vancouver Island, Hoey was 30 when he was killed. He is buried in Taukkyan Commonwealth War Graves Commission Cemetery, Burma, and is commemorated in the Soldiers' Chapel of St George, Lincoln Cathedral.

Charles Hoey's mother, Mary, in the depths of her grief back in Duncan, Vancouver Island, wrote a poem to her son's memory. It could well reflect the feelings of many parents of fallen warriors, whether or not they won the VC.

To My Son: Major C.F. Hoey, VC

I think that all is quiet where you are lying,
  The smoke and dust of battle long since gone.
Now little birds and shy small animals come freely
  About their daily life, while you sleep on—
When the first light of day touches the hilltop,
  Folding away the mist that evening laid
With careful hands to shield you from the darkness
  That you might rest there safe and unafraid,
One shining ray will light where you are lying,
  Spreading its radiance like a flag unfurled;
A memory of the glory of your passing,
  And of the courage that you gave the world.

Mary Hoey,
Duncan, BC

George Albert Cairns

Operation Thursday, an airborne action conducted by two Chindit brigades deep into the heart of Japanese-held Burma during March 1944, receives scant mention in British military history. As an airborne operation it is unique because the others were predominantly parachute operations. Also, other airborne incursions were intended to link up rapidly with ground troops. But there were no ground troops to cooperate with Operation Thursday's raiders; they were on their own behind enemy lines. The orders given to Brigadier Orde Wingate were to cut the supply routes of the Japanese 18th Division which was blocking the route of the 'Chinese Army of India', to otherwise help the Chinese enter the war in Burma against the Japanese and to 'create havoc' in the Japanese rear.

Wingate chose two landing zones for his gliders – 'Broadway' and 'Piccadilly' – about 60 miles north-east of the large centre of Indaw. Some gliders, loaded with assault boats and outboard engines, were to land on a crossing point of the Irrawaddy River.

One of Wingate's Chindit officers was Lieutenant George Cairns, of the 77th Independent Infantry Brigade, who arrived by glider on 5 March 1944. Other officers and men were not so lucky. Because of overloading and the lack of rehearsal many gliders broke away from their tows and the leading gliders at 'Broadway' suffered many accidents. Its successful defence against air and ground attack is an extraordinary event in the history of the war. Lieutenant Cairns's exploit at Henu Block – rewarded by a posthumous VC and gazetted on 20 May 1949 – makes it even more remarkable.

Lieutenant George Albert Cairns, the Somerset Light Infantry, and South Staffordshire Regiment

On the 5th March 1944, 77 Independent Infantry Brigade, of which the 1st South Staffordshire Regiment formed a part, landed by glider at Broadway (Burma).

On the 12th March, 1944, columns from the South Staffordshire Regiment and 3/6 Gurkha Rifles established a road and rail block across the Japanese lines of communication at Henu Block.

The Japanese counter-attacked this position heavily in the early morning of the 13th March, 1944, and the South Staffordshire Regiment was ordered to attack a hill-top which formed the basis of the Japanese attack.

During this action, in which Lieutenant Cairns took a foremost part, he was attacked by a Japanese officer who with his sword hacked off Lieutenant Cairns' left arm. Lieutenant Cairns killed this Officer, picked up the sword and continued to lead his men in the attack and slashing left and right with the captured sword killed and wounded several Japanese before he himself fell to the ground.

Lieutenant Cairns subsequently died from his wounds.

His action so inspired all his comrades that later the Japanese were completely routed, a very rare occurrence at that time.

The 34-year-old Cairns, a Londoner by birth, had superhuman will and strength to go on fighting after his arm had been severed from his body. He probably knew that, isolated as they were behind enemy lines, he could not possibly receive adequate treatment for his dreadful wound. The spectacle of this mortally injured officer killing or wounding enemy officers and men with an enemy sword was awesome. The date given for the citation's gazetting – 20 May 1949 and nearly four years after the end of the war against Japan – is correct. Cairns's VC was the last to be gazetted for the Second World War.

The ramifications of the award are interesting. Cairns's exploit took place on 13 March 1944 and he died of wounds six days later. He was serving with the Chindits at the time and three officers witnessed his astonishing heroism. The Chindits' commander, Brigadier Orde Wingate, was carrying their recommendation, of which he would certainly have approved, when his plane crashed in the jungle on 24 March 1944. Wingate was killed and his records were destroyed in the consequent fire. Cairns's regiment brought the recommendation to the notice of the War Office only to find that two of the three original witnesses had also been killed in Burma. Then, in 1948, Cairns's widow took the matter to her Member of Parliament and to Brigadier (later General) J.M. Calvert who had commanded the Chindit brigade of which Cairns's unit formed part. As a result, the VC was gazetted on 20 May 1949, more than five years after Cairns's act of valour. The citation illustrates how richly deserved it was.

Lieutenant Cairns is buried in the Commonwealth War Graves Commission Cemetery, Taukkyan, Burma, and he is commemorated in the Garrison Church, Whittington Barracks, Lichfield, Staffordshire.

John Pennington Harman

The garrison of Kohima under Colonel H.V. Richards DSO, numbered 3,500 against 15,000 Japanese. The enemy not only surrounded Kohima but overlooked it from all sides and from the hills they poured in a murderous destructive fire. So close were the opposing lines that a Japanese soldier deepening his foxhole heaved a shovelful of soil into a British trench. The two sides divided the district commissioner's garden between them. The Japanese held his bungalow and to take it a British tank drove up to the front door and fired shells into the building.

Colonel Young DSO, a British doctor who passed through the Japanese lines to tend the wounded in Kohima, handled about 600 casualties during the siege and amputated with a knife. To get medical supplies he and some helpers raided a ruined hospital which was in Japanese hands. That Kohima was held against overwhelming odds was due to the courage of men such as Lance-Corporal John Harman, whose posthumous VC citation was gazetted on 22 June 1944.

Lance-Corporal John Pennington Harman, the Queen's Own Royal West Kent Regiment

In Burma at Kohima on 8th April, 1944, Lance-Corporal Harman was commanding a section of a forward platoon. Under cover of darkness the enemy established a machine-gun post within 50 yards of his position, which became a serious menace to the remainder of his Company. Owing to the nature of the ground Lance-Corporal Harman was unable to bring the fire of his section on to the enemy machine-gun post. Without hesitation he went forward by himself and using a four-second grenade which he held on to for at least two seconds after releasing the lever in order to get immediate effect, threw it into the post and followed up immediately. He annihilated the post and returned to his section with the machine-gun.

Early the following morning he recovered a position on a forward slope 150 yards from the enemy in order to strengthen a platoon which had been heavily attacked during the night. On occupying his position he discovered a party of enemy digging in under cover of machine-gun fire and snipers. Ordering his Bren gun to give him covering fire he fixed his bayonet and alone charged the post shooting four and bayoneting one thereby wiping out the post.

When walking back Lance-Corporal Harman received a burst of machine-gun fire in his side and died shortly after reaching our lines.

Lance-Corporal Harman's heroic action and supreme devotion to duty were a wonderful inspiration to all and were largely responsible for the decisive way in which all attacks were driven off by his Company.

What a pity that the citation does not finish with Harman's last words to his mates as they tried to save him from bleeding to death. 'I got the lot,' he said, 'It was worth it.'

Born in Beckenham, Kent, Lance-Corporal Harman was 29 when he was killed. He is buried in the Commonwealth War Graves Commission Cemetery at Kohima.

John Neil Randle

Captain John Randle was another Kohima VC which, to those who know about the continuous and cruel fighting at the besieged position, is enough information to indicate that his decoration was hard won and well merited. A recent graduate from Oxford, Randle was called up shortly before the war. After some months with the East Surrey Regiment he attended an officers' training course and was commissioned. Married soon after this, Randle was posted to the 2nd Battalion, Royal Norfolk Regiment, which was sent to India in 1942.

After varied service in India and Burma, the battalion found itself as part of the garrison in the enemy-surrounded hill village of Kohima in the Naga Hills of Assam. The Japanese held the higher ground virtually all round the British perimeter and their snipers were bloodily effective. So, too, were their mortars, because they had the better observation.

The fighting at Kohima was as bitter as anywhere in the entire war. For a long time the Japanese and the British were on either side of the tennis court at the district commissioner's wrecked residence on Kohima Ridge. Occasionally airlifts of supplies got through to the British but nothing reached the Japanese. Starving and diseased, they continued to attack. In the end the British broke the siege, forcing the Japanese both back to the surrounding mountains and on to the Imphal plain below, where the fighting continued.

Japanese snipers were always a menace and at one point a sniper dubbed 'Little Willie' fired from a hole in a tree for three weeks, picking off eight officers. All efforts to kill him by rifle fire and mortar bombs failed and in the end he slipped away unscathed.

The British offensive had to be kept going whatever the difficulties, including the monsoon, which added its own torments to the fighting. In some places more than 15 inches of rain fell in a single day and soldiers lived in a thick mire. Swarms of black flies drove men to a tormented frenzy and after heavy rains trees and bushes were densely laden with bloodsucking leeches. No citation ever gave the slightest reference to the hideous background of a valorous exploit.

On 4 May the Norfolks were ordered to capture a ridge overlooking their positions and to drive the Japanese from it. It was here that John Randle's exploit took place. His posthumous VC award was gazetted on 12 December 1944.

Lieutenant (temporary Captain) John Neil Randle, the Royal Norfolk Regiment

On the 4th May, 1944, at Kohima in Assam, a Battalion of the Norfolk Regiment attacked the Japanese positions on a nearby ridge. Captain Randle took over command of the Company which was leading the attack when the Company Commander was severely wounded. His handling of a difficult situation in the face of heavy fire was masterly and although wounded himself in the knee by grenade splinters he continued to inspire his men by his initiative, courage and outstanding leadership until the Company had captured its objective and consolidated its position. He then went forward and brought in all the wounded men who were lying outside the perimeter.

In spite of his painful wound Captain Randle refused to be evacuated and insisted on carrying out a personal reconnaissance with great daring in bright moonlight prior to a further attack by his Company on the positions to which the enemy had withdrawn.

At dawn on 6th May the attack opened, led by Captain Randle, and one of the platoons succeeded in reaching the crest of the hill held by the Japanese. Another platoon, however, ran into heavy medium machine gun fire from a bunker on the reverse slope of the feature. Captain Randle immediately appreciated that this particular bunker covered not only the rear of his new position but also the line of communication of the Battalion and therefore the destruction of the enemy post was imperative if the operation was to succeed.

With utter disregard of the obvious danger to himself Captain Randle charged the Japanese machine gun post single-handed with rifle and bayonet. Although bleeding in the face and mortally wounded by numerous bursts of machine gun fire he reached the bunker and silenced the gun with a grenade thrown through the bunker slit. He then flung his body across the slit so that the aperture should be completely sealed.

The bravery shown by this officer could not have been surpassed and by his self-sacrifice he saved the lives of many of his men and enabled not only his own Company but the whole Battalion to gain its objective and win a decisive victory over the enemy.

Some historians of the Victoria Cross suggest that Randle's exploit could have been the most heroic act of the war by a soldier. It would be invidious to make comparisons but certainly for a soldier to seal an enemy gun slit with his body in order to prevent the Japanese from firing at his own men is a demonstration of high valour.

Born in Benares, India, Randle had lived at Radlett, Hertfordshire, and Petersham, Surrey, before his Army days; he was 25 when he was killed. He is buried in the Commonwealth War Graves Commission Cemetery, Kohima. He was the brother-in-law of Flying Officer Manser VC, killed over Belgium on 31 May 1942. Mrs Randle lost her husband and her brother, both VC winners.

On Jail Hill, Kohima, a monument to the men of the British 2nd Division was erected. On it is this inscription: 'For your tomorrow they gave their today.'

Hanson Victor Turner

Even after the Kohima siege was broken, on 18 April 1944, the Japanese made furious efforts to regain it and true to their military cult they were prepared for any amount of blood sacrifice. The British, Indians and Gurkhas gave them their death wish. One British sniper, Private Burton, shot 43 of the enemy as they tried to break out of a burning hut. Kohima Ridge was in British hands on 14 May. After 50 days the heroic siege was over.

Many of the Japanese moving south from Kohima towards Imphal strengthened the garrison which already held the village of Ningthoutong Kha Khunog. The Japanese had the advantage in the difficult country between Kohima and Imphal. The only road was carved out of a cliff, so that to get off it troops had to go down vertically or up vertically. Japanese forces were at many places along the Imphal road and every one of their strong units had to be shadowed. By early June the monsoon had set in with rain falling solidly every day; for every two steps an infantryman climbed up a hillside he slipped back one. Nominally, the Japanese were the defenders and they seemed to be comparatively unaffected by the mud and rain and occasionally they attacked British positions. Early in June 1944 the West Yorkshire Regiment was the target of a night assault. Among the defenders in the British lines was Sergeant Hanson Turner whose citation for the posthumous award of the VC, gazetted on 17 August 1944, reveals a soldier of remarkable will and leadership.

Corporal (acting Sergeant) Hanson Victor Turner, the West Yorkshire Regiment (The Prince of Wales's Own)

In Burma, at Ningthoutong soon after midnight on the night of 6th–7th June, 1944, an attack was made by a strong force of Japanese with medium and light machine-guns. In the first instance the attack largely fell on the SW corner of the position which was held by a weak platoon of about 20 men of which Sergeant Turner was one of the Section Commanders. By creeping up under cover of a nullah the enemy were able to use grenades with deadly effect against this portion of the perimeter. Three out of the four light machine guns in the platoon were destroyed and the platoon was forced to give ground. Sergeant Turner with coolness and fine leadership at once reorganized his party and withdrew 40 yards. The enemy made determined and repeated attempts to dislodge them and concentrated all fire they could produce in an effort to reduce the position and so extend the penetration. Sustained fire was kept up on Sergeant Turner and his dwindling party by the enemy for a period of two hours. The enemy, however, achieved no further success in this sector. Sergeant Turner, with a doggedness and spirit of endurance of the highest order, repelled all their attacks and it was due entirely to his leadership that the position was ultimately held throughout the night.

When it was clear that the enemy were attempting to outflank the position, Sergeant Turner determined to take the initiative in driving the enemy off and killing them. The men left under his command were the minimum essential to maintain the position he had built up with such effect. No party for a counter-attack could therefore be mustered and speed was essential if the enemy were to be frustrated. He at once boldly and fearlessly went forward from his position alone armed with all the hand grenades he could carry, and went into the attack against the enemy single handed. He used his weapons with devastating effect and when his supply was exhausted he went back for more and returned to the offensive again. During all this time the enemy were keeping up intense small arms and grenade fire.

Sergeant Turner in all made five journeys to obtain further supplies of grenades and it was on the sixth occasion still single handed, while throwing a grenade among a party of the enemy, he was killed.

His conduct on that night will ever be remembered by the Regiment. His superb leadership and undaunted will to win in the early stages of the attack was undoubtedly instrumental in preventing the enemy plan from succeeding. The number of enemy found dead the next morning was ample evidence of the deadly effect his grenade throwing had had. He displayed outstanding valour and had not the slightest thought for his own safety. He died on the battlefield in a spirit of supreme self-sacrifice.

Sergeant Turner's regiment, the 1st Battalion the West Yorkshire Regiment, was part of the 5th Indian Airborne Division, whose spectacular landings in Burma had foiled Japanese plans to capture India. Born in Andover, Hampshire, Turner was only a few weeks off his 34th birthday when he was killed. He is buried in the Commonwealth War Graves Commission Cemetery at Imphal, India.

Michael Allmand

The 'front' against the Japanese was 700 miles in length and the far right sector was near Burma's border with China. It was centred on Mogaung and ahead of that town was Myitkyina. The British thrust here was meant to sweep through the Kachin Hills and cut off large numbers of Japanese troops. Gurkha units were involved in the fighting to gain control of Mogaung in June 1944. Captain Michael Allmand, from the Indian Armoured Corps, had been attached to the 6th Gurkha Rifles at his own request. He was awarded the VC posthumously for great and sustained valour in the Mogaung operations. His citation was gazetted on 26 October 1944.

Lieutenant (acting Captain) Michael Allmand, Indian Armoured Corps, attached 6th Gurkha Rifles

Captain Allmand was commanding the leading platoon of a Company of the 6th Gurkha Rifles in Burma on 11th June, 1944, when the Battalion was ordered to attack the Pin Hmi Road Bridge.

The enemy had already succeeded in holding up our advance at this point for twenty-four hours. The approach to the Bridge was very narrow as the road was banked up and the low-lying land on either side was swampy and densely covered in jungle. The Japanese who were dug in along the banks of the road and in the jungle with machine guns and small arms, were putting up the most desperate resistance.

As the platoon came within twenty yards of the Bridge, the enemy opened heavy and accurate fire, inflicting severe casualties and forcing the men to seek cover. Captain Allmand, however, with the utmost gallantry charged on by himself, hurling grenades into the enemy gun positions and killing three Japanese himself with his kukrie.

Inspired by the splendid example of their platoon commander the surviving men followed him and captured their objective.

Two days later Captain Allmand, owing to casualties among the officers, took over command of the Company and dashing thirty yards ahead of it through long grass and marshy ground, swept by machine gun fire, personally killed a number of enemy machine gunners and successfully led his men onto the ridge of high ground that they had been ordered to seize.

Once again on June 23rd in the final attack on the Railway Bridge at Mogaung, Captain Allmand, although suffering from trench-foot, which made it difficult for him to walk, moved forward alone through deep mud and shell-holes and charged a Japanese machine gun nest single-handed but he was mortally wounded and died shortly afterwards.

The superb gallantry, outstanding leadership and protracted heroism of this very brave officer were a wonderful example to the whole Battalion and in the highest traditions of his regiment.

The citation did not go on to say that largely because of Captain Allmand's bravery Mogaung was captured. Born at Golders Green, London, Allmand was only 21 when he died; he is buried in the Commonwealth War Graves Commission Cemetery at Taukkyan, Burma.

Frank Gerald Blaker

Many raids and minor operations in Burma had relatively little influence on the great major operations but were necessary in order to gain information, to cut enemy supply routes and to capture and hold positions which, because of their height, gave good observation over major enemy positions. The end result was often an attack uphill because the Japanese, following their earlier victories in 1942–3, already held much of the high ground; one such position was the strategic summit above their base of Taungni (Taunggyi) east of Meiktila. The British commanders considered it necessary to capture this hill. The task fell to the 9th Gurkha Rifles, one of whose British officers was Major Frank Blaker MC. The citation for his posthumous VC, gazetted on 26 September 1944, vividly illustrates the risks entailed in such an operation.

Captain (temporary Major) Frank Gerald Blaker MC, the Highland Light Infantry (City of Glasgow Regiment), attached 9th Gurkha Rifles, Indian Army

In Burma on 9th July, 1944, a Company of the 9th Gurkha Rifles was ordered to carry out a wide, encircling movement across unknown and precipitous country, through dense jungle, to attack a strong enemy position on the summit of an important hill overlooking Taungni.

Major Blaker carried out this movement with the utmost precision and took up a position with his Company on the extreme right flank of the enemy, in itself a feat of considerable military skill.

Another Company, after bitter fighting, had succeeded in taking the forward edge of the enemy position by a frontal assault, but had failed to reach the main crest of the hill in the face of fierce opposition.

At this crucial moment Major Blaker's Company came under heavy and accurate fire at close range from a medium machine gun and two light machine guns, and their advance was also completely stopped.

Major Blaker then advanced ahead of his men through very heavy fire and in spite of being severely wounded in the arm by a grenade, he located the machine guns, which were the pivot of the enemy defence, and single-handed charged the position.

When hit by a burst of three rounds through the body he continued to cheer on his men while lying on the ground.

His fearless leadership and outstanding courage so inspired his

Company that they stormed the hill and captured the objective, while the enemy fled in terror into the jungle.

Major Blaker died of wounds while being evacuated from the battlefield. His heroism and self-sacrifice were beyond all praise and contributed in no small way to the defeat of the enemy and the successful outcome of the operations.

Born at Meiktila, Burma, to British parents in the Colonial Service, Major Blaker was 24 when he was killed. He is buried in the Commonwealth War Graves Commission Cemetery at Taukkyan.

George Arthur Knowland

Even into 1945 a campaign of manoeuvre-battle was still in progress in Burma, whatever the general opinion in Britain that the war in that remote country was 'as good as over'. Most history books were ignoring it as late as the 1990s, yet four remarkable VC exploits took place between January and July 1945.

The Chindwin Line no longer existed at the end of 1944 and the 14th Army was committed to a type of battle different from that which had driven the Japanese from Kohima–Imphal and from the Manipur Plain. There the emphasis had been on attritional fighting; now the British moved on to manoeuvre. Lieutenant-General Leese was the new C–in–C of the 11th Army Group and C–in–C Allied Land Forces in South-East Asia.

General Slim's orders were to destroy the enemy forces in the Mandalay area and to capture Rangoon before the monsoon broke in May. Initially he was concerned about crossing the Irrawaddy River near Mandalay, even though in some places it was 2 miles wide. He had five veteran divisions at his disposal but so did the enemy commander, General Kimura. Slim planned to feint from the north to encourage Kimura to decide that both corps of the British 14th Army were engaged. Meanwhile, he would secretly transfer the 4th Corps to the west and south to attack Kimura's Mandalay concentration of units from the rear. In the meantime Lieutenant-General A.D.I. Sultan, C–in–C Northern Combat Area Command, was clearing the Ledo Road to China, a task achieved on 22 January.

Meanwhile the 2nd Division was preparing for an attack on Gangaw (Kangkaw) on the eastern slopes of the Pondawng Range 120 miles west of Mandalay. No 1 Army Commando was part of that division and it was in action at the end of January 1945 in very difficult country. One of the Commando officers was Lieutenant George Knowland, who had been detached from the Royal Norfolk Regiment to the Commandos.

His posthumous VC citation, gazetted on 12 April 1945, describes an action of great ferocity, with the enemy determined to dislodge Knowland from his position while he was even more determined to hold it. How he survived for as long as he did is astonishing because the enemy could see that this one man was the spirit of the resistance and continuously aimed at him.

Lieutenant George Arthur Knowland, the Royal Norfolk Regiment, attached Commandos

In Burma on 31st January, 1945, near Kangaw, Lieutenant Knowland was commanding the forward platoon of a Troop positioned on the extreme North of a hill which was subjected to very heavy and repeated enemy attacks throughout the whole day. Before the first attack started, Lieutenant Knowland's platoon was heavily mortared and machine gunned, yet he moved about among his men keeping them alert and encouraging them, though under fire himself at the time.

When the enemy, some 300 strong in all, made their first assault they concentrated all their efforts on his platoon of 24 men but in spite of the ferocity of the attack, he moved about from trench to trench distributing ammunition, and firing his rifle and throwing grenades at the enemy, often from completely exposed positions.

Later, when the crew of one of his forward Bren Guns had all been wounded, he sent back to Troop Headquarters for another crew and ran forward to man the gun himself until they arrived. The enemy was then less than 10 yards from him in dead ground down the hill so in order to get a better field of fire, he stood on top of the trench, firing the light machine gun from his hip and successfully keeping them at a distance until a Medical Orderly had dressed and evacuated the wounded men behind him. The new Bren Gun team also became casualties on the way up and Lieutenant Knowland continued to fire the gun until another team took over.

Later, when a fresh attack came in he took over a 2 in[ch] Mortar and in spite of heavy fire and the closeness of the enemy, he stood up in the open to face them, firing the mortar from his hip and killing six of them with his first bomb. When all bombs were expended he went back through heavy grenade, mortar and machine gun fire to get more, which he fired in the same way from the open in front of his platoon positions. When those bombs were finished he went back to his own trench and still standing up fired his rifle at them. Being hard pressed and with the enemy closing in on him from only 10 yards away, he had no time to re-charge his magazine. Snatching up the Tommy gun of a casualty, he sprayed the enemy and was mortally wounded stemming this assault, though not before he had killed and wounded many of the enemy.

Such was the inspiration of his magnificent heroism, that, though fourteen out of twenty-four of his platoon became casualties at an early stage, and six of his positions were over-run by the enemy, his men held on through twelve hours of continuous and fierce fighting until reinforcements arrived. If this Northern end of the hill had fallen the rest of the hill would have been endangered, the beach-head dominated by the enemy and other units farther inland cut off from their source of supplies. As it was, the final successful counter-attack was later launched from the vital ground which Lieutenant Knowland had taken such a gallant part in holding.

There are references in this citation which probably only an infantryman would appreciate. A 2-inch mortar is not normally fired from the hip. Indeed, as an infantryman myself I would never have used it in this way and I have never heard of anybody else doing so. A mortar barrel rests on a base plate which is firmly placed on the ground. The barrel points upwards at an angle of anything from 45 to 75 degrees so that the bomb fired from it has a high trajectory; it lobs over low hills, walls and foliage and drops straight into enemy positions. Lieutenant Knowland had no time to use his mortar in the usual way. Japanese were charging him so he fired the bomb directly at them. This was difficult and dangerous for himself and the recoil thump would have been considerable. It was imperative for him to hold the position because, as the citation indicates, it protected a point of the Myitka River below where supplies were arriving. Taking place during daylight, everything that Knowland did was in full view of every British soldier nearby and his valour inspired them.

Lieutenant Knowland, who had been born at Catford in Kent, was only 22 when he was killed. He is buried in the Commonwealth War Graves Commission Cemetery at Taukkyan.

William Basil Weston

With the British and Gurkha regiments pressing forward through the courage and persistence of other brave soldiers, General Slim moved the 7th Division southward to where Lieutenant-General Frank Messervy was concentrating his 4th Corps around the confluence of the Chindwin and Irrawaddy Rivers, south-west of Mandalay. Here, in the area of Pakokku, opposite Meiktila, the corps in mid-February 1945 was supplied by air from Chittagong, in the Ganges Delta.

At the end of the second week in February the 19th Division crossed the Irrawaddy 40 miles north of Mandalay while the 7th crossed 10 miles south of Pakokku. Behind the 7th Division were the motorized 17th and 5th Indian Divisions waiting to break through the opening made by the 7th.

The division reached Meiktila airfield and in capturing it cut the Japanese forces in two. A phase of desperate fighting followed and while this battle developed the British 2nd Division forced the Irrawaddy below Mandalay. The struggle for Meiktila lasted almost 10 days before the town was captured and Mandalay was more exposed to the British–Indian thrust.

During the fighting for Meiktila on 3 March the Green Howards the 1st Battalion the Yorkshire Regiment was heavily engaged. One of its officers was Lieutenant William Weston, who was leading a platoon of soldiers who had never before been in action and were shocked by the severity of the fighting. The courage exhibited by the slightly built young officer was remarkable and his exploit must rank as one of the most outstanding in VC history. The award of his posthumous VC was gazetted on 15 May 1945.

Lieutenant William Basil Weston, the Green Howards (Alexandra, Princess of Wales's Own Yorkshire Regiment) attached the West Yorkshire Regiment, the Prince of Wales's Own

This officer, on 3rd March 1945, during the attack on the town of Meiktila, Burma, was commanding a platoon. The task of the company was to clear jungle from the north to the water's edge – a distance of about 1,600 yards, of which the last 800 yards was not only strongly held but was a labyrinth of tracks and well constructed buildings. The company was working with tanks and Lieutenant Weston's platoon was one of the platoons leading the attack. The assault of the last 800 yards was commenced at 1330 hours and was to be completed by dusk.

Practically every man in Weston's platoon was seeing service for the first time and under difficult conditions. From the start Lieutenant Weston realised that only by personal example on his part could he carry out the task within the time. As the advance continued the already strong opposition increased until it reached a stage when it can only be described as fanatical. Fire from light automatics was heavy from concealed positions and concrete emplacements. Each bunker position had to be taken separately. Fire from the front, including that of snipers, was accurate and throughout the day fighting was at close quarters and at times was hand to hand.

By his magnificent bravery Lieutenant Weston inspired the men of his platoon to great achievements. Without thought of his personal safety he personally led his men into position after position, exterminating the enemy wherever found.

Throughout, the leadership was superb, encouraging his Platoon to the same fanatical zest as that shown by the enemy. His bravery, his coolness under fire and enthusiasm inspired his Platoon. There was no hesitation on his part and no matter how heavy or sustained the enemy's fire he boldly and resolutely led his men on from bunker position to bunker position. It was at 1700 hours, within sight of the water's edge which marked the completion of the Platoon's task, that he was held up by a very strong bunker position. Lieutenant Weston, appreciating the limited time now at his disposal and the necessity of clearing the area before nightfall, quickly directed the fire of the tanks with him on to the position. He then led a party with bayonets and grenades to eliminate the enemy within the bunker. As on many occasions before, he was the first into the bunker. At the entrance to the bunker he was shot at by the enemy inside and fell forward wounded. As he lay on the ground and still fired by the undaunted courage that he had shown throughout the day, he withdrew the pin from a grenade in his hand and by doing so killed himself and most of the enemy in the bunker. It is possible that he could have attempted to reach safety but to do so would have endangered the lives of his men who were following him into the bunker. Throughout the final 3½ hours of battle Lieutenant Weston set an example which seldom can have been equalled. His bravery and inspiring leadership was beyond question. At no time during the day did he relax and inspired by the deeds of valour which he continually performed, he personally led on his men as an irresistible force.

The final supreme self-sacrifice of this gallant young officer within sight of victory was typical of the courage and bravery so magnificently displayed and sustained throughout the day's operation.

Basil Weston, who was only just 21 when he performed his astonishing exploit, was born in Ulverston, Lancashire. He is buried in the Commonwealth War Graves Commission Cemetery at Taukkyan, Burma. In St Mary's Roman Catholic Church, Ulverston, is a plaque to his memory.

Claud Raymond

On 20 March Mandalay was captured and the city was cleared in several days of fighting. The battle of the plain was over and those of the enemy who escaped were compelled to abandon heavy equipment and flee eastward to the Shan Hills. For General Slim the next stage was a race against time for Rangoon before the monsoon broke in April–May; when that happened all military movement would be impossible.

The Japanese still strongly held Taungup, the most southerly of their bases in the Arakan coastal area. In March an Indian infantry brigade advanced southward along the road from Letpan to Taungup. Some 40 miles ahead of this brigade was a small patrol working with a Commando unit, whose job it was to gain intelligence, create diversions and carry out demolitions. Second in command of the patrol was Lieutenant Claud Raymond of the Corps of Royal Engineers, whose immediate task was to study the enemy's defences and the condition of the routes to them. However, he was also a trained infantryman and it was as an infantry officer that on 21 March he performed an exploit that resulted in the award of a posthumous VC, gazetted on 28 June 1945.

Lieutenant Claud Raymond, Corps of Royal Engineers

In Burma, on the afternoon of 21st March, 1945, Lieutenant Raymond was second-in-charge of a small patrol which was acting in conjunction with a larger detachment of a special force whose objective was to obtain information and create a diversion in the area of Taungup, by attacking and destroying isolated enemy posts some 40 miles in advance of an Indian Infantry Brigade, pushing down the road from Letpan to Taungup.

The patrol was landed on the south bank of the Thinganet Chaung, an area known to be held by numerous enemy strong points and gun positions, and marched about five miles inland. As they were nearing the village of Talaku and moving across an open stretch of ground, they were heavily fired on from the slopes of a jungle covered hill by a strongly entrenched enemy detachment.

Lieutenant Raymond immediately charged in the direction of the fire. As he began to climb the hill he was wounded in the right shoulder, but he ignored this wound and continued up the slope firing his rifle from the hip. He had advanced only a few yards further when a Japanese threw a grenade which burst in his face and most severely wounded him. He fell but almost immediately picked himself up again and in spite of loss of blood from his wounds, which later were to prove fatal, he still continued on, leading his section under intense fire. He was hit yet a third time, his wrist being shattered by what appeared to have been an explosive bullet. In spite of this third wound he never wavered but carried on into the enemy position itself and in the sharp action which followed was largely responsible for the killing of two Japanese and the wounding of a third.

The remaining Japanese then fled in panic into the jungle, thus leaving the position in our hands together with much equipment.

The position itself was strongly fortified by foxholes and small bunkers and would have proved extremely formidable had not the attack been pressed home with great determination under the courageous leadership of Lieutenant Raymond.

Several other men were wounded during the action and Lieutenant Raymond refused all treatment until they had been attended to, insisting despite the gravity of his injuries, on walking back towards the landing craft in case the delay in treating his wounds and carrying him should endanger the withdrawal of the patrol.

It was not until he had walked nearly a mile that he collapsed and had to allow himself to be carried on an improvised stretcher. Even then he was continually encouraging the other wounded by giving the thumbs up sign and thus undoubtedly helping them to keep cheerful and minimise the extent of their injuries until the landing craft was reached. Soon after he died of his wounds.

The outstanding gallantry, remarkable endurance and fortitude of

Lieutenant Raymond, which refused to allow him to collapse, although mortally wounded, was an inspiration to everyone and a major factor in the capture of the strong point. His self-sacrifice in refusing attention to his wounds undoubtedly saved the patrol by allowing it to withdraw in time before the Japanese could bring up fresh forces from neighbouring positions for a counter attack.

Lieutenant Claud Raymond, who came from Mottistone, Isle of Wight, was only 21 when he was killed. He is buried in the Commonwealth War Graves Commission Cemetery at Taukkyan, Burma, and is commemorated in the Royal Engineers' Museum at Rochester, Kent.

P.R. Collins – the Non-VC

I have mentioned that numerous acts of great valour which might be supposed to merit the award of the VC have not been so rewarded. One instance in the Burma campaigns of 1944–5 provides an excellent and until now unpublished example. Major P.R. Collins of the 4th Battalion 2nd King Edward VII's Own Gurkha Rifles was recommended for the VC in an action in which he lost his life. The recommendation was not accepted and Major Collins received only a Mention in Despatches. Under the regulations concerning gallantry awards of the time he could not have been posthumously granted any other award, hence his Mention in Despatches. However, a number of former active-service soldiers to whom I have shown the citation consider that the action it describes should have resulted in a VC award. Unless some as yet unknown documents come to light we shall never know why it was not allowed. It was printed after the war in the privately published 50-page regimental history (Gale and Polden, 1949).

Major P.R. Collins's VC citation, of which an extract is given below, may stand in this book for all the brave soldiers and airmen who were recommended for this supreme decoration but did not receive it.

On 7th June, 1945, the 4th Battalion, 2nd Gurkha Rifles, was engaged in carrying out an attack on a strong Japanese raiding base at Tanbingon in the foothills of the Pegu Yomas. Major P.R. Collins was in command of 'B' Company.

'B' Company's task was to block the tracks running east from the village towards Ondaw, where further Japanese forces were known to be located. After an arduous night march on a compass bearing through thick jungle, Major Collins detached four sections to establish his first block and went on to take up the main blocking position with the remaining five sections and Company HQ. As dawn was breaking a burst of fire was heard from the first block and this was followed by heavy machine-gun, grenade discharger and rifle fire on Major Collins' force. In the darkness he had penetrated into a strong Japanese position consisting of five cunningly hidden bunkers. Japanese fire, including five light machine guns, was sweeping 'B' Company from the front and both flanks at a range of thirty yards and the position was critical as the bunkers were almost impossible to locate in the waist-high grass and scrub. With utter disregard of danger and supreme coolness, Major Collins walked from section to section. Standing up under a hail of bullets, he succeeded in locating all five bunkers and by firing his rifle at them was able to direct the fire of his men on to their correct targets.

He then organized an attack with two sections on the two left-hand bunkers and again under intensified fire, walked back to direct the covering fire of the remaining sections.

By this time, in the damp heat of the jungle, Major Collins was almost exhausted by his exertions and the strain of constant exposure to imminent danger. Whilst his attack was in progress, enemy reinforcements from Ondaw arrived by mechanical transport and formed up in readiness to counter-attack. It then became obvious that Major Collins would have to withdraw his small force to escape encirclement by superior numbers. The enemy launched their attack but in spite of his fatigue, Major Collins once more walked round under heavy fire to all his sections giving out orders for the evacuation of the wounded and the withdrawal of his force. Enemy pressure increased but the withdrawal was so skilfully planned and controlled that heavy casualties were inflicted on the Japanese and the wounded carried safely away. Major Collins stayed with the last section to cover the remainder and finally gave the order for it to pull out as the enemy closed in from all sides.

He was killed by light machine-gun fire at a range of fifteen yards after a sustained display of courage, determination, leadership and endurance under conditions of extreme danger which is quite beyond all praise.

As a result of his action Tanbingon was captured and consolidated by the remainder of the Battalion at negligible cost and Ondaw seized the following day against trifling opposition. When Major Collins' body was recovered, forty dead Japanese were found close to the spot where he had held off the counter-attack and covered the withdrawal. Captured documents showed later that the strength of the enemy with whom he was engaged was more than two hundred.

To Major Collins's self-sacrifice, magnificent bravery and outstanding leadership are due the heavy defeat of a strong Japanese force, the capture of two important enemy strongpoints and the safe withdrawal of his own men from a critical position.

CHAPTER NINE

The Liberation of Europe 1944–5

D-Day

Stanley Hollis

The war in North Africa had been over for 18 months before the D-Day landings in June 1944, the campaigns in Italy had been going on for nine months and the fighting in India–Burma for two and a half years. The majority of men who had won the VC were, sadly, dead and buried. The war in north-west Europe that began on 6 June 1944 and ended in May 1945 would give other soldiers the opportunity to demonstrate valour beyond the call of duty.

Planning for the invasion of Europe had been settled at conferences but when Generals Eisenhower and Montgomery arrived in Britain from the Mediterranean the planning became reality. Normandy was chosen as the invasion area because it had weaker defences than the Pas de Calais, the alternative site. Between them, the Americans, British and Canadians assembled in Britain 45 divisions, 6,000 warplanes and an armada. Three airborne divisions dropped on the early morning of 6 June and five infantry divisions arrived on the beaches from landing craft. The Germans made only one organized counter-attack that day and it was repulsed. However, the fighting was intense as the Allied infantry strove to capture blockhouses, concrete gun positions, fortified houses and communications centres.

Despite the intensity of the fighting on a 50-mile front, and behind it where the airborne units were operating, only one VC was awarded for a D-Day exploit. But what a remarkable exploit it was. The award went to Company Sergeant Major Stanley Hollis of the 6th Battalion Green Howards and the citation was gazetted on 17 August 1944.

Warrant Officer Class II (Company Sergeant Major) Stanley Elton Hollis, the Green Howards (Alexandra, Princess of Wales's Own Yorkshire Regiment) (Middlesbrough)

In Normandy on 6th June, 1944, during the assault on the beaches and the Mont Fleury Battery, CSM Hollis's Company Commander noticed that two of the pillboxes had been by-passed, and went with CSM Hollis to see that they were clear. When they were 20 yards from the pillbox, a machine-gun opened fire from the slit and CSM Hollis instantly rushed straight at the pillbox, firing his Sten gun. He jumped on top of the pillbox, re-charged his magazine, threw a grenade in through the door and fired his Sten gun into it, killing two Germans and making the remainder prisoner. He then cleared several Germans from a neighbouring trench. By his action, he undoubtedly saved his Company from being fired on heavily from the rear and enabled them to open the main beach exit.

Later the same day, in the village of Crepon, the Company encountered a field gun and crew armed with Spandaus at 100 yards range. CSM Hollis was put in command of a party to cover an attack on the gun, but the movement was held up. Seeing this, CSM Hollis pushed right forward to engage the gun with a PIAT from a house at 50 yards range. He was observed by a sniper who fired and grazed his right cheek, and at the same moment the gun swung round and fired at point-blank range into the house. To avoid the fallen masonry CSM Hollis moved his party to an alternative position. Two of the enemy gun crew had by this time been killed, and the gun was destroyed shortly afterwards. He later found that two of his men had stayed behind in the house and immediately volunteered to get them out. In full view of the enemy who were continually firing at him, he went forward alone using a Bren gun to distract their attention from the other men. Under cover of his diversion, the two men were able to get back.

Wherever fighting was heaviest, CSM Hollis appeared and in the course of a magnificent day's work, he displayed the utmost gallantry and on two separate occasions his courage and initiative prevented the enemy from holding up the advance at critical stages. It was largely through his heroism and resource that the Company's objectives were gained and casualties were not heavier, and by his own bravery he saved the lives of many of his men.

Stanley Hollis, who came from Middlesbrough, Yorkshire, was 31 at the time of his exploit. He died in February 1972. His men said that he was every inch the sergeant major, efficient, incisive and always immaculate. Photographs of the man give him these qualities. It is said that he refused the offer of a commission because he preferred the more distinctive rank of warrant officer to that of being 'just one more lieutenant'.

Normandy

Sidney Bates

By 12 June the Allies had linked their beachheads and held an unbroken front of 60 miles which was 15 miles deep at its widest. They were well and truly established but the Germans, even though they now lacked airpower, contested every position. Eisenhower and Montgomery and the other Allied leaders knew that progress would be slow – they had a schedule that would bring them to the Rhine in 11 months after the landing.

In Operation Epsom, British infantry reached the River Odon and on 8 July they occupied half of the city of Caen, which had been reduced to rubble by Allied bombings. Operation Goodwood followed, a large-scale tank battle to sweep around the east of Caen, but German Panzer units and artillery smashed many British tanks.

The Americans, in an infantry and tank offensive, broke through the German lines on 31 July and reached the large town of Avranches at the base of the Cherbourg peninsula. Hitler now overrode his generals and ordered what remained of 10 Panzer divisions in Normandy to mass for an attack through Mortain to Avranches. The Führer's idea was to cut off the spearhead of the developing American threat.

Ten miles north of Mortain lay the Normandy village of Sourdeval, a picturesque settlement of old buildings, gardens and the ubiquitous hedgerows. The Royal Norfolk Regiment was holding Sourdeval when the 10th Panzer Division hit them on 6 August as part of Hitler's drive towards Avranches. The odds were against the Norfolks but they held fast through the efforts of splendid junior leaders, one of whom was Corporal Sidney Bates, whose posthumous award of the VC was gazetted on 2 November 1944.

Corporal Sidney Bates, the Royal Norfolk Regiment

In North-West Europe on 6th August, 1944, the position held by a battalion of the Royal Norfolk Regiment near Sourdeval was attacked in strength by 10th SS Panzer Division. The attack started with a heavy and accurate artillery and mortar programme on the position which the enemy had, by this time, pin-pointed.

Half an hour later the main attack developed and heavy machine-gun and mortar fire was concentrated on the point of junction of the two forward companies.

Corporal Bates was commanding the right forward section of the left forward company which suffered some casualties, so he decided to move the remnants of his section to an alternative position whence he appreciated he could better counter the enemy thrust. However, the enemy wedge grew still deeper, until there were about 50 to 60 Germans, supported by machine-guns and mortars, in the area occupied by the section.

Seeing that the situation was becoming desperate, Corporal Bates then seized a light machine-gun and charged the enemy, moving forward through a hail of bullets and splinters and firing the gun from his hip. He was almost immediately wounded by machine-gun fire and fell to the ground but recovered himself quickly, got up and continued advancing towards the enemy, spraying bullets from his gun as he went. His action by now was having an effect on the enemy riflemen and machine gunners but mortar bombs continued to fall all around him.

He was then hit for the second time and much more seriously and painfully wounded. However, undaunted, he staggered once more to his feet and continued towards the enemy who were now seemingly nonplussed by their inability to check him. His constant firing continued until the enemy started to withdraw before him. At this moment, he was hit for the third time by mortar bomb splinters – a wound that was to prove mortal. He again fell to the ground but continued to fire his weapon until his strength failed him. This was not, however, until the enemy had withdrawn and the situation in this locality had been restored.

Corporal Bates died shortly afterwards of the wounds he had received but by his supreme gallantry and self-sacrifice he had personally restored what had been a critical situation.

Sidney Bates, who came from Camberwell, London, was not quite 23 when he was killed. He is buried in the Commonwealth War Graves Commission Cemetery at Bayeux, France. His exploit on 6 August 1944 was a classic demonstration of splendid infantry section leading. It also showed, yet again, how one determined soldier can turn almost certain local defeat into a triumph.

But his actions went further than that. The Panzer attack on Mortain was stopped and though this was hardly due solely to the courage of Corporal Bates, he set an example that day that inspired men in other units.

David Jamieson

While Corporal Bates and his company of the Norfolks were holding Sourdeval another Norfolk company was holding a bridgehead over the River Orne, Normandy. The bridges across this river had been important objectives of the British 6th Airborne Division in pre-dawn glider attacks on 6 June, D-Day.

Bridgeheads across rivers are always important, either to prevent the enemy crossing or to protect them so that allied troops may cross in safety. On 7/8 August 1944 Panzer units struggled to cross the Orne to establish a new front against the steadily advancing Allies.

Major David Jamieson's bridgehead over the Orne was south of Grimbosq, Normandy, and it was imperative that it be held. The Germans were determined to smash Jamieson's block and for 36 hours they battered at the Norfolks' positions. The award for Captain Jamieson's VC, gazetted on 26 October 1944, illustrates how sustained the enemy attack was and how continuous was Jamieson's resistance with fewer than 100 men and with all other officers wounded and out of action.

Captain David Jamieson, the Royal Norfolk Regiment

Captain Jamieson was in command of a Company of the Royal Norfolk Regiment which established a bridgehead over the River Orne, south of Grimbosq, in Normandy.

On August 7th, 1944, the enemy made three counter-attacks which were repulsed with heavy losses. The last of these took place at 1830 hours when a German Battle Group with Tiger and Panther tanks attacked and the brunt of the fighting fell on Captain Jamieson's Company. Continuous heavy fighting ensued for more than four hours until the enemy were driven off, after suffering severe casualties and the loss of three tanks and an armoured car accounted for by this Company. Throughout these actions, Captain Jamieson displayed outstanding courage and leadership which had a decisive influence on the course of the battle and resulted in the defeat of these determined enemy attacks.

On the morning of August 8th the enemy attacked with a fresh Battle Group and succeeded in penetrating the defences surrounding the Company on three sides. During this attack two of the three tanks in support of the Company were destroyed and Captain Jamieson left his trench under close range fire from enemy arms of all kinds and went over to direct the fire of the remaining tank, but as he could not get in touch with the commander of the tank by the outside telephone he climbed upon it in full view of the enemy. During this period Captain Jamieson was wounded in the right eye and left forearm but when his wounds were dressed he refused to be evacuated. By this time all the other officers had become casualties so Captain Jamieson reorganised his Company, regardless of personal safety, walking amongst his men in full view of the enemy, as there was no cover. After several hours of bitter and confused fighting the last Germans were driven from the Company position.

The enemy counter-attacked the Company three more times during that day with infantry and tanks. Captain Jamieson continued in command, arranging for artillery support over his wireless and going out into the open on each occasion to encourage his men. By the evening the Germans had withdrawn, leaving a ring of dead and burnt out tanks around the position.

Throughout this thirty-six hours of bitter and close fighting, and despite the pain of his wounds, Captain Jamieson showed superb qualities of leadership and great personal bravery. There were times when the position appeared hopeless, but on each occasion it was restored by his coolness and determination. He personally was largely responsible for the holding of this important bridgehead over the River Orne and the repulse of seven German counter-attacks with great loss to the enemy.

David Jamieson standing amid the carnage he and his men had inflicted upon the German tank units is one of the abiding images of the war. Jamieson came from Thornham, near King's Lynn, Norfolk, and he was 23 at the time of his exploit. He was later promoted major.

Tasker Watkins

The Allied plan in Normandy, as organized by Eisenhower and Montgomery, was for the Americans from the south and the British from the north to close the 'Falaise Gap' through which German units were withdrawing eastward and trap them in the 'Falaise pocket'. On the night of 14 August the two Allied wings were 15 miles on either side of the town of Falaise.

Field Marshal Rommel had been seriously wounded during an RAF attack on his car and his place had been taken by General Von Kluge who put the critical situation to Hitler whose consent was needed even to save his armies from certain destruction. Between 50 and 60 dismembered German divisions remained in Normandy. If they were to fight somewhere else, Kluge said on 15 August, they must retreat at once. Hitler angrily and reluctantly agreed and ordered the Twelfth SS Hitler Youth Division to hold open the ever tightening throat of the pocket while the rest of the once great force escaped.

But it was not as easy as it might have seemed to Hitler, a long way from the battlefield. Every objective that might assist the Germans to withdraw was attacked. The task of Lieutenant Tasker Watkins of the 1st/5th Battalion Welch Regiment was to help cut the railway line at Barfour. The exploit for which he was awarded the VC took place on 16 August and the citation was gazetted on 2 November 1944.

Lieutenant Tasker Watkins, the Welch Regiment

In North-West Europe on the evening of 16th August, 1944, Lieutenant Watkins was commanding a company of the Welch Regiment. The battalion was ordered to attack objectives near the railway at Bafour. Lieutenant Watkins's company had to cross open cornfields in which booby traps had been set. It was not yet dusk and the company soon came under heavy machine-gun fire from posts in the corn and farther back, and also fire from an 88 mm. gun; many casualties were caused and the advance was slowed up.

Lieutenant Watkins, the only officer left, placed himself at the head of his men and under short range fire charged two posts in succession, personally killing or wounding the occupants with his Sten gun. On reaching his objective he found an anti-tank gun manned by a German soldier; his Sten gun jammed so he threw it in the German's face and shot him with his pistol before he had time to recover.

Lieutenant Watkins's company now had only some 30 men left and was counter-attacked by 50 enemy infantry. Lieutenant Watkins directed the fire of his men and then led a bayonet charge which resulted in the almost complete destruction of the enemy.

It was now dusk and orders were given for the battalion to withdraw. These orders were not received by Lieutenant Watkins's company as the wireless set had been destroyed. They now found themselves alone and surrounded in depleted numbers and in failing light. Lieutenant Watkins decided to rejoin his battalion but while passing through the cornfields once more, he was challenged by an enemy post at close range. He ordered his men to scatter and himself charged the post with a Bren gun and silenced it. He then led the remnants of his company back to battalion headquarters.

His superb gallantry and total disregard for his own safety during an extremely difficult period were responsible for saving the lives of his men, and had a decisive influence on the course of the battle.

Tasker Watkins, who came from Nelson, Glamorgan, was 24 at the time of his exploit. A lawyer by profession, he had a distinguished career, became senior presiding judge for England and Wales and was knighted.

The name of the town mentioned in his citation is correctly Barfour, not Bafour. The Twelfth SS Hitler Youth Division, fighting with the fanatical bravery for which Hitler Youth units became famous, was cut to pieces but it kept the way open to the River Seine. British units and French Resistance groups had destroyed the bridges but the Germans crossed by ferries. Despite the courage of Lieutenant Tasker Watkins and others many German soldiers evaded the trap that had been set for them.

Arnhem

John Hollington Grayburn

By mid-September 1944 the Allies had freed most of the German-occupied areas of western Europe except for isolated areas of Belgium and France, while nearly all of Holland remained to be liberated. Progress since the crossing of the Seine in pursuit of the withdrawing Germans had been rapid. The principal battle line now had its left pivot at Ostend on Belgium's

North Sea coast and extended east through Antwerp and most of Belgium. Near Aachen, American troops were actually on German soil and holding a tiny portion of the Siegfried Line.

The British Second Army was nearer the coast, driving towards Nijmegen, while the First Army, keeping to the line of the Meuse River, was aiming at Aachen.

So many Allied divisions were arriving in France that Eisenhower and his Army commanders did not have enough supplies for them nor could they get what they had to the front fast enough. The priority therefore was to restore the great port of Antwerp, which had been badly damaged by the Germans, and use it as the base for the invading armies.

Eisenhower and Montgomery did not always agree but they concurred on the need for the British to thrust ahead and establish a bridgehead on the River Rhine. Montgomery suggested a daring plan which became known as Operation Market Garden, an airborne landing with Arnhem as its centre. Fundamentally, the plan was for the British 1st Airborne Division and the Polish Brigade to make a landing at Arnhem, more than 60 miles from British frontline positions east of Antwerp. While the paratroops held the bridge over the River Lek, the British XXX Corps would race northwards through Belgium and Holland to link up with them. This would cut off the German Fifteenth Army to the west.

The whole operation looked good on paper and on 17 September 1944 it began well. The first VC of the Arnhem epic was won that day by a lieutenant of the Parachute Regiment, John Grayburn, whose posthumous citation was gazetted on 23 January 1945.

Lieutenant John Hollington Grayburn, Parachute Regiment Army Air Corps

For supreme courage, leadership and devotion to duty.

Lieutenant Grayburn was a platoon commander of the Parachute Battalion which was dropped on 17th September, 1944, with the task of seizing and holding the bridge over the Rhine at Arnhem.

The North end of the bridge was captured and early in the night Lieutenant Grayburn was ordered to assault and capture the Southern end with his platoon. He led his platoon on to the bridge and began the attack with the utmost determination but the platoon was met by a hail of fire from two 20 mm. quick firing guns, and from the machine guns of an armoured car. Almost at once Lieutenant Grayburn was shot through the shoulder. Although there was no cover on the bridge, and in spite of his wound, Lieutenant Grayburn continued to press forward with the greatest dash and bravery until casualties became so heavy that he was ordered to withdraw. He directed the withdrawal from the bridge personally and was himself the last man to come off the embankment into comparative cover.

Later, his platoon was ordered to occupy a house which was vital to the defence of the bridge and he personally organized the occupation of the house.

Throughout the next day and night the enemy made ceaseless attacks on the house, using not only infantry with mortars and machine guns but also tanks and self-propelled guns. The house was very exposed and difficult to defend and the fact that it did not fall to the enemy must be attributed to Lieutenant Grayburn's great courage and inspiring leadership. He constantly exposed himself to the enemy's fire while moving among and encouraging his platoon, and seemed completely oblivious to danger.

On 19th September 1944, the enemy renewed his attacks, which increased in intensity as the house was vital to the defence of the bridge. All attacks were repulsed, due to Lieutenant Grayburn's valour and skill in organizing and encouraging his men, until eventually the house was set on fire and had to be evacuated.

Lieutenant Grayburn then took command of elements of all arms, including the remainder of his own company, and re-formed them into a fighting force. He spent the night organizing a defensive position to cover the approaches to the bridge.

On 20th September, 1944, he extended his defence by a series of fighting patrols which prevented the enemy gaining access to the houses in the vicinity, the occupation of which would have prejudiced the defence of the bridge. This forced the enemy to bring up tanks which brought Lieutenant Grayburn's positions under such heavy fire that he was forced to withdraw to an area farther North. The enemy now attempted to lay demolition charges under the bridge and the situation was critical. Realising this, Lieutenant Grayburn organised and led a fighting patrol which drove the enemy off temporarily and gave time for the fuzes to be removed. He was again wounded, this time in the back, but refused to be evacuated.

Finally, an enemy tank, against which Lieutenant Grayburn had no defence, approached so close to his position that it became untenable. He then stood up in full view of the tank and personally directed the withdrawal of his men to the main defensive perimeter to which he had been ordered.

He was killed that night.

From the evening of September 17th until the night of September 20th, 1944, a period of over three days, Lieutenant Grayburn led his men with supreme gallantry and determination. Though in pain and weakened by his wounds, short of food and without sleep, his courage never flagged. There is no doubt that had it not been for this officer's inspiring leadership and personal bravery, the Arnhem bridge could never have been held for this time.

Lieutenant Grayburn had been born in India, and came from Chalfont

St Giles, Buckinghamshire. He was 26 when he was killed. He is buried in the Commonwealth War Graves Commission Cemetery at Oosterbeek, Arnhem. His defence of the Arnhem bridge was one of the great epics of the war and was the basis for one of the major scenes of the film *A Bridge Too Far*. It seems more than usually tragic that after his three-day stand against overwhelming odds Grayburn did not know of his VC award.

Lionel Ernest Queripel

After two days the Arnhem operation faltered, though not for lack of courage among the airborne troops. The British and Poles discovered, to their surprise, that an additional German division was present in the area. It was troops from this division who had so quickly surrounded Lieutenant Grayburn and his men at the Lek bridge. By recapturing this bridge the Germans cut the British 1st Airborne Division into two groups and deprived them of unified command. Moreover, General Kurt Student, a brilliant leader and commander of the German First Parachute Army, was in Arnhem, as was General Walther Model, another dynamic leader. Their orders were incisive. The advancing British XXX Corps must be stopped by blowing up all bridges and dykes in their path. The men of 6th Airborne were on their own.

Much confused fighting took place as British and Polish units and sub-units made gallant stands against overwhelming odds. Some continued to attack. One such attack was led by Captain Lionel Queripel of the Royal Sussex Regiment. After demonstrating great valour and dedicated leadership he too was killed. His VC citation was gazetted on 1 February 1945.

Captain Lionel Ernest Queripel, the Royal Sussex Regiment (1st Airborne Division)

In Holland on the 19th September, 1944, Captain Queripel was acting as Company Commander of a composite Company composed of three Parachute Battalions.

At 14.00 hours on that day his Company was advancing along a main road which ran on an embankment towards Arnhem. The advance was conducted under continuous medium machine-gun fire which at one period became so heavy that the Company became split up on either side of the road and suffered considerable losses. Captain Queripel at once proceeded to reorganise his force, crossing and re-crossing the road whilst doing so, under extremely heavy and accurate fire. During this period he carried a wounded Sergeant to the Regimental Aid Post under fire and was himself wounded in the face.

Having reorganised his force, Captain Queripel personally led a party of men against the strong point holding up the advance. This strong point consisted of a captured British anti-tank gun and two machine-guns. Despite the extremely heavy fire directed at him, Captain Queripel succeeded in killing the crews of the machine-guns and recapturing the anti-tank gun. As a result of this, the advance was able to continue.

Later in the same day, Captain Queripel found himself cut off with a small party of men and took up a position in a ditch. By this time he had received further wounds in both arms. Regardless of his wounds and of the very heavy mortar and spandau fire, he continued to inspire his men to resist with hand grenades, pistols and the few remaining rifles.

As, however, the enemy pressure increased, Captain Queripel decided that it was impossible to hold the position any longer and ordered his men to withdraw. Despite their protests he insisted on remaining behind to cover their withdrawal with his automatic pistol and a few remaining hand grenades. This is the last occasion on which he was seen.

During the whole of a period of nine hours of confused and bitter fighting Captain Queripel displayed the highest standard of gallantry under most difficult and trying circumstances. His courage, leadership and devotion to duty were magnificent, and an inspiration to all. This officer is officially reported to be wounded and missing.

The final sentence of Queripel's citation shows the uncertainty about much of what had happened in the Arnhem pocket, even in February 1945. The war was still raging and 'This officer is officially reported to be wounded and missing' was the most accurate information available at the time. Captain Queripel had succumbed to his wounds but this was not confirmed until 4 April 1945, when the Canadians finally liberated Arnhem. He is buried in the Commonwealth War Graves Commission Cemetery at Oosterbeek, Arnhem. From Winterbourne Monkton, Dorset, Queripel was 24 when he was killed.

Robert Henry Cain

The glider-borne 2nd South Staffords had the task of securing the bridges over the final obstacle at Arnhem, the Nederijn. Insufficient aircraft were available to tow the gliders and priority was given to the American divisions, for if they failed to take their objectives the entire operation would fail. Because of the shortage only about half of the British 1st Airborne could be launched on the first day, 17 September. Furthermore, within the division the 2nd South Staffords were split between the first and second lifts, a far from ideal arrangement.

The leading half of the Staffords had a quiet enough day on 17 September but on the 18th they were sent into Arnhem to try to get through to the main road bridge, which had been secured by the 2nd Parachute Battalion. It was now cut off. The men of the second lift were to follow as soon as they landed, but against increasing enemy resistance they could only reach the town's outskirts that night. After much fighting they retired within a perimeter formed around the village of Oosterbeek and this they held for five days before withdrawing.

Major Robert Cain was commanding B Company in the first lift but something went wrong with the towing aircraft and Cain found himself landing back in Kent. He returned with the second lift and was able to resume command of his company after the advance was held up on 19 September. The citation for his VC, gazetted on 2 November 1944, picks up the story of Cain's series of exploits.

Captain (temporary Major) Robert Henry Cain, the Royal Northumberland Fusiliers, attached the South Staffordshire Regiment (1st Airborne Division)

In Holland on 19th September, 1944, Major Cain was commanding a rifle company of the South Staffordshire Regiment during the battle of Arnhem when his company was cut off from the rest of the battalion and during the next six days was closely engaged with enemy tanks, self-propelled guns and infantry. The Germans made repeated attempts to break into the company position by infiltration and had they succeeded in doing so the whole situation of the Airborne Troops would have been jeopardised.

Major Cain, by his outstanding devotion to duty and remarkable powers of leadership was to a large extent personally responsible for saving a vital sector from falling into the hands of the enemy.

On 20th September a Tiger tank approached the area held by his company and Major Cain went out alone to deal with it, armed with a PIAT. Taking up a position he held his fire until the tank was only 20 yards away when he opened up. The tank immediately halted and turned its guns on him, shooting away a corner of the house near where this officer was lying. Although wounded by machine gun bullets and falling masonry, Major Cain continued firing until he had scored several direct hits, immobilised the tank and supervised the bringing up of a 75 mm. howitzer which completely destroyed it. Only then would he consent to have his wounds dressed.

The next morning this officer drove off three more tanks by the fearless use of his PIAT, on each occasion leaving cover and taking up position in open ground with complete disregard for his personal safety.

During the following days, Major Cain was everywhere where danger threatened, moving amongst his men and encouraging them by his fearless example to hold out. He refused rest and medical attention in spite of the fact that his hearing had been seriously impaired because of a perforated eardrum and he was suffering from multiple wounds.

On the 25th September the enemy made a concerted attack on Major Cain's position using self-propelled guns, flame throwers and infantry. By this time the last PIAT had been put out of action and Major Cain was armed with only a light 2-inch mortar. However, by a skilful use of this weapon and his daring leadership of the few men still under his command, he completely demoralized the enemy who, after an engagement lasting more than three hours, withdrew in disorder.

Throughout the whole course of the Battle of Arnhem, Major Cain showed superb gallantry. His powers of endurance and leadership were the admiration of all his fellow officers and stories of his valour were being constantly exchanged amongst the troops. His coolness and courage under incessant fire could not be surpassed.

For anybody to take on a massive German Tiger tank single-handed was an audacious act. To stay on the attack and immobilize the Tiger with PIAT rounds was outstandingly brave. That Cain's VC was gazetted within six weeks of his exploits indicates that numerous officers and men were able to withdraw from Arnhem and report them. A tribute came from the divisional commander, Major-General Roy Urquhart, who visited the Staffords when they returned to Britain. He said to the CO, 'We have got to get Robert Cain a VC. He was superb!'

Robert Cain was born in Shanghai and had spent eight years with Shell in Thailand before the war. Returning to Britain soon after the outbreak of hostilities, he was commissioned and served with several units before volunteering for airborne forces. Posted to the Staffords, he led B Company in Sicily and Italy. He was 36 at the time of his VC exploit; he died at Crowborough, Sussex, in May 1974. A plaque to his memory is in the Garrison Church, Whittington Barracks, Lichfield, Staffordshire.

Cain's VC together with the beret, smock and insignia that he wore while winning his supreme award are in the regimental museum.

John Daniel Baskeyfield

Another soldier of the 2nd South Staffordshire Regiment, Lance-Sergeant John Baskeyfield, was prominent in the Arnhem epic. Having withdrawn from Arnhem after their brave attempt to reach the main bridge, the battalion took up positions at the 'Station Oosterbeek position', from which the battalion could cover the withdrawal of the airborne troops into the perimeter around the village of Oosterbeek, an attractive suburb of Arnhem.

The strength of the defence depended on the machine-gun platoon, one section of which was commanded by Lance-Sergeant Baskeyfield. On 19 September the Germans pressed no further but everybody was tense that night, ready for the certain enemy thrust next day. Sergeant Baskeyfield's posthumous VC citation, gazetted on 23 November 1944, describes his exploit.

Lance-Sergeant John Daniel Baskeyfield, the South Staffordshire Regiment (1st Airborne Division)

On 20th September, 1944, during the battle of Arnhem, Lance-Sergeant Baskeyfield was the NCO in charge of a 6–pounder anti-tank gun at Oosterbeek. The enemy developed a major attack on this sector with infantry, tanks and self-propelled guns with the obvious intent to break into and overrun the battalion position. During the early stage of the action the crew commanded by this NCO was responsible for the destruction of two Tiger tanks and at least one self-propelled gun, thanks to the coolness and daring of this NCO, who with disregard for his own safety, allowed each tank to come well within 100 yards of his gun before opening fire.

In the course of this preliminary engagement Lance-Sergeant Baskeyfield was badly wounded in the leg and the remainder of his crew were either killed or badly wounded. During the brief respite after this engagement Lance-Sergeant Baskeyfield refused to be carried to the Regimental Aid Post and spent his time attending to his gun and shouting encouragement to his comrades in neighbouring trenches.

After a short interval the enemy renewed the attack with even greater ferocity than before, under cover of intense mortar and shell fire. Manning his gun quite alone Lance-Sergeant Baskeyfield continued to fire round after round at the enemy until his gun was put out of action. By this time his activity was the main factor in keeping the enemy tanks at bay. The fact that the surviving men in his vicinity were held together and kept in action was undoubtedly due to his magnificent example and outstanding courage. Time after time enemy attacks were launched and driven off. Finally, when his gun was knocked out, Lance-Sergeant Baskeyfield crawled, under intense fire, to another 6–pounder gun nearby, the crew of which had been killed and proceeded to man it single-handed. With this gun he engaged an enemy self-propelled gun which was approaching to attack. Another soldier crawled across the open ground to assist him but was killed almost at once. Lance-Sergeant Baskeyfield succeeded in firing two rounds at the self-propelled gun, scoring one direct hit which rendered it ineffective. Whilst preparing to fire a third shot, however, he was killed by a shell from a supporting enemy tank.

The superb gallantry of this NCO is beyond praise. During the remaining days at Arnhem stories of his valour were a constant inspiration to all ranks. He spurned danger, ignored pain and, by his supreme fighting spirit, infected all who witnessed his conduct with the same aggressiveness and dogged devotion to duty which characterised his actions throughout.

To appreciate the nerve and daring required for Baskeyfield's exploit it is necessary to know something of the Tiger tank and the effect it had on troops who had to face it. The British and Americans thought it was virtually invincible and it had seemed so in Normandy. On 13 June 1944 an

SS Obersturmführer, Hans Wittmann, commanding a Tiger, destroyed 25 Allied tanks and half-tracks. This sweeping destruction blocked the way ahead and prevented an entire armoured division from advancing. A massive 56 tons in weight, the Tiger had armour 100 mm thick and was armed with the tank version of the famous 88 mm gun. It was powerful enough to knock out any Allied tank. In appearance the Tiger was massive and understandably frightening and it was this giant that Lance-Sergeant John Baskeyfield faced and defeated.

Sergeant Baskeyfield had been called up at the age of 17 and was approaching 22 when he was killed. He came from Burslem, Staffordshire. After the war his VC and other medals were put up for sale on the open market but the regiment appealed to the people of the county who subscribed in just two weeks the £1,600 needed to buy them. They are now in the regimental museum. The young sergeant's body was never found but his name is commemorated on the Groesbeek Memorial, Holland, and in the Garrison Church, Whittington Barracks, Lichfield, Staffordshire.

North-West Europe

John William Harper

For the British and Americans at Arnhem the weather was as much of an enemy as the Germans. For five days rain, low cloud and wind prevented supplies and reinforcements from being flown in. A spearhead of XXX Corps reached the River Lek by road but could not force a way across it. Within the besieged pocket casualties were heavy and the airborne medical officers were hard pressed to cope with them.

On 25 September the survivors were ordered to withdraw into the American area around Eindhoven and Nijmegen which XXX Corps had by then consolidated. The epic of Arnhem – 'the bridge too far' – had come to an end.

But elsewhere progress was being made as British and Canadian troops cleared the banks of the River Scheldt so that the great port of Antwerp could be used. And while the area occupied so briefly by 1st Airborne Division was now back in German hands, British and American units and smaller parties attacked across the low-lying fields with their many rivers, ditches and dykes. It was in this difficult terrain, near Antwerp, that Corporal John Harper of the 4th Battalion the York and Lancaster Regiment won the VC with an exploit on 29 September 1944 which involved his taking command of the platoon when its officer was seriously wounded. His posthumous award was gazetted on 2 January 1945. Throughout the citation the 'dykes' referred to are waterways, although the word also means low turf walls.

Corporal John William Harper, the York and Lancaster Regiment

In North-West Europe, on 29th September, 1944, the Hallamshire Battalion of the York and Lancaster Regiment attacked the Depot de Mendicité, a natural defensive position surrounded by an earthen wall, and then a dyke, strongly held by the enemy.

Corporal Harper was commanding the leading section in the assault. The enemy were well dug in and had a perfect field of fire across 300 yards of completely flat and exposed country. With superb disregard for the hail of mortar bombs and small arms fire which the enemy brought to bear on this open ground, Corporal Harper led his section straight up to the wall and killed or captured the enemy holding the near side.

During this operation the platoon commander was seriously wounded and Corporal Harper took over control of the platoon.

As the enemy on the far side of the wall were now throwing grenades over the top Corporal Harper climbed over the wall alone, throwing grenades, and in the face of heavy close-range small arms fire personally routed the Germans directly opposing him. He took four prisoners and shot several of the remainder of the enemy as they fled.

Still completely ignoring the heavy spandau and mortar fire which was sweeping the area, once again he crossed the wall alone to find out whether it was possible for his platoon to wade the dyke which lay beyond. He found the dyke too deep and wide to cross, and once again he came back over the wall and received orders to try and establish his platoon on the enemy side of it. For the third time he climbed over alone, found some empty German weapon pits and providing the covering fire urged and encouraged his section to scale the wall and dash for cover. By this action he was able to bring down sufficient covering fire to enable the rest of the company to cross the open ground and surmount the wall for the loss of only one man.

Corporal Harper then left his platoon in charge of his senior section commander and walked alone along the banks of the dyke, in the face of heavy spandau fire, to find a crossing place. Eventually he made contact with the battalion attacking on his right and found that they had located a ford. Back he came across the open ground and whilst directing his company commander to the ford he was struck by a bullet which fatally wounded him and he died on the bank of the dyke.

The success of the battalion in driving the enemy from the wall and back across the dyke must be largely ascribed to the superb self-sacrifice and inspiring gallantry of Corporal Harper. His magnificent courage, fearlessness and devotion to duty throughout the battle set a splendid example to his men and had a decisive effect on the course of the operations.

Corporal Harper was born at Doncaster, Yorkshire, and was 29 when he was killed. He is buried in the Commonwealth War Graves Commission Cemetery at Leopoldsville, Belgium.

George Harold Eardley

By mid-October 1944 close-encounter fighting was still in progress from the west to the east of the northern front: that is, from the Scheldt estuary to Aachen. British and Canadian troops, with significant help from the Navy and Air Force, captured the island of Walcheren, which the Germans had heavily fortified. At Aachen, the Americans were fighting inside the city while another US corps met resistance on the Moselle around Bruyères.

Units of the British Second Army were advancing towards Venlo on the Dutch–German border but first they had to capture enemy positions at Overloon and Venray in Holland. These British operations were linked to those of the Americans at Aachen and were part of a general offensive on a 5-mile front. One of the British units involved east of Overloon – that is, towards the German Siegfried Line – was the 4th Battalion the King's Shropshire Light Infantry, which on 16 October came up against defences held by formidable German paratroops. The capture of the enemy positions was achieved by one British soldier, Sergeant George Eardley. The citation for his award of the VC was gazetted on 2 January 1945.

Private (acting Sergeant) George Harold Eardley, the King's Shropshire Light Infantry

In North-West Europe, on 16th October, 1944, during an attack on the wooded area East of Overloon, strong opposition was met from well sited defensive positions in orchards. The enemy were paratroops and well equipped with machine guns. A Platoon of the King's Shropshire Light Infantry was ordered to clear these orchards and so restore the momentum of the advance but was halted some 80 yards from its objective by automatic fire from enemy machine gun posts. This fire was so heavy that it appeared impossible for any man to expose himself and remain unscathed.

Notwithstanding this, Sergeant Eardley, who had spotted one machine gun post, moved forward firing his Sten gun, and killed the occupants of the post with a grenade. A second machine gun post beyond the first immediately opened up, spraying the area with fire. Sergeant Eardley, who was in a most exposed position, at once charged over 30 yards of open ground and silenced both the enemy gunners.

The attack was continued by the Platoon but was again held up by a third machine gun post, and a section sent in to dispose of it was beaten back, losing four casualties. Sergeant Eardley, ordering the section he was with to lie down, then crawled forward alone and silenced the occupants of the post with a grenade.

The destruction of these three machine gun posts single-handed by Sergeant Eardley, carried out under fire so heavy that it daunted those who were with him, enabled his Platoon to achieve its objective and in so doing ensured the success of the whole attack.

His outstanding initiative and magnificent bravery were the admiration of all who saw his gallant actions.

Eardley's stated rank calls for some explanation. The battalion had suffered casualties and several private soldiers were acting NCOs, though it was unusual for a private to be an acting sergeant; acting lance-corporal or acting corporal was more common. However, Eardley had shown leadership qualities and had already been awarded the MM. Later he was promoted to company sergeant major. George Eardley, who came from Congleton in Cheshire, was 33 at the time of his exploit, which resulted in the capture of Venray. He died in September 1991.

Dennis Donnini

On 16 December 1944 Hitler launched a great surprise offensive in the Belgian Ardennes that soon became known as the 'Battle of the Bulge' because the attack created an enormous bulge in the Allied lines. Hitler and his generals intended it to be a breakthrough right to Antwerp, thus splitting the British and American forces. By 22 December the German generals Rundstedt, Model and Guderian were urging Hitler to call off the offensive but he refused. The Germans had made their greatest gain by 24 December but there was no enemy withdrawal and fighting continued along the front created by the bulge.

Chronological almanacs of the war devote little space to most of these operations, though one of the major published accounts* states for 16 January 1945:

Western Front There are attacks by the British XIII Corps near Roermond aimed at eliminating the small German salient west of the Maas.

The almanac's entry for 17 January merely states that the US Third Army had captured Diekirch (in Alsace) while for 18 July there is no entry at all. This is a pity because on that date British units, including the 4th/5th Battalion Royal Scots Fusiliers were still in battle west of Roermond, Holland – north of the Bulge – eliminating a troublesome pocket of resistance. In the battalion's ranks was the slightly built 19-year-old Fusilier

---

* *The Almanac of World War II*, ed. Brigadier Peter Young (Hamlyn, London, 1981).

Dennis Donnini, whose citation for the award of his posthumous VC was gazetted on 20 March 1945.

Fusilier Dennis Donnini, the Royal Scots Fusiliers

In North-West Europe on 18th January, 1945, a Battalion of the Royal Scots Fusiliers supported by tanks was the leading Battalion in the assault of the German position between the Rivers Roer and Maas. This consisted of a broad belt of minefields and wire on the other side of a stream.

As the result of a thaw the armour was unable to cross the stream and the infantry had to continue the assault without the support of the tanks. Fusilier Donnini's platoon was ordered to attack a small village.

As they left their trenches the platoon came under concentrated machine gun and rifle fire from the houses and Fusilier Donnini was hit by a bullet in the head. After a few minutes he recovered consciousness, charged down thirty yards of open road and threw a grenade into the nearest window.

The enemy fled through the gardens of four houses, closely pursued by Fusilier Donnini and the survivors of his platoon. Under heavy fire at seventy yards range Fusilier Donnini and two companions crossed an open space and reached the cover of a wooden barn, thirty yards from the enemy trenches.

Fusilier Donnini, still bleeding profusely from his wound, went into the open under intense close range fire and carried one of his companions, who had been wounded, into the barn. Taking a Bren gun he again went into the open, firing as he went.

He was wounded a second time but recovered and went on firing until a third bullet hit a grenade which he was carrying and killed him.

The superb gallantry and self-sacrifice of Fusilier Donnini drew the enemy fire away from his companions on to himself. As the result of this the platoon were able to capture the position, accounting for thirty Germans and two machine guns.

Throughout this action, fought from beginning to end at point blank range, the dash, determination and magnificent courage of Fusilier Donnini enabled his comrades to overcome an enemy more than twice their own number.

Fusilier Donnini, who came from Easington, County Durham, is buried in Sittard Commonwealth War Graves Commission Cemetery at Limburg, Holland.

Henry Eric Harden

Throughout the early part of the harsh winter of 1944–5 – that is, in January and February – the Germans put up a fierce resistance as the Allied troops drew ever nearer to the German homeland. Much of this fighting took place in Holland, which was easier to defend than to capture. The Germans had been in military occupation since 1940 and they had built many large and small fortification systems. From blockhouses and pill-boxes they covered all lines of approach, lines which they themselves had arranged to their own advantage. By using barbed wire entanglements and the countless drainage ditches and canals in low-lying Holland and by firing machine guns to predetermined ranges, the Germans inflicted many casualties on the British, Canadian and American troops who necessarily had to advance over open country.

The 45th Royal Marine Commando was faced with just such a difficult advance on 23 January 1945, close to the town of Brachterbeek. Each Royal Marine Commando troop was accompanied by one or more medics of the Royal Army Medical Corps, whose duty it was to do all they could to help wounded men. The medic on duty in the fight at Brachterbeek was Lance-Corporal Eric Harden, whose citation for a posthumous VC was gazetted on 8 March 1945.

Lance-Corporal Henry Eric Harden, RAMC

In North-West Europe on the 23rd January, 1945, the leading section of a Royal Marine Commando Troop was pinned to the ground by intense enemy machine gun fire from well concealed positions. As it was impossible to engage the enemy from the open owing to lack of cover, the section was ordered to make for some near-by houses. This move was accomplished but one officer and three other rank casualties were left lying in the open.

The whole Troop position was under continuous heavy and accurate shell and mortar fire. Lance-Corporal Harden, the RAMC orderly attached to the Troop, at once went forward, a distance of 120 yards, into the open under a hail of enemy machine gun and rifle fire directed from four positions, all within 300 yards, and with the greatest coolness and bravery remained in the open while he attended to the four casualties. After dressing the wounds of three of them, he carried one of them back to cover. Lance-Corporal Harden was then ordered not to go forward again and an attempt was made to bring in the other casualties with the aid of tanks, but this proved unsuccessful owing to the heavy and accurate fire of enemy anti-tank guns. A further attempt was then made to recover the casualties under a smoke screen, but this only increased the enemy fire in the vicinity of the casualties.

Lance-Corporal Harden then insisted on going forward again with a volunteer stretcher party and succeeded in bringing back another badly wounded man.

Lance-Corporal Harden went out a third time, again with a stretcher party, and after starting on the return journey with the wounded officer, under very heavy enemy small arms and mortar fire, he was killed.

Throughout this long period Lance-Corporal Harden displayed superb devotion to duty and personal courage of the very highest order, and there is no doubt that it had a most steadying effect upon the other troops in the area at a most critical time. His action was directly responsible for saving the lives of the wounded brought in. His complete contempt for all personal danger and the magnificent example he set of cool courage and determination to continue with his work, whatever the odds, was an inspiration to his comrades, and will never be forgotten by those who saw it.

Lance-Corporal Harden was the only member of the RAMC to be awarded the VC in the Second World War. From Northfleet, Kent, he was within a month of his 32nd birthday at the time of his exploit which, by any standard of valour, was remarkable. Armed soldiers frequently act in hot blood but Harden carried no weapons and had to rely on his Red Cross brassard for protection. In the furious exchange of fire at Brachterbeek this was no protection at all. Every one of his actions was calculated and he knew precisely the risks he was running. His actions were in the tradition of Captain Noel Chavasse of the RAMC, one of only three men ever to be awarded the VC twice. Like Harden, Chavasse had lost his life – during the First World War – while saving lives under fire.

Eric Harden is buried in Nederweert Commonwealth War Graves Commission Cemetery, Holland. On the bridge over Montforterbeek, at Brachterbeek, is a plaque to his memory and his exploit.

James Stokes

As the winter of 1944–5 wore on many British soldiers in Europe were depressed about the seeming endlessness of the war. By February, nine months had passed since the D-Day landings in Normandy, yet the Germans were still resisting and the Rhine had not been crossed. Such a crossing would have enormous psychological as well as military importance.

However, Germany was reeling from the Allied air offensive. Both RAF Bomber Command and the US Eighth Air Force increased the intensity of their attacks. Among the RAF targets were Mannheim, Kassel, Essen and Dortmund. In one raid on Dortmund 4,850 tons of bombs were dropped – the heaviest attack on any target during the war. In an attack on Bielefeld viaduct the largest bomb dropped during the war was dropped for the first time – the 22,000 lb 'Grand Slam'.

On 1 March the US Ninth Army captured München-Gladbach and Neuss and the Rhine was now a realistic target. The British First Army was attacking towards Cologne and the Third Army was near the River Kyll and south of Trier. On that same day the 2nd Battalion the King's Own Shropshire Light Infantry was attacking German positions at Kervenheim in the Rhineland. The enemy troops were holding houses and farm buildings and it was proving difficult to dislodge them, especially as they had established strongpoints. It was Private James Stokes who broke the impasse, as his posthumous VC indicates. It was gazetted on 17 April 1945.

Private James Stokes, the King's Shropshire Light Infantry

In Holland, on 1st March, 1945, during the attack on Kervenheim, Private Stokes was a member of the leading section of a Platoon. During the advance the Platoon came under intense rifle and medium machine gun fire from a farm building and was pinned down. The Platoon Commander began to reorganise the Platoon when Private Stokes, without waiting for any orders, got up and firing from the hip, dashed through the enemy fire and was seen to disappear inside the farm building. The enemy fire stopped and Private Stokes reappeared with twelve prisoners. During this operation he was wounded in the neck.

This action enabled the Platoon to continue the advance to the next objective, and Private Stokes was ordered back to the Regimental Aid Post. He refused to go and continued the advance with his Platoon.

On approaching the second objective the Platoon again came under heavy fire from a house on the left. Again without waiting for orders, Private Stokes rushed the house by himself firing from the hip. He was seen to drop his rifle and fall to the ground wounded. However, a moment later he got to his feet again, picked up his rifle and continued to advance despite the most intense fire which covered not only himself but the rest of the Platoon. He entered the house and all firing from it ceased. He subsequently rejoined his Platoon – who, due to his gallantry, had been able to advance – bringing five more prisoners.

At this stage the Company was forming up for its final assault on the objective, which was a group of buildings forming an enemy strongpoint. Again without waiting for orders, Private Stokes, although now severely wounded and suffering from loss of blood, dashed on the remaining 60 yards to the objective, firing from the hip as he struggled through intense fire. He finally fell 20 yards from the enemy position, firing his rifle until the last and as the Company passed him in the final charge he raised his hand and shouted goodbye. Private Stokes was found to have been wounded eight times in the upper part of the body.

Private Stokes' one object throughout this action was to kill the enemy, at whatever personal risk. His magnificent courage, devotion to duty and splendid example inspired all those round him and ensured the success of the attack at a critical moment; moreover, his self-sacrifice saved his Platoon and Company many serious casualties.

Private Stokes had not lived to see it, but the German bridgehead west of the Rhine was contracting and the river was crossed at Remagen on 7 March.

James Stokes was 30 at the time of his death. Born in Hutchestown, Lanark, he had spent many years in Glasgow before he joined the Army. He is buried in the Commonwealth War Graves Commission Reichswald Forest War Cemetery. His cry of 'Goodbye!' to his comrades and his wave to them as they completed the attack he had so gamely begun not only shows that he knew he was dying, it also magnifies his valour.

Edward Thomas Chapman

By April the German armies were falling back in the west, under pressure from the American and British armies, and in the east, from the Russians. But their resistance was still fierce, so much so that it astonished the Western Allies. They were not to know that the desperate Nazi generals, driven on by Hitler himself, were now throwing into the defence of the Fatherland some of the most fanatical of Nazi units. It was the misfortune of the 3rd Battalion the Monmouthshire Regiment to find itself facing, on 2 April 1945, one of the strongest enemy battalions of all, Nazi zealots to a man.

The British troops were fighting in a place of great significance to Germans, the Teutoburger Wald, where in the year AD 9 the German warrior chief Arminius defeated the Roman legion of Varus. In German military history this defeat has echoed down the centuries and generations of soldiers have been trained at camps and barracks in the Teutoburger Wald. It is doubtful if any member of the Monmouthshire Regiment knew about this ancient history and such knowledge would have made no difference to them. But it inspired the Germans and they opposed the Monmouthshire men with determined valour of their own.

It was against this background that Private Edward Chapman won the VC, his citation being gazetted on 13 July 1945.

Corporal Edward Thomas Chapman, the Monmouthshire Regiment

On 2nd April 1945, a Company of the Monmouthshire Regiment crossed the Dortmund–Ems canal and was ordered to assault the ridge of the Teutoburger Wald, which dominates the surrounding country. This ridge is steep, thickly wooded and is ideal defensive country. It was, moreover, defended by a battalion of German officer cadets and their instructors, all of them picked men and fanatical Nazis.

Corporal Chapman was advancing with his section in single file along a narrow track when the enemy suddenly opened fire with machine guns at short range, inflicting heavy casualties and causing some confusion. Corporal Chapman immediately ordered his section to take cover and seizing the Bren gun he advanced alone, firing the gun from his hip, and mowed down the enemy at point blank range, forcing them to retire in disorder.

At this point, however, his Company was ordered to withdraw but Corporal Chapman and his section were still left in their advanced position, as the order could not be got forward to them.

The enemy then began to close up to Corporal Chapman and his isolated section and under cover of intense machine gun fire they made determined charges with the bayonet. Corporal Chapman again rose with his Bren gun to meet the assaults and on each occasion halted their advance.

He had now nearly run out of ammunition. Shouting to his section for more bandoliers, he dropped into a fold in the ground and covered those bringing up the ammunition by lying on his back and firing the Bren gun over his shoulder. A party of Germans made every effort to eliminate him with grenades but with reloaded magazine he closed with them and once again drove the enemy back with considerable casualties.

During the withdrawal of his Company the Company Commander had been severely wounded and left lying in the open a short distance from Corporal Chapman. Satisfied that his section was now secure, at any rate for the moment, he went out alone under withering fire and carried his Company Commander for 50 yards to comparative safety. On the way a sniper hit the officer again, wounding Corporal Chapman in the hip and, when he reached our lines, it was discovered that the officer had been killed.

In spite of his wound Corporal Chapman refused to be evacuated and went back to his Company until the position was fully restored two hours later.

Throughout the action Corporal Chapman displayed outstanding gallantry and superb courage. Single-handed he repulsed the attacks of well-led, determined troops and gave his battalion time to reorganise on a vital piece of ground overlooking the only bridge across the canal. His magnificent bravery played a very large part in the capture of this vital ridge and in the successful development of subsequent operations.

Edward Chapman, who came from Pontlottyn, Glamorgan, was 25 at the time of his exploit, which was virtually that of one man against a battalion – and a battalion of highly motivated and skilled professionals at that. He was promoted sergeant and later he was awarded the BEM. He remains one of the least known VC winners of the war, perhaps because of his innate modesty.

Ian Oswald Liddell

Towards the end of March 1945 the Allied push into Germany became more vigorous. They were now east of the Rhine with all that this meant in terms of strategic, tactical and psychological advantage. But it also meant much to the Germans and they fought with stubborn bravery. The most impressive Allied advances were made by the American armoured units of the Ninth Army, in Field Marshal Montgomery's group, and by the First and Third Armies in General Bradley's group. On 1 April the spearheads of General Simpson's Ninth Army and General Hodge's First Army converged at Paderborn, in west-central Germany. The result was that General Model's Army Group B was encircled in an area of about 4,000 square miles.

All these massive movements were made up of many small actions, some of them significant in their tactical importance and dramatic in their operation. The exploit of Captain Ian Liddell of the Coldstream Guards near Rothenburg on 3 April 1945 was as dramatic as anything created for a fictional war film. It won him the VC, his citation being gazetted on 7 June 1945.

Lieutenant (temporary Captain) Ian Oswald Liddell, Coldstream Guards

In Germany on 3rd April, 1945, Captain Liddell was commanding a Company of the Coldstream Guards which was ordered to capture intact a bridge over the River Ems near Lingen. The bridge was covered on the far bank by an enemy strong point, which was subsequently discovered to consist of 150 entrenched infantry supported by three 88 mm. and two 20 mm. guns. The bridge was also prepared for demolition with 500 lb bombs which could plainly be seen.

Having directed his two leading platoons on to the near bank, Captain Liddell ran forward alone to the bridge and scaled the 10 feet high road block guarding it with the intention of neutralising the charges and taking the bridge intact. In order to achieve his object he had to cross the whole length of the bridge by himself under intense enemy fire, which increased as his object became apparent to the Germans. Having disconnected the charges on the far side, he re-crossed the bridge and cut the wires on the near side. It was necessary for him to kneel, forming an easy target whilst he successively cut the wires.

He then discovered that there were also charges underneath the bridge and completely undeterred he also disconnected these. His task completed he then climbed up on to the road block in full view of the enemy and signalled his leading platoon to advance.

Thus, alone and unprotected, without cover and under heavy enemy fire, he achieved his object. The bridge was captured intact and the way cleared to the advance across the river Ems. His outstanding gallantry and superb example of courage will never be forgotten by those who saw it.

As a result of Captain Liddell's remarkable initiative, the Coldstream Guards captured the bridge intact and the advance across the River Ems continued. However, in a further action Captain Liddell was mortally wounded and became yet another VC winner not to survive to read his citation. Liddell, who was 25 at the time of his death, had been born in Shanghai. He is buried in Becklingen Commonwealth War Graves Commission Cemetery at Soltau, Germany. The Liddell family had Monmouthshire connections and there are memorials to Ian Liddell in two of the county's churches, Maunton Church, Chepstow and St Thomas's Church, Shirenewton. As with all Guards VC winners, he is also commemorated in the Guards Chapel, Wellington Barracks, London.

Edward Colquhoun Charlton

When the British Army and its allies, the Americans and Canadians, moved into Germany they encountered even fiercer German resistance than in Holland and Belgium. On virtually every occasion when the Allies captured a position the Germans vigorously counter-attacked.

The Irish Guards, part of the Guards Armoured Division, was given the objective of cutting the autobahn between Hamburg and Bremen to prevent enemy movement along it. On 20 April 1945 Major Michael O'Cock, commanding 1 Squadron, cleared the autobahn between Sittensen and Elsdorf, leaving the road open to the north. Towards evening he sent one troop north-west from Elsdorf to the village of Wistedt, but it was too isolated in the darkness and was called back. Each troop consisted of three 75 mm gun Sherman tanks and one Firefly Sherman armed with a 17–pounder.

The Guards spent a quiet night but before dawn on 21 April a troop under Lieutenant Barry Quinan was ordered to re-occupy Wistedt, 2 miles away. The tanks were accompanied by a platoon of infantry led by Lieutenant William Harvey-Kelly. A short-circuit in Quinan's tank caused it to break down completely and he ordered the co-driver, Guardsman Edward Charlton, to dismount his Browning machine gun so that if the crew could not repair the tank's electrical system Charlton could at least support the accompanying infantry section. Charlton's subsequent valour, which won him the posthumous award of the VC, was gazetted on 2 May 1946.

Guardsman Edward Colquhoun Charlton, the Irish Guards

On the morning of 21st April, 1945, Guardsman Charlton was co-driver in one tank of a troop, which, with a platoon of infantry seized the village of Wistedt.

Shortly afterwards, the enemy attacked this position under cover of an artillery concentration and in great strength, comprising as it later transpired a battalion of the 15th Panzer Grenadiers supported by six self-propelled guns.

All the tanks, including Guardsman Charlton's, were hit; the infantry were hard pressed and in danger of being over-run.

Thereupon, entirely on his own initiative, Guardsman Charlton decided to counter-attack the enemy. Quickly recovering the Browning from his damaged tank, he advanced up the road in full view of the enemy, firing the Browning from his hip.

Such was the boldness of his attack and the intensity of his fire that he halted the leading enemy company, inflicting heavy casualties on them. This effort at the same time brought much needed relief to our own infantry.

For ten minutes Guardsman Charlton fired in this manner until wounded in the left arm. Immediately, despite intense enemy fire, he mounted his machine gun on a nearby fence which he used to support his wounded left arm. He stood firing thus for a further ten minutes until he was again hit in the left arm, which fell away shattered and useless.

Although twice wounded and suffering from loss of blood, Guardsman Charlton again lifted his machine-gun on to the fence, now having only one arm with which to fire and reload. Nevertheless, he still continued to inflict casualties on the enemy until finally he was hit for the third time and collapsed. He died later of his wounds, in enemy hands. The heroism and determination of this Guardsman in his self-imposed task were beyond all praise. Even his German captors were amazed at his valour. Guardsman Charlton's courageous and self-sacrificing action not only inflicted extremely heavy casualties on the enemy and retrieved his comrades from a desperate situation, but also enabled the position to be speedily recaptured.

Charlton was not mentioned in the battalion's war diary because apart from the troop commander all the tank commanders had been either captured or killed and most other witnesses close to the site of Charlton's exploit were also captured. The Germans who made them prisoner were sailors who had been based on the Kiel Canal. The first indication of the extent of Charlton's bravery came to light when several of the guardsmen taken prisoner were released from POW camps on 28 April and confirmation of his death came when his grave was discovered after the war.

When Sergeant Jim Connolly, one of Charlton's comrades, was released from the POW camp he reported Charlton's gallantry to a staff liaison officer, repeating what a German officer had told him after Charlton's capture. His daring and bravery had astonished the enemy. Back in Britain, Connolly made a further report to the OC Guards Depot at Tring and for good measure repeated it to Captain Parker at No 9 RAOC Company at Thetford.

A condition of the award, as earlier described, is that an exploit must have been witnessed by at least two other individuals. Proof of Charlton's exploit was found in accounts taken from German prisoners of war who spoke of a lone guardsman who stood in front of three burning tanks and held up a battalion of German infantry, obviously buying time for his comrades to reorganize themselves.

Before his death was confirmed, Charlton had been recommended for the immediate award of the MM. On 10 May this request was marked 'unsuccessful', as it had to be once his death in action was known. Gradually the full story of Charlton's valour came out and was recognized. His VC was gazetted in what was to be the final wartime honours list, on 2 May 1946.

On 28 May 1946, at the opening of the Household Brigade War Memorial Cloister at the Guards Chapel, Wellington Barracks, London, Charlton's mother presented his VC to the Irish Guards for permanent safekeeping.

Eddie Charlton had been born in Rowlands Gill, County Durham, but the family moved to Old Trafford, Manchester, in 1935. He was 24 when he was killed in his splendid action. He is buried in the Commonwealth War Graves Commission Cemetery at Soltau, Germany, close to the grave of Captain Ian Liddell VC. In St John's Church, Old Trafford, is a plaque to Charlton's memory and in the town there is an 'Edward Charlton Road'.

I have already quoted a letter sent by a soldier to the widow of a VC winner (Mrs Moira Anderson). It is interesting to read what another soldier wrote to the parents of Eddie Charlton. It was written in May 1946 by Sergeant Hughie Gallagher, Irish Guards, to Mrs Charlton.

I am writing this letter to you in reference to your son Eddie. I am one of the happiest men in England after I had seen in the paper of his reward, the VC. It was only through his gallantry that saved my life that I am able to write this to you. The work he did that day is indescribable, he saved quite a lot of lives, though badly wounded. You asked me to tell you all that happened that day but I'm afraid I couldn't do it. You must forgive me for that but if the same had happened to me I would not like anybody to describe it to my mother. I was the last person with him. Unfortunately he was badly wounded and I very slightly and we were both taken to the same German aid post. He was in great spirit all the time but not allowed to be taken to the prison camp with me so with his old saying 'Up the Micks!' we parted company.

Irish Guardsman James Mendes DCM wrote a tribute to Eddie Charlton for the magazine *John Bull* in June 1946, at the time of the Victory Day Parade in London.

There is a man who will march with me on the Victory Day parade, a man you will not see. He will not be photographed by the cameras that record the great parade, twelve thousand strong, of men and women who made victorious war by land, sea and air. He will not hear the roaring of the mechanized columns, the steadily marching feet, the overhead drone as the RAF flies past. Not for him the slow-rolling cheers of the crowds, the sharp words of command, the music and the flags. He is just one of the greater invisible host that will be on parade that day. The men who never came back, the fellows who had the bad luck, the marchers who ought to be there. And *are* there, in the hearts of those who fought alongside them. For I shall see him alright. Not dressed for a ceremonial parade, clean-shaven, bright as to boots, meticulously clothed. I shall see him as he fell – tackling a battalion of Panzer Grenadiers on his own.

Ed was my pal. Funny that an Englishman should have to win the VC for an Irish regiment but that's the way it is. Yet after five years in the Irish Guards Ed was more Irish than English, in fact, more Irish than many of us. He had the blarney all right, and the temper with a physique to make it dangerous. But he had a heart of gold. He was a man, the way real men are and should be. He liked his beer and his fun. He lived the British way and died the British way.

That was Ed, who goes down in the ruddy annals of military history for one of the greatest bits of heroism in this war. . . .

The citation just says he recovered the Browning from his damaged tank. That alone was something. Not only was he in full view of the enemy and in the line of their sights, but his Sherman was *brewing up*. Anybody who is familiar with Shermans will tell you they have nasty habits when they're hit. They burst into flames and the ammo starts popping. It's uncomfortable to be near one, must less on it; the citation just says that he recovered the Browning!

This story might never have been told, had he not made it possible for some of his comrades to come back alive and report it. In Ed's case there were not only his pals, but the enemy, too, who saw to it that he will never be forgotten. Ed died in a German field hospital and captured Germans told interrogating officers the amazing story of a man who stood in front of three blazing Shermans and held up a battalion of Panzer Grenadiers.

To me, Ed still lives. He will march with us through London. You won't see him, but he'll be there.

The Royal Air Force VCs

General Analysis

To understand the backdrop of war against which men of the RAF won Victoria Crosses it is first necessary to sketch the vast conflict in which British airmen took part. The RAF came into being as an independent service only on 1 April 1918, as a result of the amalgamation of the Royal Flying Corps and the Royal Naval Air Service. After 1933 Britain faced a growing threat from Germany under the Nazi regime as well as a possible war in the Far East against Japan and in the Mediterranean against Italy. The RAF had to undergo a rapid expansion in aircraft and manpower but it was not even on a war footing until 1936 when various commands were established, such as Fighter Command and Bomber Command.

As late as 1938 the RAF's *Manual of Air Tactics* stated that air-to-air combat between attacking and defending fighters was 'not practicable' because of the speed of the aircraft – up to 400 mph. Interceptions would be too fleeting for either machine to loose off destructive fire and too fast for pilots to survive the 'acrobatic manoeuvres' that would be required. The bomber would be the dominant type of aircraft but enemy bombers could readily be shot down – according to RAF doctrine – by fighters, which would need just one pass to destroy a bomber.

When war was declared in September 1939 the RAF had a total of 1,911 aircraft, which might in itself seem a respectable number. However, at the same time the Luftwaffe, the German air force, had 4,161 aircraft. British designers and manufacturers needed to work hard to make up the deficiency and to produce ever better aircraft.

Many fighters were obsolescent, notably the Gloster Gladiator, a single-engine biplane which had a closer affinity to First World War flying conditions than to those of the Second. It saw active service in Norway and France in 1940, it helped defend Plymouth during the Battle of Britain and in the Mediterranean it performed well against Italian aircraft which were no more advanced than itself. Had the RAF planned sufficiently far ahead, they would never have needed to use the Gloster Gladiator.

In the opening years of the war the best fighters were the Spitfire and the Hurricane. Coastal aircraft were a mixture of land-based Ansons, Hudsons and Blenheims with some flying-boats, the best of which was the Sunderland I. In the beginning bombers were mainly of the two-engine variety, but four-engine Stirlings and Halifaxes were appearing.

At the outbreak of war the RAF had a personnel strength of 20,033 aircrew and 153,925 ground crew, with 1,734 members of the WAAF. The aircrew total grew to 144,488 by May 1945, reinforced by 33,976 Dominion aircrew. The WAAF strength reached 157,286. The overall strength of men and women in the RAF was 1,208,853.

Even in summary, the RAF's contribution to the war effort was immense. Its operations were continuous over Europe, the North Atlantic and the seas around the British Isles. During the Battle of Britain it prevented the Luftwaffe from controlling the skies as a prelude to the planned invasion of Britain in 1940. In lengthy campaigns it supported the Army in North Africa, the Mediterranean and Levant, Italy, the Balkans, South-East Asia and the Far East. With the American Army Air Forces, the RAF played a major role in the air offensive against German targets in Germany itself and elsewhere. It was ceaselessly active during the Normandy landings and in support of the Allied armies as they fought across France and the Low Countries and into Germany.

In the bomber offensive the RAF made an enormous logistic effort and suffered heavily for it. The RAF's official history of Bomber Command records that of a total of 70,353 officers, non-commissioned officers and men killed or missing on operations between 3 September 1939 and 14 August 1945, 47,293 lost their lives or disappeared. Of course, 'disappeared' meant that the men so listed had been killed. A further 7,000 bomber aircrew from the Dominions, Poland and Czechoslovakia were also killed while flying with the RAF.* Nearly 60 per cent of Bomber Command aircrew became casualties; 85 per cent of this total were sustained on operations and 15 per cent in training and other accidents. The total number of wounded was 8,403, other than as prisoners of war. In the Army and Navy the proportion of casualties is the other way around – more wounded than killed. When a bomber crashed or blew up few of the crew survived. Similarly, most fighter pilots shot down were killed.

Bomber crews were expected to fly 30 sorties before they were entitled to a 'rest'. The chances of surviving 30 sorties – known as a tour of operations – were so slender that many members of bomber crews fully expected to lose their lives. Under RAF regulations men were liable to a second tour of 30 sorties. After that they could be used on operations again only if they volunteered. Many did volunteer, quite without coercion and persuasion.

Between 3 September 1939 and 8 May 1945 – the end of the war in Europe – Bomber Command lost 8,325 aircraft on operations in Europe. In addition, thousands of other planes returned to Britain as near wrecks after being mauled by flak and by enemy fighter pilots.

Fighter Command also sustained many casualties, though with only one man to a plane instead of the six or eight to a bomber the overall total was less. Churchill was speaking of the men of Fighter Command when he said, 'Never in the field of human conflict was so much owed by so many to so

---

* 'Enough fatal casualties to form seventy battalions of infantry or the crews of thirty modern battleships', as Martin Middlebrook and Chris Everitt so graphically put it in *The Bomber Command War Diaries*.

few.' During the Battle of Britain, in the period 24 August to 5 September, the Luftwaffe nearly broke Fighter Command. More than 450 British fighters were destroyed, 103 pilots killed and 128 wounded. The RAF was for a time in crisis since it could not replace pilots or planes fast enough and some of the airfields were out of action from severe damage caused by Luftwaffe bombers.

Hitler and Goering saved the day for Britain. Britain's air defence was at its weakest and a German victory was possible but at that very moment the Luftwaffe was ordered to bomb London. This was the Blitz. With the enemy concentrating on one target the RAF was able to concentrate its slender resources for defence. While they were doing this the airfields were rebuilt.

Between 14/15 September Bomber Command, with the help of light naval craft, destroyed 200 German barges waiting on the European coast to begin Operation Sea Lion, the invasion of Britain. They inflicted enough damage to show Hitler and his generals that no invasion fleet could ever get across the Channel. Sea Lion was cancelled.

Considering the large number of RAF aircraft and their crews in action and the 330,000 sorties they flew, the number of VCs awarded to airmen was minute – 32 in all to the RAF, RAAF, RNZAF, RCAF and SAAF. Of this total 22 were won by RAF men. Remarkably, only one fighter pilot was awarded the VC.

CHAPTER TEN

Fighter Command VC

Eric James Brindley Nicolson

In what became known as the Battle of Britain, one of the fateful battles of history, Hitler intended that the Luftwaffe should defeat the Royal Air Force so that he could neutralize the Royal Navy. After that his invasion of Britain could proceed. The Luftwaffe began with the Germans' Adlerangriff (Eagle Attack), attacks on coastal towns and shipping in July 1940. By August the Luftwaffe's chief, Hermann Goering, had gathered 2,800 aircraft in three fleets, operating from northern France, Belgium and Holland, Norway and Denmark. Air Marshal Sir Hugh Dowding's Fighter Command had only 650 operational Spitfires and Hurricanes in 52 squadrons. About 800 pilots were available to fly them.

German strategy was to lure the RAF planes into combat against a superior force that would destroy them. However, immediately before the war the British had built a chain of radar warning stations – largely at Dowding's urging – and this radar enabled him to concentrate superior numbers of his own fighters at vital points to counter the Luftwaffe attacks.

Goering set 10 August as the opening day of his all-out offensive but bad weather forced postponement of Adlertag (Eagle Day) until 13 August. On this day the Luftwaffe flew 1,485 sorties and at the end of it had lost 45 planes. The RAF had lost 13 but, more crucially, only seven pilots.

Over southern England near Salisbury on 16 August was stationed the RAF's 249 Squadron, one of whose pilots, Eric Nicolson, was to become the only Battle of Britain VC and the only fighter pilot to be so decorated. His citation was gazetted on 15 November 1940.

Flight Lieutenant James Brindley Nicolson, No 249 Squadron

In recognition of most conspicuous bravery during an engagement with the enemy near Southampton on 16th August, 1940, Flight Lieutenant Nicolson's aircraft was hit by four cannon shells, two of which wounded him whilst another set fire to the gravity tank. When about to abandon his aircraft owing to flames in the cockpit he sighted an enemy fighter. This he attacked and shot down, although as a result of staying in his burning aircraft he sustained serious burns to his hands, face, neck and legs.

Flight Lieutenant Nicolson has always displayed great enthusiasm for air fighting and this incident shows that he possesses courage and determination of a high order. By continuing to engage the enemy after he had been wounded and his aircraft set on fire, he displayed exceptional gallantry and disregard for the safety of his own life.

(Nicolson's first name was actually Eric but it was not shown in the *London Gazette*.)

Because of his injuries Nicolson saw no more of the Battle of Britain or the Luftwaffe's last attack, which took place on 30 September. The 23-year-old pilot, in his first experience of air combat, had shown down an enemy Messerschmitt, nearly lost his life in the air, been shot and further wounded by a stupid farmer firing a shotgun at him from the ground – and won the VC. However, he fared better than Pilot Officer M.A. King, flying with him, whose Hurricane had been set on fire. As King descended in his parachute a gunner officer took him for an enemy flier and ordered his men to open fire. They shot his parachute to pieces and King fell to his death. King's friends would gladly have formed a firing squad for the gunner officer for this 'murder'. Even if the descending flier had been a German, he had no business shooting at an enemy who posed no threat.

Nicolson's citation was all too succinct and it was left to others, notably Chaz Bowyer, to give more details of his ordeal. Bowyer says that Nicolson had great difficulty in pulling back the hood cover and then in dropping from his shattered Hurricane. When the parachute opened a Messerschmitt flashed past and turned to come back again. Bowyer says 'Fearing that the German might try to machine-gun him, Nicolson let himself hang limply, simulating death, and the German roared by him without further trouble.'

Some of Nicolson's doctors virtually gave him up for dead but willpower brought him through and in September 1941 he was again in the air. Early in 1942 he was posted to India and between August 1943 and August 1944 he led a squadron in Burma. In this period he was awarded the DFC. He was killed on 2 May 1945 when a Liberator in which he was flying as an observer caught fire and crashed into the Bay of Bengal.

The award of the VC to Flight Lieutenant (finally Wing Commander) Nicolson is an interesting one. During the Battle of Britain several fighter pilots shot down a succession of enemy aircraft and a large number flew more missions than Nicolson's single one, while some were operational for the entire period of the Battle of Britain. All of them showed great courage and there was some resentment – never stated publicly – that others were not also awarded the VC. Nobody ever questioned Nicolson's valour.

However, from the way in which Nicolson himself stubbornly insisted on further flying duties and really active service it is reasonable to speculate that he felt that he had to live up to his great award and the reputation it had given him. In this decision he may have been showing even greater courage than he had displayed in the air on 16 August 1940.

Without in any way devaluing Nicolson's VC, and viewing events with the benefit of hindsight, it is difficult to understand why certain other fighter pilots were not also decorated with the VC. This omission applies to four airmen in particular – Flight Lieutenant R.R. Stanford Tuck, Squadron Leader J.E. ('Johnnie') Johnson, Sergeant Pilot James ('Ginger') Lacey and Group Captain Douglas Bader. Their exploits are worth summarizing here in order to illustrate how much valour a pilot might display and yet *not* be awarded a VC.

R.R. Stanford Tuck

Tuck learned to fly only with difficulty and some of his instructors despaired of him. But he concentrated, as they had urged him to, and in various courses he was finally rated as exceptional, though some senior officers considered him over-confident and cocky. During the early months of the war and despite having clocked up 700 hours of flying, he was not sent into combat. Tuck was a member of a Spitfire squadron and Fighter Command was at that time relying on Hurricanes.

As a flight lieutenant member of 92 Squadron, Tuck first saw action on 23 May 1940 when his squadron of 12 Spitfires was sent to fly patrol over Dunkirk. On this day the evacuation from Dunkirk was under way and the RAF pilots' orders were simple: 'Go in and attack any aircraft attacking our troops or ships.' They were also warned that they might encounter German gaggles (swarms) of up to 40 planes.

After a time the squadron was bounced by a formation of Messerschmitts and at once one Spitfire went down in flames. In a masterful manoeuvre, Tuck caught the enemy leader and opened up with his eight .303 Brownings. He was perhaps the RAF's best marksman and he made sure of his victim. One of the last to return to base, Tuck had little time to rest before the squadron was again scrambled. Over Dunkirk once more 92 Squadron was attacked by Me.110s, twin-engined German fighters and especially formidable since they had a rear gunner to add to the pilot's firepower.

The Spitfires were outnumbered and several dogfights developed. Tuck's plane was hit but he maintained his own attack and brought down his second victim of the day. Holding his nerve when an enemy pilot flew straight at him, Tuck followed the Me. down almost to ground level – the German pilot actually flew under some high tension cables. His own plane again hit several times by the rear gunner, Tuck still maintained his attack and saw the rear gunner slump over his gun. Soon afterwards the Me. crashed. With his Spitfire in tatters and the engine dead, Tuck was lucky to land safely at his airfield.

From this beginning – three enemy planes destroyed in one day – Tuck continued to fight the Luftwaffe relentlessly. His squadron leader had been brought down, though he lived, and Tuck was promoted to command

No 92, soon becoming one of the RAF's best known pilots. The squadron was not involved in the air battles of July and August 1940 so Tuck made German bombers over Wales his targets. Without regard for his own safety, he regularly went in so close that on one occasion he had to bale out at 500 feet, a dangerously low altitude.

In September, as leader of 257 Squadron, flying Hurricanes, Tuck was embroiled in the Battle of Britain and on 15 September he shot down an Me.110. By the end of the year he had notched up 18 confirmed kills. Promoted in July 1941, he led a wing of Spitfires and later was sent to the US to advise on combat techniques. At the end of 1941, he was leading the 'Biggin Hill wing' but in January 1942 he was shot down by anti-aircraft fire while strafing ground targets near Boulogne. Even then he was not finished; as his plane fell, he attacked the guncrew that had hit him, destroying the gun and killing the men.

After many attempts to escape from captivity he succeeded in January 1945 and finally, weak and starving, he met the Russians. They forced him to fight the Germans for two weeks before he escaped.

Tuck had shot down 29 enemy aircraft and, although he had been a prisoner for three years, at the war's end he was still the RAF's eighth ranking pilot. He finished his wartime career with the DSO, the DFC and 2 Bars and the American DFC. It was generally felt within the RAF that one or more of his exploits warranted the VC, especially that of 23 May 1940.

J.E. 'Johnnie' Johnson

J.E. Johnson had his first chance to engage in combat in January 1941 when he and a comrade from 616 Squadron shared a claim to having damaged a German bomber. The great Douglas Bader, as wing leader at Tangmere, recognized Johnson's potential as a combat pilot and chose him to fly in his leading section. Johnson brought off his first kill in June 1941 and was promoted to flight commander. He reached a tally of 6½ kills, won the DFC and was appointed squadron leader to lead 610 Squadron. In a period of six months in 1943 he brought down 19 more enemy planes. He achieved his last victory, his 38th, on 27 September 1944, while the RAF was supporting the Arnhem operation. This was his 515th sortie over enemy territory and the first and only time enemy bullets had hit his plane. It says much for Johnson's courage and sustained determination that every one of his victims was an enemy fighter.

For many years the mission which Johnson flew as a squadron leader on 19 August 1942 was regarded in the RAF as a classic example. He shot down three Messerschmitts in an outstanding exhibition of valour. As a group captain, Johnson finished the war with a DSO and 2 Bars, the DFC and Bar, the American DFC, the Belgian Order of Leopold and the Belgian Croix de Guerre. Later he was awarded the CB and CBE and he retired with the rank of air vice marshal. There were some other US awards too but such is the mystique of the VC that all 12 of Johnson's decorations cannot equal it. He was the RAF's leading British scorer with 38 victories, though Squadron Leader M.T. St J. Pattle, a South African, is credited with 41 victories in North Africa and Greece.

James Henry 'Ginger' Lacey

James Harry ('Ginger') Lacey learnt to fly before he was 20 and became a member of the RAFVR in January 1939. First he flew the Hawker Fury and then the Hurricane. He was called to the RAF on 2 September 1939, the day before war was declared, and joined 501 Squadron which moved to France in May 1940. During the confused fighting of that early summer he shot down five Me.109 fighters, enough to give him a high reputation in the RAF, though he was still only a sergeant pilot.

On 14 September a German Heinkel bombed Buckingham Palace and the RAF commanders considered it essential that the attacker should not be allowed to get away. Hitler had to be shown that Buckingham Palace could not be attacked with impunity. However, the weather was so foul that only a volunteer pilot could be asked to go after the Heinkel. Lacey, standing by at Kenley Fighter Station, south of London, volunteered by racing at once for his Spitfire. Amazingly, considering the poor visibility, he found the Heinkel, closed behind it and killed the rear gunner with a burst of fire. At once another German took over the turret gun and opened up on the Spitfire, which was hit. Lacey killed this opponent too and his bullets set the Heinkel afire. Turning away, Lacey dropped from his own burning Spitfire and was nearly shot by a Home Guard sentry as he descended by parachute.

He had suffered burns to the legs, later described as 'bad enough', but he hid them with a new pair of trousers before reporting to his CO. He was so anxious to stay on duty that he had his burns treated privately.

Next day 501 Squadron was scrambled to meet a '50–plus' enemy raid. This was 15 September – later to become the date for the Battle of Britain – and the Germans were making a great effort.

Desperately manoeuvring to get above the oncoming enemy bombers, Lacey's plane lost 5,000 feet of height before he could set off to rejoin his squadron, which was now out of sight. While doing so he found himself flying towards a dozen Me.109s, which were above him. Discretion and the rules of combat engagement required that against such odds he should 'disappear', but that would not have been Ginger Lacey. By zooming upwards and looping the loop he finished upside down behind the last Messerschmitt in the German squadron. From this unpromising and unusual position, he opened fire and sent the enemy down in flames.

The rest of the flight had seen neither the destruction of their comrade nor Lacey's attack and flew on eastwards. Lacey worked his way in behind an Me.109 and opened fire, sending it down spewing white smoke. The other German pilots now noticed their challenger and broke left and right into two groups, circling at high speed to trap him. At this point Lacey really should have run, but he noticed that one Me. 109 was trailing behind and he himself still had some ammunition – so he closed in for an attack. He fired off all his ammunition at the target and then, through brilliant flying, he extricated himself from the German envelopment. Overall, he could claim one enemy fighter shot down, one probable, one possible and a bomber. That afternoon 501 Squadron was scrambled again to intercept an enemy bomber force protected by fighters. In a dogfight with the Messerschmitts Lacey shot off an enemy's tail and shortly afterwards brought down a Heinkel bomber.

Lacey, who already held the DFM, was merely awarded a second DFM. Commissioned in 1941, he was seldom out of the action over France and, late in the war, over Burma where he shot down his 28th – and last – confirmed victim. Lacey finished the war as the 12th ranking fighter pilot of the RAF. He was a great hero of the Battle of Britain and his exploits on 14–15 September surely warranted the award of the VC.

Douglas Robert Stewart Bader

Group Captain Douglas Bader, the legless hero immortalized in the book and film *Reach for the Sky*, was awarded the DSO and Bar, the DFC and Bar, the French Legion d'Honneur and the Croix de Guerre. Edward H. Sims, author of *The Fighter Pilots*, says of Bader: 'He was unquestionably an expert on tactics, exceptional at controls of a fighter, a natural leader and endowed with almost unlimited courage.'

He had scored 22½ victories when his fighter was rammed and he baled out over occupied France. Sims continues:

> Had it not been for the enforced end of his career it is hard to estimate how many enemy aircraft he would have shot down. It is also difficult to estimate the value, to his country and to the RAF, of a man who would not accept physical handicap or defeat and who possessed such determination. His example – and legend – was an inspiration to wartime fighter pilots.

For all his tremendous reputation, Bader was not awarded the VC. Was he not considered to have performed some 'signal act of valour', the defining criterion for the award of the VC? But consider his actions on 20 August 1940, in the midst of the Battle of Britain. Bader and his 242 Squadron of 12 Hurricanes were waiting impatiently at Duxford when they were scrambled at 4.45 p.m. Having sent one section to reconnoitre, Bader had nine Hurricanes when confronted by more than 70 enemy

Dornier bombers together with Messerschmitt fighters. Ordering one section of three to attack the upper 'box' of bombers, Bader himself led his Hurricanes in a slashing attack designed to break up the enemy formations. Bader shot down a twin-engine fighter, his first victim in the Battle of Britain. Pressing on in a manoeuvring chase, he shot down a second Me.110 and was then himself nearly surprised by an enemy fighter on his tail. Although the skilful Bader turned the tables on the German and finished up behind him, he could not catch him.

On that day Bader's 12 Hurricanes shot down 12 of the enemy without loss to themselves. It was an accomplished performance of leadership. On 7 September his squadron claimed 11 victories and two days later, with three squadrons, Bader could claim 20 victims. On 15 September his wing claimed 52 victories, later confirmed. In all cases the RAF planes had been outnumbered. Bader claimed that his tactics, which were controversial at the time, were largely responsible for these victories. On 1 October he was awarded the DSO for his work. And it was a DSO of high quality, not one of many which merely states, 'For outstanding services'.

Appointed a Companion of the Distinguished Service Order, Acting Squadron Leader Douglas Robert Stewart Bader

This officer has displayed gallantry and leadership of the highest order. During three recent engagements he has led his squadron with such skill and ability that thirty-three enemy aircraft have been destroyed. In the course of these engagements Squadron Leader Bader has added to his previous successes by destroying six enemy aircraft.

Here were all the elements of a VC citation. Edward Sims states that Bader 'contributed an aggressiveness unsurpassed in the RAF. He flew almost daily in good weather and was advised to take a rest but he rejected the advice.'

Bader flew his last sortie on 9 August 1941. He had shot down two Me.109s when another rammed him. Because of his 'tin legs' he was lucky to get out of the cockpit and parachute to safety. He was confined to a hospital under guard but was so respected that Oberst Adolf Galland, the great German fighter pilot, sent a car for him so that he could visit the fliers of Jagdgeschwader (fighter wing) 26. Soon after this he escaped from the hospital but was caught. He kept on trying to escape and in the end he was sent to Colditz prison, where the most incorrigible escapers were confined.

In the 1960s I met Bader when we were both living in Sussex and on one social occasion when we were alone I said, 'Be frank with me, confidentially, were you disappointed you didn't receive the VC?' All he would say was, 'I thought that at one time I may have deserved it.' And then he changed the subject. I have not broken that confidence until now, many years after Bader's death.

Why Bader, Lacey, Johnson and Tuck did not receive the VC is a matter of conjecture. No doubt there were other fighter pilots of comparable stature, and about whose exploits I am less well informed, who might also have deserved the supreme decoration. In the first place, somebody had to 'witness' their exploits, but witnesses to air combat were often lacking. Their deeds had to be described and written down and indeed this happened; the debriefing officer at an RAF station was usually the intelligence officer whose duty it was to record each pilot's report. Then somebody had to recommend that a high decoration be awarded. There followed an assessment at various levels. Inevitably, if regrettably, personalities played a part. For instance, Bader was regarded as abrasive and critical of some of his superiors. Also, there was a perceived need to satisfy the demands and expectations of various Groups and of Fighter Command itself. We will probably never know why some fighter pilots were not awarded the VC or why some recommendations were disallowed. I am prepared to concede that Tuck, Johnson and Bader *may* have been borderline cases but James Lacey's exploits should certainly have been regarded as 'signal acts of valour' warranting the VC. I suspect that his own modesty militated against him – he was never a man to sell himself as a hero. But then neither was Eric Nicolson. He was astounded when he learnt of his VC award. We come, in the end, to 'luck' – the luck of being selected from among so many bravest of the brave.

I must admit that Chaz Bowyer, to whom I defer as the most authoritative historian of the war in the air, does not agree with me that Lacey, Johnson, Tuck or Bader might have merited a VC. He says, 'I have nothing but admiration for such individual achievements but could name dozens of other men with equal (if not greater) "qualifications".'

However, these achievements, which did *not* result in the award of a VC, do serve to indicate the very demanding standards required to win the award.

CHAPTER ELEVEN

Bomber Command VCs

An intelligent man of limited experience – he had no Services background – once asked me what a member of a bomber crew could possibly do to merit his being awarded the Victoria Cross. He said, 'The pilot takes his bomber up to a certain altitude, flies it until he is over the target, drops his bombs and flies home. I know that he can be shot at by the enemy but this applies to anybody in a war. I don't know what men can do with or in a bomber that can deserve the VC.'

I thought, 'Oh God, such ignorance!' but patiently I explained the many risks that an entire bomber crew, not just the pilot, had to face in order to carry out a mission, together with all the tensions and strains and discomforts. In the first place they had to get their heavily laden plane off the ground, often in atrocious weather conditions. An aircraft could crash on take-off, the bombs would detonate and the entire crew would be killed. During the long and tiring trip, at high altitude, the crew would need to wear oxygen masks and they were often very cold. There was the added risk that in the crowded sky, with perhaps a thousand bombers taking part in a single raid, two planes could collide in heavy cloud – another disaster.

From the moment the bombers crossed the enemy coast they were vulnerable to anti-aircraft fire and attacks by German fighters. Over some targets the anti-aircraft fire was so intense that the crews saw close up shellburst after shellburst while splinters from the exploding shells peppered the aircraft. At any time a bomber might be set on fire – the great hazard for all aircraft crews. Bombers used high octane and highly inflammable fuel. A small fire, fanned by the bomber's windrush and fed by the oxygen within its system could quickly become a disastrous one. Somehow the fire had to be contained or everybody died. Bombers carried weapons for their own protection and they were manned by skilled gunners but the gunners themselves were in exposed positions; some bombers returned to base safely but with all their gunners killed or wounded.

Flying over a long distance or for a long period in a bomber was extremely uncomfortable. Meals were basic, generally for each crew member a picnic lunch packed in a brown paper bag and consisting of sandwiches, chocolate, a square of cheese, chewing gum and perhaps a piece of fruit. They drank tea or coffee from a thermos flask. The chocolate, cheese, and chewing gum were welcome but many bomber crew members returned to base with their sandwiches uneaten; the tension during the mission seemed to inhibit hunger.

To my knowledge nobody has ever pointed out in a book that the men needed to urinate and defecate. In an aircraft with just one pilot this flier simply had to grit his teeth and stand the strain, unless he was confident enough to put his aircraft on automatic pilot – or 'George', as it was called. In the Hampden bomber there was no way the pilot could get to the Elsan portable toilet that many larger bombers carried; he urinated into a bottle. This was a difficult manoeuvre to negotiate in a tight space and in cumbersome flying gear. In a Whitley some crew members had to crawl along a 'tunnel' under and between petrol tanks to reach the Elsan. One member of a bomber crew told me, 'Lots of us just pissed in our pants because it was less bother than any other way of doing it. And sometimes we dirtied our pants. We did that anyway when we were really scared. Of course, we didn't tell other people.'

Assuming that the aircraft reached their targets and dropped their bombs, they were even more vulnerable to fighter attack on their way home because their formation would be much more fragmented. They might have lost fuel following damage caused by enemy bullets or flak and not be able to reach England. This could lead to a ditching in the sea. Moreover, when airmen baled out they were by no means safe. In the air, as they descended by parachute, they could be killed by pieces of exploding aircraft or by anti-aircraft and machine-gun fire from the ground. Once on the ground many aircrew faced a hostile reception from angry civilians and trigger-happy soldiers. Numerous fliers were killed or wounded under such circumstances.

There was yet another hazard. British barrage balloons, intended to deflect enemy bombers from their course and perhaps to bring some of them down, were anchored to the ground by steel cables. Several RAF pilots were killed when they ran into these cables. One hit a balloon cable at Harwich and crashed into a grain silo.

Apart from all the risks run by bomber pilots, the idea that they reached a certain height, flew dead level to drop their bombs and then turned round and headed for home is absurd. Many bombing runs were made while diving, others at dangerously low levels, yet others required a manoeuvrable aircraft and a daring pilot. Long before he won his VC, Guy Gibson, flying a Hampden, perfected a dive-bombing attack. It consisted of a 60-degree dive from 6,000 feet and pulling out at 2,000 feet. He and other pilots found that such a technique produced great accuracy, even though it was hazardous.

In an amazing night raid near Aachen, Gibson and Pilot Officer Pit flew along railway lines and bounced bombs into railway tunnels, where they blew up. But a tunnel goes under a hill and the instant that the bombs were 'away' the pilots had to pull their Hampdens sharply upwards to avoid crashing into the hillside. The job was to be done with the help of a flare but

Gibson, on a second run, could not operate the mechanism which released the flare. He turned on his landing light which lit up the rail track enough for him to see the sleepers rushing by. At the same time his navigator held the Aldis signalling light straight forward as a spotlight while they waited for the tunnel to loom up in its light.

Gibson described what happened:

On the word 'Gone!' [from his navigator bomb aimer] I slammed the throttles forward and saw the tunnel spotlighted by our Aldis before I yanked back the stick. The old Hampden, relieved of her bombs, went up like an elevator and we cleared a 400-foot cliff by a few feet. I remember this well because it was a white cliff with a chalk face and we could see it quite clearly. Eleven seconds later came that pleasant muffled crump showing that we had reached our mark.

Pilot Officer Pit's raid was even more daring. When he found his tunnel – again by night – he noticed a train steaming into it. Quickly he flew around to the other end and 'sealed it up' by bombing the exit. Then he went back to the entrance and wrecked that too.

It was Gibson who dropped the first 2,000 lb bomb of the war. He released it on his sixth shallow dive-bombing attempt to sink the *Scharnhorst* in Kiel harbour.

As their citations for VCs and other decorations show, bomber crews well deserved their awards. Their lives were on the line during every mission.

When the German armies overran Poland, France, Belgium and Holland in 1940 their operations were popularly referred to as blitzkriegs or *the* Blitzkrieg. It was not a new term; General Hans von Seeckt had adopted it in the 1920s when he commanded the small German Army. He believed that an armoured force operating independently could achieve victory swiftly and cheaply. But von Seeckt had reservations about the theory, foreseeing that the ascendancy of armour would lead to the growth of mass armies.

On 10 May 1940 the German armour and follow-up infantry moved so incisively and vigorously that the 'phoney war' came to an end in an hour and the British Expeditionary Force (BEF) was soon heavily engaged as the German thrust gained momentum, particularly where the less well-trained divisions of the French Army manned the front.

The RAF, constantly in action, was now demonstrating its primary role of supporting British troops. It strafed enemy columns, bombed bridges to block the path of the onrushing Germans, attacked enemy railways and trains, and all the while its pilots had to fight off attacks on their own airfields; often they were forced to change bases daily. Whatever they did they could only delay, not stop, the German advance. In order to give some relief to the British and French Army the RAF squadrons were expected to press home their attacks whatever the risks.

One of the forward squadrons was No 12, flying Fairey Battle two-seater bombers. The squadron was committed to battle on 12 May 1940, being ordered to destroy two bridges, at Vroehoven and Veldwezelt, across the strategic Albert Canal. It was to be a 'volunteer job' and when the entire squadron offered themselves the CO decided to use the six crews on the ready roster. As it happened, five aircraft took part in the raid.

Flying Officer Norman Thomas, leading one section of three aircraft to bomb the Vroehoven bridge, and Flying Officer Donald Garland, whose target was the Veldwezelt bridge, well knew that a mission requiring 'volunteers' would be particularly hazardous. They took some comfort from the fact that eight Hurricanes would be protecting them from enemy fighters.

Donald Edward Garland and Thomas Gray

Each section commander could choose his method of approach. Thomas planned a diving attack from about 6,000 feet while Gray chose a low-level run. Unfortunately, the expected protection from the Hurricanes did not materialize. The Hurricane pilots fought valiantly but a swarm of Messerschmitts overwhelmed them and, fighting for their lives, the fighter pilots were unable to protect the Fairey Battles. Thomas and one of his section, Pilot Officer T.D. Davy, reached their target, where Thomas was shot down. Davy, his aircraft ablaze, ordered his crew of two to bale out and crash landed his plane in the French lines.

What happened to Pilot Officer Garland and his crew, Sergeant Thomas Gray, observer, and Leading Aircraftman Lawrence Reynolds, rear gunner, is described in a joint VC citation for two of them, gazetted on 11 June 1940.

Flying Officer Donald Edward Garland, No 12 Squadron RAF
Sergeant Thomas Gray, No 12 Squadron RAF

In recognition of most conspicuous bravery. Flying Officer Garland was the pilot and Sergeant Gray the observer of the leading aircraft of a formation of five aircraft that attacked a bridge over the Albert Canal which had not been destroyed and was allowing the enemy to advance into Belgium. All the aircrews of the squadron concerned volunteered for the operation and after five crews had been selected by drawing lots [this is an error], the attack was delivered at low altitude against this vital target. Orders were issued that this bridge was to be destroyed at all costs. As had been anticipated, exceptionally intense machine-gun and anti-aircraft fire was encountered, and the bridge area was heavily protected by enemy fighters.

In spite of this the formation successfully delivered a dive bombing attack from the lowest practicable altitude and British fighters in the vicinity reported that the target was obscured by the bombs bursting on it and in its vicinity. Only one aircraft returned from this mission out of the five concerned. The pilot of this aircraft reports that in addition to the extremely heavy anti-aircraft fire, through which our aircraft dived to attack the objective, they were also attacked by a large number of enemy fighters after they had released their bombs on the target. Much of the success of this vital operation must be attributed to the formation leader, Flying Officer Garland, and to the coolness and resource of Sergeant Gray, who navigated Flying Officer Garland's aircraft under most difficult conditions in such a manner that the whole formation was able successfully to attack the target in spite of subsequent heavy losses. Flying Officer Garland and Sergeant Gray unfortunately failed to return from the mission.

The citation refers to the mission crews being chosen by drawing lots but Bowyer, that thorough RAF researcher, states that the entire squadron volunteered while the five crews that made the raid were those on stand-by.

Donald Garland, approaching the age of 22 when he died, was the first of four brothers to be killed or to die while serving during the war. Thomas Gray was nearly 26. They are buried in the Commonwealth War Graves Commission Cemetery at Haverlee, Belgium, together with Leading Aircraftman Lawrence Reynolds, the gunner, who was not decorated. Indeed, he was not even mentioned in the citation for Garland and Gray. Under the rules governing decorations at the time Reynolds could only have been awarded the VC and no doubt the authorities considered that three VCs for a single exploit was one too many. Nevertheless, logic must ask – if the observer, Gray, was considered worthy of the VC, why not the gunner? The three men are buried side by side.

Their mission was ill-conceived – not their fault – and was, in fact, a suicide attack. It would have been more justified, in the desperate circumstances of the time, had it been made 48 hours earlier. The Germans had captured the bridge on a Friday but it was not until Saturday night that enemy air defences were in place. Garland's attack was made on Sunday morning. The RAF was buying time for the Army and any real damage caused to the bridges would slow the enemy and allow Army units to take up better positions or to disengage and withdraw. It is a sad fact of history that the two bridges damaged by the Hampdens were repaired the very next day.

The British Army and with it the RAF was forced to retreat, a retrogressive movement that culminated in the evacuation from Dunkirk and St Valery-en-Caux.

With the British Army out of Europe, the RAF went on the direct offensive against the Germans. During the latter half of 1940 enemy communications were particular objectives. In August the target of one particular raid was an old aqueduct carrying the Dortmund–Ems Canal across the River Ems north of Münster. It was of great importance to the industrial areas of the Ruhr, being a principal waterway for moving munitions manufactured there. During an earlier RAF raid a newer aqueduct had been blown up and the Germans had diverted all traffic to the old one. Thus, it had become an object of military importance.

Roderick Alastair Brook Learoyd

On 12 August 1940 five Hampden bombers were ordered to destroy this target. The raid resulted in a VC for Flight Lieutenant Roderick Learoyd, aged 27, of 49 Squadron. The citation, gazetted on 20 August, is more than usually descriptive.

Acting Flight Lieutenant Roderick Alastair Brook Learoyd, No 49 Squadron RAF

In recognition of most conspicuous bravery. This officer, as first pilot of a Hampden aircraft, has repeatedly shown the highest conception of his duty and complete indifference to personal danger in making attacks at the lowest altitudes regardless of opposition. On the night of 12th August 1940, he was detailed to attack a special objective on the Dortmund–Ems Canal. He had attacked this objective on a previous occasion and was well aware of the risks entailed. To achieve success it was necessary to approach from a direction well known to the enemy, through a lane of especially disposed anti-aircraft defences, and in the face of the most intense point blank fire from guns of all calibres. The reception of the preceding aircraft might well have deterred the stoutest heart, all being hit and two lost. Flight Lieutenant Learoyd nevertheless made his attack at 150 feet, his aircraft being repeatedly hit and large pieces of the main plane torn away. He was almost blinded by the glare of many searchlights at close range but pressed home this attack with the greatest resolution and skill. He subsequently brought his wrecked aircraft home and, as the landing flaps were inoperative and the undercarriage indicators out of action, waited for dawn in the vicinity of his aerodrome before landing, which he accomplished without causing injury to his crew or further damage to the aircraft. The high courage, skill and determination which this officer has invariably displayed on many occasions in the face of the enemy, sets an example which is unsurpassed.

Roderick Learoyd became a wing commander and survived the war. He died in January 1996.

John Hannah

The exploit which won the VC for Sergeant John Hannah was very different from those which involved pilots. He was a wireless operator/air gunner of

83 Squadron, flying Hampdens, and he was only 18 years of age. Fully to appreciate his 'act of signal valour' it is necessary to visualize the interior of the Hampden bomber. To begin with, it was nothing like the great and relatively spacious Wellingtons and Halifaxes which followed it, the bombers generally seen in wartime films. The crew of four had tightly cramped quarters. The navigator sat in a nose cupola, with the pilot above and behind him. The wireless operator/gunner sat in what was inappropriately called a 'cabin' and beneath that was the lower gunner. These two and the navigator could crawl from one end of the aircraft to the other but not stand upright. Much was stowed into every bit of available space, including a collapsible dinghy, should the Hampden ditch, and two fire extinguishers. The wireless operator/gunner sat facing the tail, ready to carry out either of his duties, as occasion demanded. Close by was his radio but even closer to his hands were the twin .303 Vickers machine guns. Usually there was also a basket containing carrier pigeons for sending emergency messages.

On 15 September 1940 Pilot Officer C.A. Connor was one of the pilots of 83 Squadron ordered to bomb German invasion barges at Antwerp. His crew consisted of John Hannah, as wireless operator/gunner, Sergeant D.A. Hayhurst, navigator and bomb aimer and Sergeant G. James, the lower gunner. Connor took off at 10.30 p.m. Hannah's subsequent exploit is described in the citation for the VC, gazetted on 12 October 1940.

Sergeant John Hannah, No 83 Squadron RAF

In recognition of most conspicuous bravery on the night of 15th September, 1940. Sergeant Hannah was the wireless operator/air gunner in an aircraft engaged in a successful attack on enemy barge concentrations at Antwerp. It was then subjected to intense anti-aircraft fire and received a direct hit from a projectile of an explosive and incendiary nature, which apparently burst inside the bomb compartment. A fire started which quickly enveloped the wireless operator's and rear gunner's cockpits, and as both the port and starboard petrol tanks had been pierced, there was grave risk of the fire spreading. Sergeant Hannah forced his way through the fire to obtain two extinguishers and discovered that the rear gunner had had to leave the aircraft. He could have acted likewise, through the bottom escape hatch or forward through the navigator's hatch, but remained and fought the fire for ten minutes with the extinguishers, beating the flames with his log book when these were empty. During this time thousands of rounds of ammunition exploded in all directions and he was almost blinded by the intense heat and fumes, but had the presence of mind to obtain relief by turning on his oxygen supply. Air admitted through the large holes caused by the projectile made the bomb compartment an inferno and all the aluminium sheet metal on the floor of this airman's cockpit was melted away, leaving only the cross bearers. Working under these conditions, which caused burns to his face and eyes, Sergeant Hannah succeeded in extinguishing the fire. He then crawled forward, ascertained that the navigator had left the aircraft, and passed the latter's log and maps to the pilot.

This airman displayed courage, coolness and devotion to duty of the highest order and, by his action in remaining and successfully extinguishing the fire under conditions of the greatest danger and difficulty, enabled the pilot to bring the aircraft safely to its base.

The citation is adequately descriptive but Pilot Officer Connor, a witness throughout to Hannah's courage, added some interesting details. When Hannah saw the flames and molten metal eating up the bomber he called Connor on the intercom system and said calmly, 'The aircraft is on fire.'

'Is it very bad?' Connor asked.

'Bad – but not too bad,' Hannah said with the same coolness.

In fact, the situation could not have been worse. Sergeant Hayhurst, ordered back from the nose to check the situation, could not see Sergeant James but Hannah seemed to be alight all over. Understandably, Hayhurst considered that James was dead – in fact he had baled out – and that Hannah must inevitably die so he slithered back to the Hampden's nose and baled out, sure that Connor would follow him.

Knowing that Hannah was doing his best to put out the fire, Connor stayed in his seat, all too aware that his blazing plane was a splendid target for enemy flak gunners. Finally, Hannah reported over the intercom, 'The fire is out, sir.' When the sergeant crawled forward to him, Connor was appalled by his appearance, with his face and hands badly burnt. His radio destroyed and the carrier pigeons dead, Hannah helped to navigate the crippled Hampden home to RAF Scampton.

The many officers who inspected the Hampden were astonished that such a wreck could have been flown back, amazed that such a fire could have been successfully fought.

Three crew members were decorated – Hannah with the VC, Connor with the DFC and Hayhurst with the DFM. Hannah's health deteriorated, he was discharged on full pension in 1942 and he died in June 1947, aged 26. He remains the youngest airman ever to have been awarded the VC.

Hughie Idwal Edwards

Bombing certain targets in Germany required not merely persistence but sustained determination, especially at low altitudes. At strategic targets, German air defences were so formidable that even the most daring of British – and later American – pilots considered some places just too dangerous to tackle. Nevertheless, their strategic importance required that an attempt be made to penetrate those defences. One such objective was the port of Bremen, where German ships provided a tempting but difficult target. A night raid on Bremen on 17/18 June 1941 had been a failure, with 11 Whitleys and 3 Wellingtons lost, the heaviest night losses of the war to date. Then, on 30 June, a daylight raid was only moderately successful.

A further raid was planned for 4 July, to be led by Wing Commander Hughie Edwards DFC, a 28-year-old Australian, but a member of the RAF, not the RAAF. Edwards himself planned the details of the attack by 12 Blenheims of 105 and 107 Squadrons. He was awarded a VC for his gallantry. There is reference in his citation, gazetted on 22 July 1941, to his 'physical disability'. During an earlier parachute descent his leg had been so severely damaged that it was paralysed below the knee and he had spent nine months in hospital.

Acting Wing Commander Hughie Idwal Edwards DFC, No 105 Squadron RAF

In recognition of most conspicuous bravery. Wing Commander Edwards, although handicapped by a physical disability resulting from a flying accident, has repeatedly displayed gallantry of the highest order in pressing home bombing attacks from very low heights against strongly defended objectives.

On 4th July, 1941, he led an important attack on the Port of Bremen, one of the most heavily defended towns in Germany. This attack had to be made in daylight and there were no clouds to afford concealment. During the approach to the German coast several enemy ships were sighted and Wing Commander Edwards knew that his aircraft would be reported and that the defences would be in a state of readiness. Undaunted by this misfortune he brought his formation 50 miles overland to the target, flying at a height of little more than 50 feet, passing under high-tension cables, carrying away telegraph wires and finally passing through a formidable balloon barrage. On reaching Bremen he was met with a hail of fire, all his aircraft being hit and four of them being destroyed. Nevertheless he made a most successful attack, and then with the greatest skill and coolness withdrew the surviving aircraft without further loss.

Throughout the execution of this operation which he had planned personally with full knowledge of the risks entailed, Wing Commander Edwards displayed the highest possible standard of gallantry and determination.

Four Blenheims were shot down during the raid and the crews killed but the loss was considered to be justified by the great damage wrought.

Edwards, who had joined the RAF in 1936, remained in the Air Force after the war, became an Air Commodore and finished his active career in 1963. When he died in 1982 he held not only the VC but was a KCMG with the CB, DSO, OBE and DFC.

Kenneth Campbell

The names of the great German battleships and pocket battleships, *Bismarck, Tirpitz, Gneisenau, Scharnhorst, Admiral Graf Spee*, crop up so frequently in histories of the Second World War that people of subsequent generations could easily gain the impression that the British High Command, political and military, had an obsessive fixation about them. This is true – they had. For as long as they were operational, these formidable fighting ships posed a terrible threat. In effect, they threatened Britain's very existence because in conjunction with the U-boats, they were cutting the oceanic supply lines which provided Britain with food, petrol, raw materials for war production, troop reinforcements from abroad and armaments from the United States.

British spies and the French Resistance knew that any information about the movements of the battleships was important and must be communicated at once to London. Churchill himself, frustrated and exasperated by what he saw as the 'inability' of the RAF and Navy to trap and destroy the destructive *Gneisenau* and *Scharnhorst*, ordered that 'serious risks and sacrifices' had to be made. He was being less than fair to his fighting men – they had already made sacrifices – but his rebuke indicated the level of menace the capital ships posed.

In the last week of March 1941 the two ships arrived in Brest. French Resistance radioed the news to London and an RAF reconnaissance Spitfire confirmed that the report was true. On 4/5 April, 54 bombers – 39 Wellingtons, 11 Hampdens and 4 Manchesters – raided Brest docks and a direct hit was claimed on one of the German ships. This was probably the bomb which fell but did not explode in the dry dock in which the *Gneisenau* was lying. Other bombs hit the hotel being used by German naval officers and several of them were killed. With the prospect of further attacks, the *Gneisenau*'s captain decided his ship would be safer if moored in the harbour; he was fearful that the unexploded bomb lying next to *Gneisenau* might be set off in another raid. He took her to a deepwater buoy.

Brest was as heavily defended as any target throughout the war, in any country. In addition, there were the natural defences of the hills around it. RAF Coastal Command was given the task of making a torpedo run against *Gneisenau* with Bristol Beauforts, in conjunction with a raid by 71 bombers – Wellingtons, Manchesters and Whitleys. Because of bad weather only 47 aircraft located the target and they caused no damage to the big ships. The three Bristol Beauforts were piloted, respectively, by Flying Officer Kenneth Campbell, Flying Officer John Hyde and Sergeant H. Camp, all of 22 Squadron and all veterans. Flying independently, they were to rendezvous near Brest but poor weather prevented this and Campbell made the strike alone. It brought him a posthumous VC, gazetted on 13 March 1942.

Flying Officer Kenneth Campbell, No 22 Squadron RAFVR

In recognition of most conspicuous bravery. This officer was the pilot of a Beaufort aircraft of Coastal Command which was detailed to attack an enemy battle cruiser in Brest Harbour at first light on the morning of 6th April 1941. The aircraft did not return but it is now known that a torpedo attack was carried out with the utmost daring.

The battle cruiser was secured alongside the wall on the north shore of the harbour, protected by a stone mole bending around it from the west. On rising ground behind the ship stood protective batteries of guns. Other batteries were clustered thickly round the two arms of land which encircle the outer harbour. In this outer harbour near the mole were moored three heavily-armed anti-aircraft ships, guarding the battle cruiser. Even if an aircraft succeeded in penetrating these formidable defences, it would be almost impossible after delivering a low-level attack, to avoid crashing into the rising ground beyond. This was well known to Flying Officer Campbell who, despising the heavy odds, went cheerfully and resolutely to the task. He ran the gauntlet of the defences. Coming in almost at sea level, he passed the anti-aircraft ships at less than mast-height in the very mouths of their guns, and skimming over the mole launched a torpedo at point-blank range. The battle cruiser was severely damaged below the water-line and was obliged to return to the dock whence she had come only the day before.

By pressing home his attack at close quarters in the face of a withering fire on a course fraught with extreme peril, Flying Officer Campbell displayed valour of the highest order.

From the beginning there was little prospect that the 24-year-old Campbell and his crew of three would survive the attack on *Gneisenau*. It was merely a matter of getting a torpedo to run true before they were brought down. The battered Beaufort crashed into the harbour, from where the Germans recovered it. They buried the RAF men in the Brest cemetery. The VC citation is interesting because, gazetted one year after the exploit, it showed that intelligence was indeed coming back from occupied France. While Flying Officer Hyde, far above Campbell's Beaufort, saw something of the action only French Resistance observers could have seen Campbell coming in 'almost at sea level' and passing the Germans' flak ships 'at less than mast height'. It was also the Resistance which reported that the *Gneisenau* was crippled and that repairs would take 'many months'. In fact, *Gneisenau* was out of action for nearly nine months. Overall, intelligence must have been very good for the authorities to decide on the award of a VC to Campbell, without waiting for an investigation after the war. But there remains one puzzling note. It appears that the Germans found the body of Sergeant James Scott, the navigator, in the pilot's seat normally occupied by Campbell.*

---

* *Scharnhorst and Gneisenau* by Richard Garrett (David & Charles, Newton Abbot, 1978).

Arthur Stewart King Scarf

When the Japanese began their war against Britain, its Commonwealth Allies and the US, on 7 December 1941, the air defences of Singapore were in a serious state. The RAF had a station at Butterworth but it was ill-defended and only a handful of planes were based there. The Japanese effort to capture Singapore began on 8 December when the 25th Army landed troops on the east coast of Malaya at Kota Bharu and on the eastern shores of Thailand at Singapore and Patini. On 9 December there occurred one of the most remarkable deeds of valour and determination of the war. It resulted in a posthumous VC for Squadron Leader Arthur Scarf but because of the rapid defeat of the British forces in Malaya, the consequent confusion and the loss and destruction of records it was not gazetted until 21 June 1946, nearly a year after the war ended.

Squadron Leader Arthur Stewart King Scarf, No 62 Squadron RAF

In recognition of most conspicuous bravery. On 9th December, 1941, all available aircraft from the Royal Air Force Station, Butterworth, Malaya, were ordered to make a daylight attack on the advanced operational base of the Japanese Air Force at Singora, Thailand. From this base, the enemy fighter squadrons were supporting the landing operations.

The aircraft detailed for the sortie were on the point of taking off when the enemy made a combined dive-bombing and low level machine-gun attack on the airfield. All our aircraft were destroyed or damaged with the exception of the Blenheim piloted by Squadron Leader Scarf. This aircraft had become airborne a few seconds before the attack started.

Squadron Leader Scarf circled the airfield and witnessed the disaster. It would have been reasonable had he abandoned the projected operation, which was intended to be a formation sortie. He decided, however, to press on to Singora in his single aircraft. Although he knew that this individual action could not inflict much material damage on the enemy, he nevertheless appreciated the moral effect which it would have on the remainder of the squadron, who were helplessly watching their aircraft burning on the ground.

Squadron Leader Scarf completed his attack successfully. The opposition over the target was severe and included attacks by a considerable number of enemy fighters. In the course of these encounters, Squadron Leader Scarf was mortally wounded.

The enemy continued to engage him in a running fight, which lasted until he had regained the Malayan border. Squadron Leader Scarf fought a brilliant evasive action in a valiant attempt to return to his base. Although he displayed the utmost gallantry and determination, he was, owing to his wounds, unable to accomplish this. He made a successful forced-landing at Alor Star without causing any injury to his crew. He was received into hospital as soon as possible, but died shortly after admission.

Squadron Leader Scarf displayed supreme heroism in the face of tremendous odds and his splendid example of self-sacrifice will long be remembered.

The 27-year-old Scarf knew exactly what he was doing and what he was facing during every minute of his exploit. His twin-engine Blenheim, the RAF's fastest medium-range bomber at the beginning of the war – it had a maximum speed of 280 mph – could in theory outrun the Japanese Mitsubishis of the time but Scarf was swamped by them, coming as they did from all directions. He must have used his own forward-firing guns to good effect, as did his turret gunner, Flight Sergeant C. Rich. And somehow the bomb aimer, Flight Sergeant F. Calder, dropped his bombs on target.

Despite dreadful wounds, Scarf's determination was so great that he managed to land the stricken Blenheim. He was still alive when Rich and Calder lifted him out of his cockpit and he lived long enough to greet his wife, an Army nurse, as he reached the operating theatre. He died soon afterwards from multiple wounds, loss of blood and shock. Scarf may be the least known of RAF Second World War VC winners, perhaps because his recognition came so late. However, this in itself shows that the award system works, despite its many deficiencies. It shows also, in Scarf's case, that his heroism was so great that numerous people, in captivity throughout the war, were determined to remember it and bring him due recognition, no matter how belated.

Leslie Thomas Manser

The exploit for which Flying Officer Leslie Manser RAFVR was awarded the VC was of the 'self-sacrifice' type common during the war. In Manser's case it was considered exceptional even by the high standards of the RAF.

In the earlier months of 1942 the RAF had mounted massive raids against Lubeck and Rostock and the chief of Bomber Command, Sir Arthur Harris, approached Winston Churchill and the RAF's Chief of Staff, Sir Charles Portal, with the idea of making 1,000–bomber raids on selected German cities. Some raids were markedly successful and, despite the complexities of organizing the streams of bombers flowing towards the targets, there was never a serious collision.

On the night of 30/31 May 1942, 1,047 bombers, a mixture of Wellingtons, Stirlings, Halifaxes, Whitleys, Manchesters and Hampdens was sent to raid Cologne. Immense damage was inflicted: nearly 500 people were killed, 5,000 injured and 45,000 bombed out. In addition, 150,000 of the populace fled the city. The large numbers of bombers over the target despite the anti-aircraft defences, and the destruction wrought in the old city, shocked the Germans.

However, 43 aircraft were lost. One of them, a Manchester, was under the command of 20-year-old Flying Officer Leslie Manser, of 50 Squadron, with Sergeant P. Baveystock as co-pilot. The difficulty of getting a lumbering, stricken bomber back to Britain is illustrated in the posthumous citation for Flying Officer Manser, gazetted on 23 October 1942.

Flying Officer Leslie Thomas Manser, No 50 Squadron RAFVR

In recognition of most conspicuous bravery. Flying Officer Manser was captain and first pilot of a Manchester aircraft which took part in the mass raid on Cologne on the night of May 30th, 1942.

As the aircraft was approaching its objective it was caught by searchlights and subjected to intense and accurate anti-aircraft fire. Flying Officer Manser held on his dangerous course and bombed the target successfully from a height of 7,000 feet.

Then he set course for base. The Manchester had been damaged and was still under heavy fire. Flying Officer Manser took violent evasive action, turning and descending to under 1,000 feet. It was of no avail. The searchlights and flak followed him until the outskirts of the city were passed. The aircraft was hit repeatedly and the rear gunner was wounded. The front cabin filled with smoke; the port engine was over-heating badly.

Pilot and crew could all have escaped safely by parachute. Nevertheless, Flying Officer Manser, disregarding the obvious hazards, persisted in his attempt to save aircraft and crew from falling into enemy hands. He took the aircraft up to 2,000 feet. Then the port engine burst into flames. It was ten minutes before the fire was mastered, but then the engine went out of action for good. Part of one wing was burnt, and the air-speed of the aircraft became dangerously low.

Despite all the efforts of pilot and crew, the Manchester began to lose height. At this critical moment, Flying Officer Manser once more disdained the alternative of parachuting to safety with his crew. Instead, with grim determination, he set a new course for the nearest base, accepting for himself the prospect of almost certain death in a firm resolve to carry on to the end.

Soon, the aircraft became extremely difficult to handle and, when a crash was inevitable, Flying Officer Manser ordered the crew to bale out. A sergeant handed him a parachute but he waved it away, telling the non-commissioned officer to jump at once as he could only hold the aircraft steady for a few seconds more. While the crew were descending to safety they saw the aircraft, still carrying the gallant captain, plunge to earth and burst into flames.

In pressing home his attack in the face of strong opposition, in striving, against heavy odds, to bring back his aircraft and crew and, finally, when in extreme peril, thinking only of the safety of his comrades, Flying Officer Manser displayed determination and valour of the highest order.

There was no shortage of witnesses to Manser's courage because the crew had baled out over Belgium and with one exception they were picked up by a Resistance escape line and, by stages, returned to Britain. Baveystock, the co-pilot, described the episode vividly, while Pilot Officer N. Horsley, the radio operator, the bomb aimer, Flying Officer R. Barnes and the front gunner, Sergeant A. Mills, all spoke of Manser's heroism. In later years Baveystock, who was promoted to flight lieutenant, said that Manser's example had inspired him. This was evidently so, since he finished the war with the DSO, DFC and DFM. Flying Officer Manser is buried in the Commonwealth War Graves Commission Cemetery at Haverlee, Belgium.

Hugh Gordon Malcolm

During the 1940–3 campaigns in North Africa the RAF's main function was to support the Army. There were two principal ways of doing this – by strafing the Italian and German troops, their positions and their lines of communications and by raiding the airfields in order to make it more difficult for enemy aircraft to attack British troops. It was a different war from that in Europe where the principal targets were German and Italian industrial centres and cities, at least until after the Allied invasion of Europe.

At the end of the Battle of El Alamein, which had begun on 23 October 1942, Field Marshal Rommel's lines were broken west of El Alamein and the German and Italian forces began a retreat to Tunisia. They were still strong, because of General Montgomery's failure to pursue the defeated enemy army with as much vigour as his original assault. The enemy established the Mareth Line which was supported by many squadrons of aircraft operating from Bizerte and other bases. Enemy air superiority surprised the Allied commanders and determined efforts were ordered to destroy enemy planes on the ground.

The RAF squadron most heavily engaged was No 18, flying Blenheims, under Wing Commander Hugh Malcolm. His valour and determination led to his being awarded the VC. Unfortunately, it was yet another posthumous award. Malcolm was 26 when killed in action. Unusually, his citation, gazetted on 27 April 1943, covers exploits on three separate dates.

Acting Wing Commander Hugh Gordon Malcolm (deceased), No 18 Squadron RAF

In recognition of most conspicuous bravery. This officer commanded a squadron of light bombers in North Africa. Throughout his service in that theatre his leadership, skill and daring were of the highest order.

On 17th November, 1942, he was detailed to carry out a low-level formation attack on Bizerte airfield, taking advantage of cloud cover. Twenty miles from the target the sky became clear but Wing Commander Malcolm carried on, knowing well the danger of proceeding without a fighter escort. Despite fierce opposition, all bombs were dropped within the airfield perimeter. A Junkers 52 and a Messerschmitt 109 were shot down: many dispersed enemy aircraft were raked by machine-gun fire. Weather conditions became extremely unfavourable and as a result two of his aircraft were lost by collision; another was forced down by enemy fighters. It was due to this officer's skilful and resolute leadership that the remaining aircraft returned safely to base.

On 28th November, 1942, he again led his squadron against Bizerta airfield which was bombed from a low altitude. The airfield on this occasion was heavily defended and intense and accurate anti-aircraft fire was met. Nevertheless, after his squadron had released their bombs, Wing Commander Malcolm led them back again and again to attack the airfield with machine gun fire.

These were typical of every sortie undertaken by this gallant officer; each attack was pressed to an effective conclusion however difficult the task and however formidable the opposition.

Finally, on 4th December, 1942, Wing Commander Malcolm, having been detailed to give close support to the First Army, received an urgent request to attack an enemy fighter airfield near Chouigui. Wing Commander Malcolm knew that to attack such an objective without a fighter escort – which could not be arranged in the time available – would be to court almost certain disaster; but believing the attack to be necessary for the success of the Army's operations, his duty was clear. He decided to attack.

He took off with his squadron and reached the target unmolested but when he had successfully attacked it his squadron was intercepted by an overwhelming force of enemy fighters. Wing Commander Malcolm fought back, controlling his hard-pressed squadron and attempting to maintain formation. One by one his aircraft were shot down until only his own aircraft remained. In the end, he, too, was shot down in flames.

Wing Commander Malcolm's last exploit was the finest example of the valour and unswerving devotion to duty which he constantly displayed.

Hugh Malcolm, who came from Broughty Ferry, Dundee, was 24 when he died. He is buried in the Commonwealth War Graves Commission Cemetery at Beja, Tunisia.

Guy Penrose Gibson

The Ruhr was one of RAF Bomber Command's most important targets. The valley of the Ruhr, the heart of the German iron and steel industry, was a place of great strategic significance and any major damage that could be inflicted upon it was a serious blow to the German war effort. A notable series of raids became known as 'The Battle of the Ruhr'. Forty-three large-scale attacks were made between March and July 1943, most of them directed against Essen, Cologne, Bochum, Duisburg, Wuppertal, Dusseldorf and Dortmund.

In the same period some of the great dams from which much of the Ruhr's heavy industry derived its electric power were attacked. The best known of them were the Möhne and Eder Dams. Bomber Command's 617 Squadron, under the command of Wing Commander Guy Gibson, was specially trained in low-level and skip-bombing techniques and used a new rotating bomb designed by Barnes Wallis. On the night of 16 May 1943 Lancasters from 617 Squadron carried out a precision-bombing raid which breached the Möhne and Eder Dams.

On 28 May Gibson's VC was gazetted, but his citation covered much more than his 'dam-busting' operation. Few citations in VC history have dealt with such a long period of exploits. In effect, the operational background to Gibson's DSO and DFC is implicit in the VC citation.

Nineteen Lancasters had set out on the raid. Of these only eight took part in the actual attack *and* returned. Thirty-three members of the crews were decorated. Guy Gibson had been pushing his luck for many months; he had done more than any one pilot could reasonably have been expected to do and his chief, 'Bomber' Harris, should have insisted that his most famous pilot finish operational flying. Indeed, for some time Gibson's superiors had refused his requests to be allowed to take part in raids. It was Harris himself who gave permission for 'one last sortie', on 19 September 1944. It was made by a mixed force of 230 Lancasters and Mosquitoes and Gibson was Master Bomber – in effect the raid commander. The raid completed, Gibson spoke to his crews by radio: 'Nice work chaps, now beat it home.' Everybody who has ever written about Gibson quotes these final words – for they *were* final. On the way home Gibson's Mosquito went down in flames. His remains were not identified until after the war and he was buried in Steenbergen, Holland.

Gibson was 26 when he was killed. He held the VC, DSO and Bar, DFC and Bar and the American Legion of Merit, a remarkable collection of decorations. Marshal of the Royal Air Force Arthur Harris was a strong leader with a powerful personality; it is a pity that he could not say 'No' to Guy Gibson.

Acting Wing Commander Guy Penrose Gibson DSO, DFC, Reserve of Air Force Officers, No 617 Squadron

In recognition of most conspicuous bravery.

This officer served as a night bomber pilot at the beginning of the war and quickly established a reputation as an outstanding operational pilot. In addition to taking the fullest possible share in all normal operations, he made single-handed attacks during his 'rest' nights on such highly defended objectives as the German battleship *Tirpitz*, then completing in Wilhelmshaven.

When his tour of operational duty was concluded, he asked for a further operational posting and went to a night-fighter unit instead of being posted for instructional duties. In the course of his second operational tour, he destroyed at least three enemy bombers and contributed much to the raising and development of new night-fighter formations.

After a short period in a training unit, he again volunteered for operational duties and returned to night bombers. Both as an operational pilot and as a leader of his squadron, he achieved outstandingly successful results and his personal courage knew no bounds. Berlin, Cologne, Danzig, Gdynia, Genoa, Le Creusot, Milan, Nuremberg and Stuttgart were among the targets he attacked by day and by night.

On the conclusion of his third operational tour, Wing Commander Gibson pressed strongly to be allowed to remain on operations and he was selected to command a squadron then forming for special tasks. Under his inspiring leadership, this squadron has now executed one of the most devastating attacks of the war – the breaching of the Möhne and Eder dams.

The task was fraught with danger and difficulty. Wing Commander Gibson personally made the initial attack on the Möhne dam. Descending to within a few feet of the water and taking the full brunt of the anti-aircraft defences, he delivered his attack with great accuracy. Afterwards he circled very low for 30 minutes, drawing the enemy fire on himself in order to leave as free a run as possible to the following aircraft which were attacking the dam in turn.

Wing Commander Gibson then led the remainder of his force to the Eder dam where, with complete disregard for his own safety, he repeated his tactics and once more drew on himself the enemy fire so that the attack could be successfully developed.

Wing Commander Gibson has completed over 170 sorties, involving more than 600 hours operational flying. Throughout his operational career, prolonged exceptionally at his own request, he has shown leadership, determination and valour of the highest order.

Arthur Louis Aaron

Germany's industrial regions were not the only targets for Bomber Command in 1942–4. Italy's war production centres were also heavily hit and on the night of 12 August 1943, 656 RAF night bombers flew from their British bases to attack Turin and Milan. A Stirling bomber in this great air fleet was captained by 21-year-old Flight Sergeant Arthur Aaron, every member of whose crew was also a sergeant – navigator, bomb aimer, engineer, radio operator and the gunners. Their target was Turin. What happened on that flight won a posthumous VC award for Arthur Aaron, gazetted on 5 November 1943.

Acting Flight Sergeant Arthur Louis Aaron DFM, No 218 Squadron RAFVR (deceased)

In recognition of most conspicuous bravery. On the night of 12th August, 1943, Flight Sergeant Aaron was captain and pilot of a Stirling aircraft detailed to attack Turin. When approaching to attack, the bomber received devastating bursts of fire from an enemy fighter. Three engines were hit, the windscreen shattered, the front and rear turrets put out of action and the elevator control damaged, causing the aircraft to become unstable and difficult to control. The navigator was killed and other members of the crew were wounded.

A bullet struck Flight Sergeant Aaron in the face, breaking his jaw and tearing away part of his face. He was also wounded in the lung and his right arm was rendered useless. As he fell forward over the control column, the aircraft dived several thousand feet. Control was regained by the flight engineer at 3,000 feet. Unable to speak, Flight Sergeant Aaron urged the bomb aimer by signs to take over the controls. Course was then set southwards in an endeavour to fly the crippled bomber, with one engine out of action, to Sicily or North Africa.

Flight Sergeant Aaron was assisted to the rear of the aircraft and treated with morphia. After resting for some time he rallied and mindful of his responsibility as captain of aircraft insisted on returning to the pilot's cockpit, where he was lifted into his seat and had his feet placed on the rudder bar. Twice he made determined attempts to take control and hold the aircraft to its course but his weakness was evident and with difficulty he was persuaded to desist. Though in great pain and suffering from exhaustion, he continued to help by writing directions with his left hand.

Five hours after leaving the target the petrol began to run low, but soon afterwards the flare path at Bone airfield was sighted. Flight Sergeant Aaron summoned his failing strength to direct the bomb aimer in the hazardous task of landing the damaged aircraft in the darkness with undercarriage retracted. Four attempts were made under his direction; at the fifth Flight Sergeant Aaron was so near to collapsing that he had to be restrained by the crew and the landing was completed by the bomb aimer.

Nine hours after landing, Flight Sergeant Aaron died from exhaustion. Had he been content, when grievously wounded, to lie still and conserve his failing strength, he would probably have recovered but he saw it as his duty to exert himself to the utmost, if necessary with his last breath, to ensure that his aircraft and crew did not fall into enemy hands. In appalling conditions he showed the greatest qualities of courage, determination and leadership, and though wounded and dying, he set an example of devotion to duty which has seldom been equalled and never surpassed.

The author of this citation must have known that it contained a serious untruth. He wrote that Aaron's Stirling had been attacked by 'an enemy fighter', but this was not so. The rear gunner of another Stirling had opened fire on Aaron's bomber, killing the navigator, Sergeant Brennan, mortally wounding Aaron and badly damaging the Stirling. He could not have mistaken the Stirling for an enemy aircraft because the two Stirlings were close together and flying in a steady formation of many British bombers. The raiders were not yet under attack.

Half a century later this type of incident would be called 'casualties caused by friendly fire'. This disgusting phrase was not in use during the Second World War, although 'Allied fire' was sometimes mentioned. In 1943, with the war at its height, it was felt inappropriate to disclose the true circumstances of the attack on Sergeant Aaron's bomber, even though his closest comrades knew what had happened, as did the entire 218 Squadron before long. The name of the gunner who had fired to such devastating effect on another Stirling was never disclosed, though it was probably known. It would not have helped Aaron's family to have been told his name. The cover-up continued into the RAF official history – Aaron was severely wounded 'in an encounter with a night fighter. . . .'*

In other respects the citation was accurate. The young pilot's fortitude and devotion to duty might have been equalled by other heroes of the war but it was certainly not surpassed.

Arthur Aaron was buried in the British military cemetery at Bone, Tunisia, later the Commonwealth War Graves Commission Cemetery. Flight Sergeant Allan Larden, the bomb aimer was awarded the CGM, the engineer, Sergeant M. Mitcham and the radio operator, Sergeant T. Guy, each received the DFM.**

William Reid

The citation accompanying the award of the VC to Flight Lieutenant William Reid is rare because it says enough to give its readers a clear idea of the exploit concerned. A lengthy citation does not necessarily indicate a

---

* *Royal Air Force 1939–1945*, Denis Richards and Hilary St George Saunders (HMSO, London, 1954, Vol. II, p. 325).
** The detailed story of Sergeant Aaron's last flight is graphically described by Chaz Bowyer in *For Valour – The Air VCs* (Grub Street, London, 1992).

'better' VC, but in the case of a bomber pilot it does reflect the long and difficult mission. The first four lines of the final paragraph show the desperate plight Reid was in before he even began his last 200 miles to the target. His VC was gazetted on 14 December 1943.

Acting Flight Lieutenant William Reid, No 61 Squadron RAFVR

In recognition of most conspicuous bravery. On the night of November 3rd, 1943, Flight Lieutenant Reid was pilot and captain of a Lancaster aircraft detailed to attack Dusseldorf.

Shortly after crossing the Dutch coast, the pilot's windscreen was shattered by fire from a Messerschmitt 110. Owing to a failure in the heating circuit, the rear gunner's hands were too cold for him to open fire immediately or to operate his microphone and so give warning of danger; but after a brief delay he managed to return the Messerschmitt's fire and it was driven off.

During the fight with the Messerschmitt, Flight Lieutenant Reid was wounded in the head, shoulders and hands. The elevator trimming tabs of the aircraft were damaged and it became difficult to control. The rear turret, too, was badly damaged and the communications system and compasses were put out of action. Flight Lieutenant Reid ascertained that his crew were unscathed and, saying nothing about his own injuries, he continued his mission.

Soon afterwards, the Lancaster was attacked by a Focke Wulf 190. This time, the enemy's fire raked the bomber from stem to stern. The rear gunner replied with his only serviceable gun but the state of his turret made accurate aiming impossible. The navigator was killed and the wireless operator fatally injured. The mid-upper turret was hit and the oxygen system put out of action. Flight Lieutenant Reid was again wounded and the flight engineer, though hit in the forearm, supplied him with oxygen from a portable supply.

Flight Lieutenant Reid refused to be turned from his objective and Dusseldorf was reached some 50 minutes later. He had memorized his course to the target and had continued in such a normal manner that the bomb-aimer, who was cut off by the failure of the communications system, knew nothing of his captain's injuries or of the casualties to his comrades. Photographs show that, when bombs were released, the aircraft was right over the centre of the target.

Steering by the pole star and the moon, Flight Lieutenant Reid then set course for home. He was growing weak from loss of blood. The emergency oxygen supply had given out. With the windscreen shattered, the cold was intense. He lapsed into semi-consciousness. The flight engineer, with some help from the bomb-aimer, kept the Lancaster in the air despite heavy anti-aircraft fire over the Dutch coast.

The North Sea crossing was accomplished. An airfield was sighted.

The captain revived, resumed control and made ready to land. Ground mist partially obscured the runway lights. The captain was also much bothered by blood from his head wound getting into his eyes. But he made a safe landing although one leg of the damaged undercarriage collapsed when the load came on.

Wounded in two attacks, without oxygen, suffering severely from cold, his navigator dead, his wireless operator fatally wounded, his aircraft crippled and defenceless, Flight Lieutenant Reid showed superb courage and leadership in penetrating a further 200 miles into enemy territory to attack one of the most strongly defended targets in Germany, every additional mile increasing the hazards of the long and perilous journey home. His tenacity and devotion to duty were beyond praise.

Flight Lieutenant Reid, approaching his 22nd birthday when he received his VC, flew many other sorties, some of them against V1 rocket sites in France. His Lancaster was shot down on 31 July 1944 and he and the radio operator were the only survivors of the crash. They were captured and put in POW camps but they survived the war. Two of the crew who had flown with him during his VC exploit were decorated: Flight Sergeant James Norris, the engineer, was awarded the CGM and Flight Sergeant Alfred Emerson, a gunner, the DFM.

Cyril Joe Barton

As I have mentioned elsewhere, bombers were sitting ducks for the enemy's fast fighters and once the latter had killed or wounded the bomber's gunners or badly damaged the guns themselves the aircraft became even more vulnerable. Unable to shoot back, the crew had to depend on the captain's skill and on luck to bring them through. Night after night hundreds of bombers took off from British airfields to make the hazardous flight to Berlin, Essen, Frankfurt, Nuremberg, Magdeburg and many other places. Some of the targets were in France, especially the centres where the Germans had taken over French factories for war production, as at Lille and Limoges.*

Bomber Command suffered its greatest loss of the war in the raid of 30/31 March 1944 when 795 aircraft set off to bomb Nuremberg – 572 Lancasters, 214 Halifaxes and 9 Mosquitoes. The raid should never have taken place because a Mosquito crew which flew a special weather reconnaissance reported that the bombers could not expect cloud cover over the target or during the flight to it. This information should have resulted in the raid being cancelled.

---

* For summaries of practically all Bomber Command raids consult *The Bomber Command War Diaries* by Martin Middlebrook and Chris Everitt (Viking, London, 1985).

The RAF planners had arranged some diversionary attacks on other targets but the German air defence staff were not deceived and assembled their fighters at strategic locations – so strategic on this particular night that it must be wondered if they had advance intelligence information. The fighters' attacks were so fierce that they shot down 82 bombers before they reached Nuremberg or on their approach run. According to Middlebrook and Everitt, 120 aircraft mistakenly bombed Schweinfurt. The raid on Nuremberg was a disaster for the RAF. That they caused practically no damage to strategic targets was largely because the German fighters mercilessly harried the bombers.

In all, 85 bombers were lost and about 600 aircrew and pilots, the worst Bomber Command losses of the war in a single raid and a great blow to Bomber Command.

One of the Halifaxes which took part in the ill-fated raid was piloted by 22-year-old Pilot Officer Cyril Joe Barton, who was posthumously awarded the VC, gazetted on 27 June 1944. His citation is more than usually interesting because each paragraph is numbered, probably to draw attention to the sequence of crises which confronted the young pilot on his last mission.

Pilot Officer Cyril Joe Barton, 578 Squadron RAFVR (deceased)

In recognition of most conspicuous bravery. On the night of 30 March, 1944, Pilot Officer Barton was captain and pilot of a Halifax aircraft detailed to attack Nuremberg. When some 70 miles short of the target, the aircraft was attacked by a Junkers 88. The first burst of fire from the enemy made the intercommunication system useless. One engine was damaged when a Messerschmitt 210 joined the fight. The bomber's machine guns were out of action and the gunners were unable to return the fire.

2.   Fighters continued to attack the aircraft as it approached the target area and in the confusion caused by the failure of the communications system at the height of the battle a signal was misinterpreted and the navigator air bomber and wireless operator left the aircraft by parachute.

3.   Pilot Officer Barton faced a situation of dire peril. His aircraft was damaged, his navigational team had gone and he could not communicate with the remainder of the crew. If he continued his mission, he would be at the mercy of hostile fighters when silhouetted against the fires in the target area and if he survived, he would have to make a 4½ hours journey home on three engines across heavily-defended territory. Determined to press home his attack at all costs, he flew on and, reaching the target, released the bombs himself.

4.   As Pilot Officer Barton turned for home the propeller of the damaged engine, which was vibrating badly, flew off. It was also discovered that two of the petrol tanks had suffered damage and were

leaking. Pilot Officer Barton held on to his course and, without navigational aids and in spite of strong head winds, successfully avoided the most dangerous defence areas on his route. Eventually he crossed the English coast only 90 miles north of his base.

5. By this time the petrol supply was nearly exhausted. Before a suitable landing place could be found the port engines stopped. The aircraft was now too low to be abandoned successfully. Pilot Officer Barton therefore ordered the three remaining members of his crew to take up their crash stations. Then, with only one engine working he made a gallant attempt to land clear of the houses over which he was flying. The aircraft finally crashed and Pilot Officer Barton lost his life but his three comrades survived.

6. Pilot Officer Barton had previously taken part in 4 attacks on Berlin and 14 other operational missions. On one of these two members of his crew were wounded during a determined effort to locate the target despite appalling weather conditions. In gallantly completing his last mission in the face of almost impossible odds this officer displayed unsurpassed courage and devotion to duty.

A few points made in the citation need clarification. Pilot Officer Barton released his bombs but neither he nor anybody else had any means of knowing how effective they were, probably not at all. But this had nothing to do with the merit of his award. Mention is made of the navigator, bomber and radio operator baling out. They did this in good faith, believing that the captain had flashed the Morse code signal for P (parachute) on the lamp which was in front of each of them. In fact, the rear gunner, Sergeant F. Brice had signalled R, meaning 'resume course'. Having seen no further sign of attacking fighters Brice was entitled to give this signal. Mention is also made of Barton's desperate attempt to avoid some houses in his path. He did not succeed. The crippled Halifax hit a house and momentum took it on crazily through other buildings. Much of the wreckage finished up in a colliery at Ryhope, County Durham. Miners from the colliery pulled the survivors from the rubble but Cyril Barton died in hospital. Many other Bomber Command captains performed similar exploits but what made Barton's worthy of the supreme award was his extraordinary persistence. It was similar to that which Flight Lieutenant Reid had demonstrated, but Reid had been lucky. Barton's luck had run out.

Cyril Joe Barton is buried in Kingston upon Thames cemetery, Surrey.

John Dering Nettleton

The chief of Bomber Command, Sir Arthur Harris, was prepared to try anything in order to inflict further damage on German industry. Obviously, this meant putting the lives of bomber crews in danger and the acceptance of heavy losses. Sometimes Harris knew full well that many of his raiders would not return. In planning the operation that became known as 'the Augsburg Raid' in April 1942 he was prepared to lose every plane of the two squadrons involved if, in so doing, he found out that the type of raid would or would not work.

In Augsburg, southern Germany, was a diesel engine factory, an important target. It was nearly 600 miles from base, requiring British aircraft to fly over enemy territory for almost the entire distance and Harris proposed to send two squadrons of the then new Lancaster bombers – in daylight and at very low level, even street level. Twelve crews were chosen, divided equally between 44 and 97 Squadron, and for more than a week they practised low flying. On the day of the raid, 17 April, a larger force of Bostons, covered by many fighters, attacked targets in northern France as a diversion for the Lancaster incursion. Nevertheless, four Lancasters were shot down during the long flight and another three near the target.

In command of 44 (Rhodesia) Squadron was 24-year-old Squadron Leader John Nettleton. The dangers of the daylight flight are indicated in the citation to the VC awarded to Nettleton, gazetted on 28 April 1942.

Acting Squadron Leader John Dering Nettleton, No 44 (Rhodesia) Squadron RAF

In recognition of most conspicuous bravery. Squadron Leader Nettleton was the leader of one of two formations of six Lancaster heavy bombers detailed to deliver a low-level attack in daylight on the diesel engine factory at Augsburg in Southern Germany on April 17th, 1942. The enterprise was daring, the target of high military importance. To reach it and get back, some 1,000 miles had to be flown over hostile territory.

Soon after crossing into enemy territory his formation was engaged by 25 to 30 fighters. A running fight ensued. His rear guns went out of action. One by one the aircraft of his formation were shot down until in the end only his own and one other remained. The fighters were shaken off but the target was still far distant. There was formidable resistance to be faced.

With great spirit and almost defenceless, he held his two remaining aircraft on their perilous course and after a long and arduous flight, mostly at only 50 feet above the ground, he brought them to Augsburg. Here anti-aircraft fire of great intensity and accuracy was encountered. The two aircraft came low over the roof tops. Though fired at from point blank range, they stayed the course to drop their bombs true on the target. The second aircraft, hit by flak, burst into flames and crash-landed. The leading aircraft, though riddled with holes, flew safely back to base, the only one of the six to return.

Squadron Leader Nettleton, who has successfully undertaken many other hazardous operations, displayed unflinching determination as well as leadership and valour of the highest order.

The Augsburg raid was a suicide attack and this must have been known in advance by everybody involved with it. Bomber Command publicists made much of the damage done to the diesel engine factory but in fact it was trivial. The statement in Nettleton's citation that the bombs dropped 'true on the target' was not correct. It was amazing that Nettleton brought his aircraft back because every German fighter that could be scrambled for hundreds of miles around Augsburg was in the air that day. Some of the great Luftwaffe aces saw the raid as an opportunity to add to their score.

In Britain, the Ministry of Economic Warfare complained that Harris should have chosen a more important target in southern Germany, if he was so determined to mount such a risky raid. The Air Ministry and even the Prime Minister became embroiled in the controversy, but subsequent great raids soon covered over the losses over Augsburg. Of the 85 crew members who took part probably 50 were killed.

No 44 was called the Rhodesia Squadron of the RAF because some of its members, but by no means the majority, had come from Rhodesia and South Africa. Nettleton, of English parentage, had been born in Natal. He was killed during a bombing flight to Turin in February 1944. He has no known grave and his name appears on the Runnymede Memorial, Surrey.

Norman Cyril Jackson

Anybody who still thinks that decorations came easily to members of bomber crews during the Second World War might change their mind if told the story of Sergeant Norman Jackson, a flight engineer of 106 Squadron. His exploit may have been the most amazing of the war and certainly it was the most unusual. It happened on the night of 26/27 April 1944 when 215 Lancasters and 11 Mosquitoes raided Schweinfurt. The pathfinding aircraft inaccurately marked the target, strong headwinds upset the bombing schedule and enemy fighters incessantly attacked the bombers. Even the terse official language of Jackson's citation, gazetted on 26 October 1945, cannot mask the high drama of his exploit and half a century later it still has the power to horrify an 'ordinary' reader.

Sergeant (now Warrant Officer) Norman Cyril Jackson, 106 Squadron RAFVR

In recognition of most conspicuous bravery. This airman was the flight engineer in a Lancaster detailed to attack Schweinfurt on the night of 26th April, 1944. Bombs were dropped successfully and the aircraft was climbing out of the target area. Suddenly it was attacked by a fighter at about 20,000 feet. The captain took evading action at once but the enemy secured many hits. A fire started near a petrol tank on the upper surface of the starboard wing, between the fuselage and the inner engine.

Sergeant Jackson was thrown to the floor during the engagement. Wounds which he received from shell splinters in the right leg and shoulder were probably sustained at that time. Recovering himself, he remarked that he could deal with the fire on the wing and obtained his captain's permission to try to put out the flames.

Pushing a hand fire-extinguisher into the top of his life-saving jacket and slipping on his parachute pack, Sergeant Jackson jettisoned the escape hatch above the pilot's head. He then started to climb out of the cockpit and back along the top of the fuselage to the starboard wing. Before he could leave the fuselage his parachute pack opened and the whole canopy and rigging lines spilled into the cockpit.

Undeterred, Sergeant Jackson continued. The pilot, bomb aimer and navigator gathered the parachute together and held on to the rigging lines, paying them out as the airman crawled aft. Eventually he slipped and, falling from the fuselage to the starboard wing, grasped an air intake on the leading edge of the wing. He succeeded in clinging on but lost the extinguisher, which was blown away.

By this time, the fire had spread rapidly and Sergeant Jackson was involved. His face, hands and clothing were severely burnt. Unable to retain his hold, he was swept through the flames and over the trailing edge of the wing, dragging his parachute behind. When last seen it was only partly inflated and was burning in a number of places.

Realising that the fire could not be controlled, the captain gave the order to abandon aircraft. Four of the remaining members of the crew landed safely. The captain and rear gunner have not been accounted for.

Sergeant Jackson was unable to control his descent and landed heavily. He sustained a broken ankle, his right eye was closed through burns and his hands were useless. These injuries, together with the wounds received earlier, reduced him to a pitiable state. At daybreak he crawled to the nearest village, where he was taken prisoner. He bore the intense pain and discomfort of the journey to Dulag Luft with magnificent fortitude. After 10 months in hospital he made a good recovery, though his hands require further treatment and are only of limited use.

This airman's attempt to extinguish the fire and save the aircraft and crew from falling into enemy hands was an act of outstanding gallantry. To venture outside, when travelling at 200 miles an hour, at a great height and in intense cold, was an almost incredible feat. Had he succeeded in subduing the flames, there was little or no prospect of his regaining the cockpit. The spilling of his parachute and the risk of grave damage to its canopy reduced his chances of survival to a minimum. By his ready willingness to face these dangers he set an example of self-sacrifice which will ever be remembered.

The Lancaster's captain, Flying Officer F. Mifflin, and the rear gunner were killed in the crash, the others spent the rest of the war as prisoners.

Jackson, aged 25 at the time of his exploit, had completed 30 missions and the 'Schweinfurt job' was to have been his last. And so it was. Despite his dreadful condition, his first captors treated him badly, even forcing him to walk on his broken ankle. His natural fitness and determination brought him through this and later ordeals. His astonishing experience did not become known until after the war when the members of the Lancaster's crew were repatriated. Jackson had said nothing about his courage but the navigator, Flight Lieutenant F. Higgins, and the others unanimously recommended him for a high decoration. Norman Jackson died in March 1994.

Robert Anthony Maurice Palmer

Throughout the war Bomber Command made enemy rail marshalling yards one of its principal targets. The more locomotives, trucks and carriages that could be destroyed the more difficulty the Germans would have in moving troops and their equipment to the battlefront. Even by December 1944 the German forces were far from beaten and the 'Battle of the Bulge', in the Ardennes, was being fought. On 23 December of that month 27 Lancasters and three Mosquitoes were sent to attack the marshalling yards at Gremberg, Cologne. Almost from the beginning the raid was jinxed. Two Lancasters collided over the English coast, with all crew members killed. As the raiders approached Cologne their cloud cover dissipated and the decision was taken to order the pilots to break formation and bomb at will rather than to the pre-set plan. This order may not have reached Squadron Leader Robert Palmer, who was to mark the target. The difficulties that the 24-year-old Palmer faced are described in his VC citation, gazetted on 23 March 1945.

Acting Squadron Leader Robert Anthony Maurice Palmer DFC, No 109 Squadron RAFVR (Missing)

In recognition of most conspicuous bravery. This officer has completed 110 bombing missions. Most of them involved deep penetration of heavily defended territory; many were low-level 'marking' operations against vital targets; all were executed with tenacity, high courage and great accuracy.

He first went on operations in January, 1941. He took part in the first 1,000 bomber raid against Cologne in 1942. He was one of the first pilots to drop a 4,000 lb bomb on the Reich. It was known that he could be relied on to press home his attack whatever the opposition and to bomb with great accuracy. He was always selected, therefore, to take part in special operations against vital targets.

The finest example of his courage and determination was on 23rd December, 1944, when he led a formation of Lancasters to attack the marshalling yards at Cologne in daylight. He had the task of marking the target and his formation had been ordered to bomb as soon as the bombs had gone from his, the leading aircraft.

The leader's duties during the final bombing run were exacting and demanded coolness and resolution. To achieve accuracy he would have to fly at an exact height and airspeed on a steady course, regardless of opposition.

Some minutes before the target was reached, his aircraft came under heavy anti-aircraft fire, shells burst all around, two engines were set on fire and there were flames and smoke in the nose and in the bomb bay.

Enemy fighters now attacked in force. Squadron Leader Palmer disdained the possibility of taking avoiding action. He knew that if he diverged the least bit from his course, he would be unable to utilise the special equipment to the best advantage. He was determined to complete the run and provide an accurate and easily seen aiming-point for the other bombers. He ignored the double risk of fire and explosion in his aircraft and kept on. With its engines developing unequal power, an immense effort was needed to keep the damaged aircraft on a straight course. Nevertheless, he made a perfect approach and his bombs hit the target.

His aircraft was last seen spiralling to earth in flames. Such was the strength of the opposition that more than half of his formation failed to return.

Squadron Leader Palmer was an outstanding pilot. He displayed conspicuous bravery. His record of prolonged and heroic endeavour is beyond praise.

The citation states Palmer as missing but he did not survive the crash of his Lancaster. It also shows him as having only one DFC; in fact, he had two. The second one was a highly justified award for having completed 100 missions, a remarkable tally. Perhaps there should have been a regulation that prevented any member of an aircrew from taking part in operational flying after a certain number of sorties. After so many missions a pilot was living on luck – and Palmer flew on operations 110 times. His career was a classic illustration of the all-too-common attitude among senior commanders that if a pilot was really good he had to be used again and again. A sentence in the citation emphasizes this attitude: 'He was always selected, therefore, to take part in special operations against vital targets.' Special operations were always dangerous and vital targets were inevitably defended strongly. It would have been possible for Palmer – and other pilots who had flown so many missions – to get himself taken off operations, but a young man's pride was involved and it would have taken an older and more senior officer to *order* him to take over a training squadron. In fact, he had been instructing for some time but he had been importuning his superiors to be allowed to return to operations and they gave way.

The citation neglected to say that Palmer was a pilot of the élite Path

Finder Force, whose task it was to lead raiders to their targets. He would normally have been flying a Mosquito bomber but on his last mission he was flying a Lancaster. It was fitted with the OBOE radar system which automatically signalled to the pilot when he should release his bombs. Only one of Palmer's crew, the rear gunner, survived. Out of the 30 aircraft which took part in the raid at least six and possibly eight failed to return. Every other bomber was damaged.

Squadron Leader Palmer is buried in the Commonwealth War Graves Commission Cemetery at Rheinberg, Germany.

Geoffrey Leonard Cheshire

On the night of 24/25 April 1944, 244 Lancasters and 10 Mosquitoes raided Munich. Although one of Germany's major cities, Munich was not in itself important as an industrial or military target, but it possessed great psychological significance as the original centre of Nazism. To strike at the city and inflict grievous damage would give all Germans a signal that the Allies were intent on destroying Hitler's political roots.

The raid was important for another reason. Marking the targets for the attack was Wing Commander Geoffrey Cheshire DSO, DFC, aged 26 and one of Bomber Command's greatest pilots. Cheshire, a flier of an innovative frame of mind, had a theory that targets could be accurately marked from low level and with relative safety. His squadron, No 617, made some successful raids in March and April 1944 and it also had some failures. However, Cheshire persevered and for the raid on Munich he was allotted four Mosquitoes, including the one he himself flew. Because of limited fuel capacity the Mosquitoes had to fly by the most direct route, even over known German defences. Under the best of conditions they would have no longer than 20 minutes over the target before they had to head for home again by the shortest route.

Cheshire and the other three marker pilots reached the target area at an altitude of only 200 feet and dropped their special fire-plume markers as intended, in the centre of Munich. The damage done by the following Lancasters was immense. If German official archives are to be believed – and they are generally accurate – 2,467 buildings were destroyed or badly damaged, only 18 of which were of military importance. About 90 people were killed and 3,000 injured while many lost their homes. None of the details were known to the bombers at the time; aerial photographs merely showed much devastation. However, it is known that Hitler was furious at the RAF's success and that must count as a bonus.

It was the Munich raid, perhaps more than any of his other 100 missions, which brought Cheshire the Victoria Cross. However, the citation, gazetted on 8 September 1944, made it clear that the award covered Cheshire's four years of active service.

Wing Commander Geoffrey Leonard Cheshire DSO, DFC, No 617 Squadron RAFVR

In recognition of most conspicuous bravery. This officer began his operational career in June, 1940. Against strongly-defended targets he soon displayed the courage and determination of an exceptional leader. He was always ready to accept extra risks to ensure success. Defying the formidable Ruhr defences, he frequently released his bombs from below 2,000 feet. Over Cologne in November, 1940, a shell burst inside his aircraft, blowing out one side and starting a fire; undeterred, he went on to bomb his target. About this time, he carried out a number of convoy patrols in addition to his bombing missions.

At the end of his first tour of operational duty in January, 1941, he immediately volunteered for a second. Again, he pressed home his attacks with the utmost gallantry. Berlin, Bremen, Cologne, Duisburg, Essen and Kiel were among the heavily-defended targets which he attacked. When he was posted for instructional duties in January, 1942, he undertook four more operational missions.

He started a third operational tour in August, 1942, when he was given command of a squadron. He led the squadron with outstanding skill on a number of missions before being appointed in March, 1943, as a station commander.

In October 1943, he undertook a fourth operational tour, relinquishing the rank of group captain at his own request so that he could again take part in operations. He immediately set to work as the pioneer of a new method of marking enemy targets involving very low flying. In June, 1944, when marking a target in the harbour at Le Havre in broad daylight and without cloud cover, he dived well below the range of the light batteries before releasing his marker-bombs, and he came very near to being destroyed by the strong barrage which concentrated on him.

During his fourth tour which ended in July, 1944, Wing Commander Cheshire led his squadron personally on every occasion, always undertaking the most dangerous and difficult task of marking the target alone from a low level in the face of strong defences.

Wing Commander Cheshire's cold and calculated acceptance of risks is exemplified by his conduct in an attack on Munich in April, 1944. This was an experimental attack to test out the new method of target marking at low level against a heavily-defended target situated deep in Reich territory. Munich was selected, at Wing Commander Cheshire's request, because of the formidable nature of its light anti-aircraft and searchlight defences. He was obliged to follow, in bad weather, a direct route which took him over the defences of Augsburg and thereafter he was continuously under fire. As he reached the target, flares were being released by our high-flying aircraft. He was illuminated from above and below. All guns within range opened fire on him. Diving to 700 feet, he dropped his markers with great precision and began to climb away. So blinding were the searchlights that he almost lost control. He then flew over the city at 1,000 feet to assess the accuracy of his work and direct other aircraft. His own was badly hit by shell fragments but he continued to fly over the target area until he was satisfied that he had done all in his power to ensure success. Eventually, when he set course for base, the task of disengaging himself from the defences proved even more hazardous than the approach. For a full twelve minutes after leaving the target area he was under withering fire but he came safely through.

Wing Commander Cheshire has now completed a total of 100 missions. In four years of fighting against the bitterest opposition he has maintained a record of outstanding personal achievement, placing himself invariably in the forefront of the battle. What he did in the Munich operation was typical of the careful planning, brilliant execution and contempt for danger which has established for Wing Commander Cheshire a reputation second to none in Bomber Command.

After the actions covered by the VC citation, Cheshire continued to mark targets in the face of great danger and because of his accuracy the bombers caused enormous damage to German military targets. Pulled 'out of the line', in July he spent a period in India before being posted, as a group captain, to the United States. On 9 August he was in one of the B-29s over Nagasaki when the second atom bomb was dropped. On medical grounds he was discharged from the RAF in January 1946. Undoubtedly the best known RAF pilot of 1939–45, with the possible exceptions of Douglas Bader and Guy Gibson, Cheshire possessed a special kind of cold, deliberate courage. Close reading of his citation reveals this – such phrases as 'marking the target alone', 'pioneer of a new method', 'invariably in the forefront of battle'. He was as distinctive in his postwar life, establishing the Cheshire Foundation homes for the incurably sick. Lord Cheshire died in July 1992.

Ian Willoughby Bazalgette

Following the success of the Allied landing in Normandy in June 1944 the Germans slowly pulled back, fighting all the way. Hitler's scientists had developed the German V-bomb rockets, with which the dictator intended to inflict as much damage as possible on Britain, if not to defeat the Allies then to bring about better terms for a possible surrender, though this had not yet been mentioned. During July and August 1944 Bomber Command continued to bomb targets in the German heartland but it was also necessary to attack military sites in Belgium and France. Among them were flying-bomb sites at Bois de Cassan, Trossy-St-Maximin and Forêt de Nieppe. These sites were not easy targets. On Hitler's direct orders, they were massively defended by flak guns but more than this the launching ramps and the flying bombs themselves were buried under several metres of reinforced concrete. Pinpoint attacks were needed to drop bombs into the small apertures visible from the air, though the French Resistance was able to help with maps smuggled out to London.

Large forces of bombers were assembled for the bomb site attacks and on 4 August 1944, 169 Halifaxes, 112 Lancasters and 10 Mosquitoes were used to attack the sites in Bois de Cassan and Trossy-St-Maximin. One of the markers for the raid on Trossy-St-Maximin was 25-year-old Squadron Leader Ian Bazalgette DFC, who was posthumously awarded the VC, gazetted on 17 August 1945.

Acting Squadron Leader Ian Willoughby Bazalgette DFC, No 635 Squadron RAFVR (deceased)

In recognition of most conspicuous bravery. On 4th August, 1944, Squadron Leader Bazalgette was 'master bomber' of a Pathfinder squadron detailed to mark an important target at Trossy St Maximin for the main bomber force.

When nearing the target his Lancaster came under heavy anti-aircraft fire. Both starboard engines were put out of action and serious fires broke out in the fuselage and the starboard main-plane. The bomb aimer was badly wounded.

As the deputy 'master bomber' had already been shot down, the success of the attack depended on Squadron Leader Bazalgette and this he knew. Despite the appalling conditions in his burning aircraft, he pressed on gallantly to the target, marking and bombing it accurately. That the attack was successful was due to his magnificent effort.

After the bombs had been dropped the Lancaster dived, practically out of control. By expert airmanship and great exertion Squadron Leader Bazalgette regained control. But the port inner engine then failed and the whole of the starboard main-plane became a mass of flames.

Squadron Leader Bazalgette fought bravely to bring his aircraft and crew to safety. The mid-upper gunner was overcome by fumes. Squadron Leader Bazalgette then ordered those of his crew who were able to leave by parachute to do so. He remained at the controls and attempted the almost hopeless task of landing the crippled and blazing aircraft in a last effort to save the wounded bomb aimer and helpless air gunner. With superb skill, and taking great care to avoid a small French village nearby, he brought the aircraft down safely. Unfortunately, it then exploded and this gallant officer and his two comrades perished.

His heroic sacrifice marked the climax of a long career of operations against the enemy. He always chose the more dangerous and exacting roles. His courage and devotion to duty were beyond praise.

The citation erred in describing Bazalgette as the master bomber, the officer with the principal task of marking the target. This makes no difference to his award since all pathfinders ran equal risks. The citation should have noted that Bazalgette could have baled out with safety but he obviously felt that he should try to get his bomb aimer, Flight Lieutenant Ian Hibberd, and gunner, Flight Sergeant Leeder, both of them helpless, down to safety. It was this self-sacrifice which so impressed the 'authorities' when, after this area of France had been liberated, the four survivors returned to their base and reported their captain's heroism. These four were not captured because Resistance people hid them. They also concealed Ian Bazalgette's body until after the Germans had run from the advancing British. Bazalgette, Hibberd and Leeder are buried at Senantes, Pas de Calais, France. The bombing raid on the Trossy-St-Maximin V-1 site was successful and it was put out of action for the loss of two Lancasters.

George Thompson

The Dortmund–Ems Canal crops up many times in Bomber Command records from 1940 until 1945. Crossing the industrial Ruhr, it was a vital waterway for German communications and over and over again bombers attacked it. On 4/5 November 1944, for instance, the banks of both branches of the canal were breached so that the water drained away, leaving it unusable and with laden barges lying stranded on the bottom. Coke from the Ruhr mines could not reach several important steel-works until the Germans, using slave labour, could repair the frequent breaches. On 1 January 1945 Bomber Command went on the offensive again, the objective being to attack the canal near Ladbergen, at a point which the Germans had just repaired. In broad daylight, 102 Lancasters and two Mosquitoes flew the mission, with the crews knowing, as always, that the angry Germans would have strengthened their defences still further since the previous raid. One of the Lancaster captains for the New Year's Day raid was Flying Officer Harry Denton, whose radio operator was Flight Sergeant George Thompson, a 24-year-old Scot. Thompson's exploit on this flight was reminiscent of that by John Hannah four years earlier and it earned him, posthumously, a VC that was gazetted on 20 February 1945.

Flight Sergeant George Thompson, No 9 Squadron RAFVR (deceased)

In recognition of most conspicuous bravery. This airman was the wireless operator in a Lancaster aircraft which attacked the Dortmund–Ems Canal in daylight on the 1st January, 1945.

The bombs had just been released when a heavy shell hit the aircraft in front of the mid-upper turret. Fire broke out and dense smoke filled the fuselage. The nose of the aircraft was then hit and an inrush of air, clearing the smoke, revealed a scene of utter devastation. Most of the Perspex screen of the nose compartment had been shot away, gaping holes had been torn in the canopy above the pilot's head, the inter-communication wiring was severed, and there was a large hole in the floor of the aircraft. Bedding and other equipment were badly damaged or alight; one engine was on fire.

Flight Sergeant Thompson saw that the gunner was unconscious in the blazing mid-upper turret. Without hesitation he went down the fuselage into the fire and the exploding ammunition. He pulled the gunner from his turret and, edging his way round the hole in the floor, carried him away from the flames. With his bare hands, he extinguished the gunner's burning clothing. He himself sustained serious burns on his face, hands and legs.

Flight Sergeant Thompson then noticed that the rear gun turret was also on fire. Despite his own severe injuries he moved painfully to the rear of the fuselage where he found the rear gunner with his clothing alight, overcome by flames and fumes. A second time Flight Sergeant Thompson braved the flames. With great difficulty he extricated the helpless gunner and carried him clear. Again, he used his bare hands, already burnt, to beat out flames on a comrade's clothing.

Flight Sergeant Thompson, by now almost exhausted, felt that his duty was yet not done. He must report the fate of the crew to the captain. He made the perilous journey back through the burning fuselage, clinging to the sides with his burnt hands to get across the hole in the floor. The flow of cold air caused him intense pain and frost-bite developed. So pitiful was his condition that his captain failed to recognise him. Still, his only concern was for the two gunners he had left in the rear of the aircraft. He was given such attention as was possible until a crash-landing was made some forty minutes later. When the aircraft was hit, Flight Sergeant Thompson might have devoted his efforts to quelling the fire and so have contributed to his own safety. He preferred to go through the fire to succour his comrades. He knew that he would then be in no position to hear or heed any order which might be given to abandon aircraft. He hazarded his own life in order to save the lives of others. Young in years and experience, his actions were those of a veteran.

Three weeks later Flight Sergeant Thompson died of his injuries. One of the gunners unfortunately also died, but the other owes his life to the superb gallantry of Flight Sergeant Thompson, whose signal courage and self-sacrifice will ever be an inspiration to the Service.

Flying Officer Denton's Lancaster was so badly damaged in the air that after the crash-landing it broke apart. Despite his own intense suffering and amid the destruction all around him, Thompson murmured jokingly to Denton, 'Jolly good landing, skipper.'*

For a time it seemed that Thompson might recover but, as with so many other badly burned aircrew, he contracted pneumonia which proved fatal. A comrade, one of the gunners, also died. It is interesting that the language of the citation refers to Thompson's 'signal' courage, quoting the key word of the original VC warrant, for 'some signal act of valour'. It is rarely mentioned in VC citations. Thompson's valour was undoubtedly 'signal' in that it stood out like a beacon of self-sacrifice. The citation also comments: 'Young in years and experience, his actions were those of a veteran.' Nearly all the RAF recipients of the VC were young and several were younger than Thompson. He was certainly not a veteran of combat flying, but a flier became a veteran very quickly. Flight Sergeant George Thompson is buried in Évere-les-Brizelles cemetery, Brussels.

---

*   Reported by Chaz Bowyer in *For Valour – The Air VCs* (Kimber, London, 1978).

CHAPTER TWELVE

Coastal and Transport Command VCs

Coastal Command VCs*

John Alexander Cruickshank

By general consent among aircrews flying anti-submarine patrols was one of the most boring jobs of the war. For long hours in a Catalina flying boat, or in a Hudson or Liberator, the crew flew over vast stretches of ocean, occasionally sighting British convoys and warships but rarely, ever so rarely, a U-boat. This was only natural for U-boat captains were not inclined to surface during daylight hours and their aerial hunters did not patrol at night because the chance of actually seeing a surfaced sub in the dark was negligible. Nevertheless, the anti-sub patrols were useful – U-boat captains knew that Catalinas and other aircraft were in the air and this kept them submerged.

The aircraft flew over all the ocean tracks known to be used by U-boats and that meant long missions over the North Sea, the Atlantic and the Western Approaches.

Flight Lieutenant John Cruickshank, RAFVR, first flew operationally with Coastal Command, in 210 Squadron, in March 1943. It was not until 17 July 1944 and his 48th mission that he saw an enemy submarine. What then happened is described in his VC citation, gazetted on 1 September 1944.

Flying Officer John Alexander Cruickshank, No 210 Squadron RAFVR

In recognition of most conspicuous bravery. This officer was the captain and pilot of a Catalina flying boat which was recently engaged on an anti-submarine patrol over northern waters. When a U-boat was sighted on the surface, Flying Officer Cruickshank at once turned to the attack. In the face of fierce anti-aircraft fire he manoeuvred into position and ran in to release his depth charges. Unfortunately they failed to drop.

---

* See also Flying Officer Trigg, pp. 12–13.

Flying Officer Cruickshank knew that the failure of this attack had deprived him of the advantage of surprise and that his aircraft offered a good target to the enemy's determined and now heartened gunners.

Without hesitation, he climbed and turned to come in again. The Catalina was met by intense and accurate fire and was repeatedly hit. The navigator/bomb aimer was killed. The second pilot and two other members of the crew were injured. Flying Officer Cruickshank was struck in seventy-two places, receiving two serious wounds in the lungs and ten penetrating wounds in the lower limbs. His aircraft was badly damaged and filled with the fumes of exploding shells. But he did not falter. He pressed home his attack, and released the depth charges himself, straddling the submarine perfectly. The U-boat was sunk.

He then collapsed and the second pilot took over the controls. He recovered shortly afterwards and, though bleeding profusely, insisted on resuming command and retaining it until he was satisfied that the damaged aircraft was under control, that a course had been set for base and that all the necessary signals had been sent. Only then would he consent to receive medical aid and have his wounds attended to. He refused morphia in case it might prevent him from carrying on.

During the next five and a half hours of the return flight he several times lapsed into unconsciousness owing to loss of blood. When he came to, his first thought on each occasion was for the safety of his aircraft and crew. The damaged aircraft eventually reached base but it was clear that an immediate landing would be a hazardous task for the wounded and less experienced second pilot. Although able to breathe only with the greatest difficulty, Flying Officer Cruickshank insisted on being carried forward and propped up in the second pilot's seat. For a full hour, in spite of his agony and ever-increasing weakness, he gave orders as necessary, refusing to allow the aircraft to be brought down until the conditions of light and sea made this possible without undue risk.

With his assistance the aircraft was safely landed on the water. He then directed the taxiing and beaching of the aircraft so that it could easily be salvaged. When the medical officer went on board, Flying Officer Cruickshank collapsed and he had to be given a blood transfusion before he could be removed to hospital.

By pressing home the second attack in his gravely wounded condition and continuing his exertions on the return journey with his strength failing all the time, he seriously prejudiced his chance of survival even if the aircraft safely reached its base. Throughout, he set an example of determination, fortitude and devotion to duty in keeping with the highest traditions of the Service.

Even by the demanding standards of exploits worthy of VC consideration, John Cruickshank's skill, courage, fortitude and leadership were remarkable. A U-boat was difficult to hit, partly because it was a small target and also because its gunners were well trained and brave. The U-347's gunners put up such spirited resistance that they badly damaged the Catalina and killed one of its crew and wounded three others. Only masterly flying by Cruickshank and his second pilot, Flight Sergeant Garnett, brought the aircraft down safely. Garnett was awarded the DFM. Few men of any of the British fighting Services received as many wounds, 72 in all, some of them serious. That Cruickshank would receive a VC was never in doubt. Just as Flight Lieutenant Lloyd Trigg VC had done in August the previous year, Cruickshank had sunk a U-boat and that was a spectacular feat. Despite his serious wounds and much loss of blood, he remained in active command and finally his determination brought the Catalina home to Sullom Voe, Shetlands. Trigg's death at the hands of a sub's gunners had shown how difficult it was to demolish a surfaced U-boat. Cruickshank did not again fly operationally, partly because he was slow to recover from the more serious of his wounds. His superiors in Coastal Command thought that he had done enough.

Transport Command VC

David Samuel Anthony Lord

The RAF's Transport Command and its aircrews have never received the publicity they deserve. Thousands of men served in this Command and many lost their lives, often while supporting the Army. The aerial workhorse was the Douglas Dakota, a rugged twin-engine plane whose top speed was 230 mph with a maximum range of 1,600 miles. Fitted with bucket seats and a large loading door, the Dakota could carry 27 people – though in emergencies it sometimes carried many more – or five tons of cargo. When used as a flying ambulance it could accommodate 18 to 24 litter patients.

Unarmed and not built for manoeuvring, Dakotas were easy prey for enemy fighters and good targets for flak gunners, hence dedicated and courageous pilots were needed to fly them. One such pilot was Flight Lieutenant David ('Lumme') Lord who, aged 33 in 1944, was older than most pilots in Fighter Command or Bomber Command.

He had qualified as a pilot before the war and had then been sent to the India–Burma theatre, where he amassed several hundred flying hours before seeing active service over Iraq. He dropped supplies, evacuated the wounded and ferried freight – the daily grind of a Transport Command pilot. By March 1942 he was back in Burma, flying supplies for Brigadier Wingate's Chindits behind Japanese lines. Soon after this Lord was awarded the DFC.

After four years of flying over inhospitable and dangerous terrain, Lord was posted back to Britain in January 1944 to join 271 Squadron. The squadron was supporting the 1st and 6th Airborne Divisions so Lord and his crew practised the dropping of paratroops, jeeps and guns. He took part in the Normandy invasion operations by dropping para-medical sections near the fighting that was raging for the city of Caen. On other occasions he dropped shells for the artillery and landmines for use by combat engineers. Lord was one of many Dakota pilots admired by the troops because, apart from combat supplies, they brought in mail from home. As the Army moved forward so did Transport Command.

In August a great operation was in its planning and training stage – Operation Market Garden, the airborne landing at Arnhem. David Lord, with others, practised the difficult task of towing the giant Horsa gliders which would carry soldiers and their gear into battle. In addition, the Dakotas would do their usual job of dropping supplies. On 18 September Lord towed his particular Horsa to Arnhem and released it as planned to make its own descent into the developing maelstrom.

His mission on 19 September was to drop urgently needed supplies to the Airborne men, who were under attack from all sides. The citation for the VC which he won that day, though it was not gazetted until 13 November 1945, describes David Lord's courage over Arnhem.

Flight Lieutenant David Samuel Anthony Lord DFC, No 271 Squadron RAF (deceased)

In recognition of most conspicuous bravery. Flight Lieutenant Lord was pilot and captain of a Dakota aircraft detailed to drop supplies at Arnhem on the afternoon of the 19th September 1944. Our airborne troops had been surrounded and were being pressed into a small area defended by a large number of anti-aircraft guns. Air crews were warned that intense opposition would be met over the dropping zone. To ensure accuracy they were ordered to fly at 900 feet when dropping their containers.

While flying at 1,500 feet near Arnhem the starboard wing of Flight Lieutenant Lord's aircraft was twice hit by anti-aircraft fire. The starboard engine was set on fire. He would have been justified in leaving the main stream of supply aircraft and continuing at the same height or even abandoning his aircraft. But on learning that his crew were uninjured and that the dropping zone would be reached in three minutes he said he would complete his mission, as the troops were in dire need of supplies.

By now the starboard engine was burning furiously. Flight Lieutenant Lord came down to 900 feet, where he was singled out for the concentrated fire of all the anti-aircraft guns. On reaching the dropping zone he kept the aircraft on a straight and level course while supplies were dropped. At the end of the run, he was told that two containers remained.

Although he must have known that the collapse of the starboard wing could not be long delayed, Flight Lieutenant Lord circled, rejoined the stream of aircraft and made a second run to drop the remaining supplies. These manoeuvres took eight minutes in all, the aircraft being continuously under heavy anti-aircraft fire.

His task completed, Flight Lieutenant Lord ordered his crew to abandon the Dakota, making no attempt himself to leave the aircraft, which was down to 500 feet. A few seconds later, the starboard wing collapsed and the aircraft fell in flames. There was only one survivor, who was flung out while assisting other members of the crew to put on their parachutes.

By continuing his mission in a damaged and burning aircraft, descending to drop the supplies accurately, returning to the dropping zone a second time and finally, remaining at the controls to give his crew a chance of escape, Flight Lieutenant Lord displayed supreme valour and self-sacrifice.

The only survivor of the crash was Pilot Officer Harry King, the navigator. Lord, the two other members of his crew and four Army despatchers whose job had been to actually drop the supplies, all died. Many soldiers had seen the Dakota in her death throes and they saw Pilot Officer King survive his low-level parachute drop. King was the only man who could describe the events in the air – but the Germans took him prisoner after their victory at Arnhem. Following the end of the war King made his delayed report of David Lord's last flight and the CO of 271 Squadron recommended that he be awarded the VC. The recommendation went through the usual channels but there never was any doubt that the decoration would be awarded. It only remains to say that Lord's nickname, 'Lumme', came from the expression he invariably used when other men might swear.

He is buried in the Commonwealth War Graves Commission Cemetery at Arnhem; close by lie the other two members of his Dakota crew. The Chief of the Air Staff, Marshal of the RAF Lord Portal, wrote to his parents:

I have read of many great deeds for which the Victoria Cross has been awarded but I do not remember one which surpassed in gallantry the action of your son. The whole of the Royal Air Force will share my admiration and will be deeply sensible of the honour your son has brought to the Service. His gallantry and sacrifice will have an illustrious place in the annals of the Royal Air Force.

Indeed, they have a unique place, for David Lord remains the only Transport Command member to be awarded the VC.

60. CSM Peter Wright, 3rd Battalion
Coldstream Guards, 25 September 1943
(pp. 102–4)

61. Major William Sidney, 5th Battalion
Grenadier Guards, 7–8 February 1944
(pp. 104–6)

62. Private George Mitchell, London
Scottish, 23–4 January 1944 (pp. 106–8)

63. Lieutenant Richard Wakeford, 2/4th
Battalion Hampshire Regiment, 13 May
1944 (pp. 108–10)

64. Fusilier Francis Jefferson, 2nd Battalion Lancashire Fusiliers, 16 May 1944 (pp. 110-11)

65. Lieutenant Gerard Norton, 1/4th Battalion Hampshire Regiment, 31 August 1944 (pp. 111–13)

66. An artist's depiction of the action in which Jefferson won his VC

67. Private Richard Burton, 1st Battalion Duke of Wellington's (West Riding) Regiment, 8 October 1944 (pp. 113–14)

68. Captain John Brunt, Sherwood Foresters attached 6th Battalion Lincolnshire Regiment, 9 December 1944 (pp. 114–16)

69. Major Anders Lassen, Special Boat Service, 8 April 1945 (pp. 116–21)

70. The first grave (left) of Major Lassen at Comacchio, Italy

71. Lieutenant-Colonel Arthur Cumming,
2/12th Frontier Force Regiment, Indian Army,
3 January 1942 (pp. 122–3)

72. Lieutenant Alec Horwood, Queen's
Royal Regiment (West Surrey),
18–20 January 1944 (pp. 125–7)

73. Major Charles Hoey, Lincolnshire
Regiment, 16 February 1944
(pp. 127–9)

74. Lieutenant George Cairns, Scottish
Light Infantry attached South Staffordshire
Regiment, 12–13 March 1944 (pp. 129–31)

75. Lance Cpl John Harman, Queen's Own Royal West Kent Regiment, 8–9 April 1944 (p. 131–2)

76. Captain John Randle, 2nd Battalion Norfolk Regiment, 4–6 May 1944 (pp. 132–4)

77. Sergeant Hanson Turner, 1st Battalion West Yorkshire Regiment (Prince of Wales's Own), 6–7 June 1944 (pp. 134–5)

78. Captain Michael Allmand, Indian Armoured Corps attached 6th Gurkha Rifles, 11 June 1944 (pp. 136–7)

79. Major Frank Blaker, Highland Light Infantry attached 9th Gurkha Rifles, 9 July 1944 (pp. 137–8)

80. Lieutenant George Knowland, Royal Norfolk Regiment attached No 1 Commando, 31 January 1945 (pp. 138–40)

81. Lieutenant William Weston, Green Howards and 1st Battalion Yorkshire Regiment, 3 March 1945 (pp. 140–2)

82. Lieutenant Claud Raymond, Royal Engineers, 21 March 1945 (pp. 142–4)

83. CSM Stanley Hollis, 6th Battalion Green Howards, 6 June 1944 (pp. 146–7)

84. Corporal Sidney Bates, Royal Norfolk Regiment, 6 August 1944 (pp. 148–9)

85. Captain David Jamieson, Royal Norfolk Regiment, 7–8 August 1944 (pp. 149–51)

86. Lieutenant Tasker Watkins, 1/5th Battalion the Welch Regiment, 1 6 August 1944 (pp. 151–2)

87. Lieutenant John Grayburn, Parachute Regiment, 17–20 September 1944 (pp. 152–5)

88. Captain Lionel Queripel, Royal Sussex Regiment attached 10th Parachute Battalion, 19 September 1944 (pp. 155–6)

89. Major Robert Cain, Royal Northumberland Fusiliers attached South Staffordshire Regiment, 19–25 September 1944 (pp. 156–8)

90. Lance-Sergeant John Baskeyfield, South Staffordshire Regiment, 1st Airborne Division, 20 September 1944 (pp. 158–60)

91. Corporal John Harper, York and Lancaster Regiment, 29 September 1944 (pp. 160–2)

92. FM Montgomery pins the ribbon of the VC on Sergeant George Eardley, King's Shropshire Light Infantry. His exploit took place on 16 October 1944 (pp. 162–3)

93. Fusilier Dennis Donnini, Royal Scots Fusiliers, 18 January 1945 (pp. 163–4)

94. L/Corporal Henry Harden, Royal Army Medical Corps attached 45 Royal Marine Commando, 23 January 1945 (pp. 164–6)

95. Private James Stokes, King's Shropshire Light Infantry, 1 March 1945 (pp. 166–8)

96. Corporal Edward Chapman, Monmouthshire Regiment, 2 April 1945 (pp. 168–9)

97. Captain Ian Liddell, 5th Battalion Coldstream Guards, 3 April 1945 (pp. 169–71)

98. Guardsman Edward Charlton, Irish Guards, 21 April 1945 (pp. 171–4)

99. Flt Lieutenant Eric Nicolson, RAF, 16 August 1940 (pp. 181–3)

100. Flg Officer Donald Garland, RAF, 12 May 1940 (pp. 192–4) (via Chaz Bowyer)

101. Sergeant Thomas Gray, RAF, 12 May 1940 (pp. 192–4) (via Chaz Bowyer)

102. Flt Lieutenant Roderick Learoyd, RAF, 12 August 1940 (p. 194)

103. Sergeant John Hannah, RAF, 15 September 1940 (pp. 194–6)

104. Wg Commander Hughie Edwards, RAF, 4 July 1941 (pp. 196–7) (via Jim Taylor/Stuart Scott)

105. An example of the flak (anti-aircraft fire) through which bombers had to fly to reach enemy targets.

106. Flg Officer Kenneth Campbell, RAF,
6 April 1941 (pp. 198–9)

107. Sqn Leader Arthur Scarf, RAF,
9 December 1941 (pp. 200–1)

108. Flg Officer Leslie Manser, RAFVR,
30 May 1942 (pp. 201–3)

109. Wg Commander Hugh Malcolm,
RAF, November–December 1942
(pp. 203–4)

110. Wg Commander Guy Gibson, RAF, 16–17 May 1943 (pp. 205–6)

111. Flt Sergeant Arthur Aaron, RAFVR, 12 August 1943 (pp. 206–8)

112. Flt Lieutenant William Reid, RAFVR, 3 November 1943 (pp. 208–10)

113. Plt Officer Cyril Barton, RAFVR, 30 March 1944 (pp. 210–12)

114. Sqn Leader John Nettleton, RAF,
17 April 1942 (pp. 212–14)

115. Sergeant Norman Jackson, RAFVR,
26 April 1944 (pp. 214–16)

116. Sqn Leader Robert Palmer, RAFVR,
23 December 1944 (pp. 216–18)

117. Wg Commander Leonard Cheshire,
RAFVR, 1940–4 (pp. 218–20)

118. Sqn Leader Ian Bazalgette, RAFVR, 4 August 1944 (pp. 220–2)

119. Flt Sergeant George Thompson, RAFVR, 1 January 1945 (pp. 222–4)

120. Flg Officer John Cruickshank, RAFVR, 17–18 July 1944 (pp. 225–7)

121. Flt Lieutenant David Lord, RAF, 19 September 1944 (pp. 227–9)

Photographs of Heroes and a Batman's Posthumous Testimonial

As each Victoria Cross was gazetted during the war there was an instant need for a photograph of him. In the case of posthumous awards this was often a difficult task. The families of some deceased VC winners could not find a photograph and in other cases it was only possible to obtain one by enlarging a single head from a family group or a party of men. In yet other cases while photographs were available they showed the fallen hero in civilian dress. Naturally, the Service concerned would have preferred to see their man in uniform.

The Royal Navy, the Army regiments and the Royal Air Force made every effort to take photographs of each VC exploit survivor because of the very real possibility that he might be killed in a subsequent action, and indeed several men were lost between the time of their exploit and the gazetting of their VC award.

In many cases portraits of VC winners were commissioned. Among them were those of Lieutenant Commander David Wanklyn, Flight Lieutenant Roderick Learoyd, Sergeant Thomas Gray RAF, Flying Officer Donald Garland, Major John Anderson, CSM Stanley Hollis and Lance-Corporal John Kenneally. These paintings add to what a study of the faces of these mostly young men reveals.

While many look like the professionals they were, others impress more by their gentle unmilitary appearance; they certainly do not look like warriors. Lieutenant Claud Raymond, Royal Engineers, looks more like a young academic posing as a soldier. Yet this slight and pale 21-year-old showed the most remarkable courage and fortitude. Flight Sergeant Aaron, who already held the DFM before the event in which he lost his life, was another who lacked the conventional stamp of the warrior, but his fortitude after suffering grievous wounds was amazing. Nineteen-year-old Fusilier Donnini's features show an impish, devil-may-care youth, which apparently he was, but he was capable of charging heavily armed enemy infantry and forcing them out of their positions. Pilot Officer Cyril Joe Barton, aged 22, who would not permit his crew to swear and who was naturally peaceable, pressed on with a difficult bombing attack and on the way home, in a crippled aircraft, crashed it while trying to avoid the houses of a village.

Photographs of the older career naval officers show professionals dedicated to their task. There is no mistaking the authority of Commander John Linton, aged 38 and holder of the DSO and DFC, or of Lieutenant-Commander Stephen Beattie, aged 34, or of Captain Bernard Warburton-Lee, who was 44. Warburton-Lee's was the first VC to be awarded in the Second World War.

Sergeant Majors always look their rank. There is no mistaking the sergeant major quality in photographs of CSM George Gristock, CSM Stanley Hollis and CSM Peter Wright.

The same practised authority is evident in the bearing of the older Army officers, such as Brigadier John Campbell, DSO and Bar and MC, earned before his VC. Commanding 7th Armoured Division, he was 48 years of age. Lieutenant-Colonel Lorne MacLaine Campbell VC, DSO and Bar, TD, commanded a battalion of Highlanders and 'his personality dominated the battlefield'. He was 38 at the time of his exploit. Lieutenant-Colonel Victor Buller Turner VC, CVO, mild-mannered by nature but strong and purposeful as a battalion commander of the Rifle Brigade, was 42 at the time of his exploit. It is interesting that he was the brother of another VC winner, Second-Lieutenant Alexander Turner, killed in France in 1915.

Several photographs survive of Major Anders Lassen VC, MC and two Bars. It was known that he naturally dominated any group of warriors and photographs show this to be so. A modest man – he rarely wore the ribbon of his MC – he had strong features and it is easy to see that he would make a successful raider.

It is among RAF crews that youth is generally evident. The RAF had no 'old' VC winners. Squadron Leader Arthur Scarf, at 28, was one of the oldest and he was a pre-war, highly professional 'RAF type'. Wing Commander Guy Gibson was only 22 at the time of his exploit and before his death at the age of 24 held the VC, DSO and Bar, DFC and Bar. In uniform Gibson looked the flying hero; in civvies he had the appearance of a bright, intelligent younger banker or accountant. He is one of the most highly and frequently decorated warriors in history and he should not have been allowed to go on flying operationally as late as September 1944, though he himself insisted on doing so.

How did their comrades regard VC winners? Undoubtedly, some fighting men disliked officers and NCOs who had a taste for combat. A score of soldiers, a few seamen and one former member of an aircrew in essence made this comment to me about their immediate commanders who had been decorated: 'My attitude was that if the silly bugger wanted to risk his life that was his business. I was ready to do my duty but not to the point of almost certain suicide.'

But large numbers of soldiers did readily follow their leaders and, despite casualties, succeeded in their attack. Seamen and airmen had no option about 'following'. They necessarily went where their commander steered or piloted them. All knew the risks and the vast majority accepted them. When a commander was awarded a VC – or any other decoration – they were pleased for him and, sometimes, even more pleased for their ship or squadron.

Since the function of every historian should be to tell the truth, I must admit that numerous officers and other ranks were jealous of comrades who were decorated while others, though not jealous, spent the rest of the war smarting under a sense of injustice that they too had not been decorated. Undoubtedly, other men deserved the VC and indeed were recommended for it only to be granted a lesser decoration during the evaluation process. The saddest cases of all were those men who were heroic and self-sacrificing but had no chance of being awarded the VC because of the lack of witnesses to their bravery.

In the Army, private soldiers who were awarded the VC were perhaps more famous than officers and NCOs with the decoration because, in many cases, they had assumed command on the death or disablement of their officers, sergeants and corporals. This in itself was commendable and when they then performed heroically it was doubly noteworthy. Many citations say of a particular serviceman, 'His leadership' (or example or action) 'was beyond all praise'. Not quite beyond *all* praise; the award of the VC is the ultimate praise.

Some NCOs and private soldiers had immense respect for officers who demonstrated not only high bravery but consideration for their men and I have no doubt that this respect existed in the Royal Navy and Royal Air Force. Some 'ordinary' soldiers wrote letters of condolence to the parents of a fallen officer or to his widow. One of the most eloquent, sincere, articulate and informative was sent by Private W. Irving MM to Moira Anderson, the widow of Major John (Jack) Anderson VC, DSO, only six days after Anderson was killed at Termoli, Italy. Officer and private soldier were both aged 25. With Mrs Anderson's permission (on remarriage she became Mrs Few) I publish the unedited letter here in full:

11.10.43

Dear Mrs. Anderson,
I take upon myself the privilege of writing to you. First of all I had better explain who I am and why I'm writing.

I was with your late husband from the time of my arrival out here in November. Was his batman, went through all the battles with him. Was with him when he won the DSO and later the VC on 'Longstop Hill'. To me he was the finest lad I've ever met. Although I'm only a private and he a major he treated me as a friend and not a batman we had faith in one another while in action.

Such a friendship grew up between us. He was a great fellow among the lads, we all thought the world of him. No one ever spoke against his fairness and consideration for others was well known in all the ranks. Everyone was sorry to hear of his passing. No one will ever take his place in the eyes of the men he led into battle. To me he was the finest, I'll never do batman to another.

On the day of the dreadful affair I was with him all the while. Jerry trapped us, but after he met his end I managed to get back to my own lines. The following day six of us went for his body and gave him a decent burial. The boys of the Pioneer Plt. made a lovely cross for his grave also a small one for me to put on.

His personal kit was handed in and in due course will reach you. Major Taylor one of his officer friends has been looking after things. No doubt you will have received news from him before this reaches you.

Being his batman and having gone through all the battles by his side I may say that no one in the unit knew your husband like I did. He was a hero and soldier to the end. One cannot describe by correspondence all his actions of fearlessness and bravery but after I return to England I will visit you (if you wish so) and will tell you all he done, and only then will you realise what a fine fellow he was.

If there is anything I can give you information, able [*sic*] or help I'll be glad to. Good luck and smile, although he has gone his name will live on the lips of all who knew him and his spirit will live throughout the battalion. We were both the same age and of the same spirit. He was with me when I won the Military Medal.

Yours sincerely,
W. Irving

Private Irving's assertion that he 'would never do batman' to another officer was evidence enough that he regarded Jack Anderson as incomparable.

Sergeant T. O'Neil, platoon sergeant to Second-Lieutenant Richard Annand, who won the VC in Belgium in May 1940, was inspired to write to *The Journal and North Mail*, County Durham newspaper, about his officer's courage and leadership. I have abbreviated Sergeant O'Neil's letter which in effect adds to Annand's VC citation.

On the night of 15 May Mr Annand came to me at platoon headquarters and asked for a box of grenades as he could hear Jerry trying to repair the bridge. Off he went and he sure must have given them a lovely time because it wasn't a great while before he was back for more. Just like giving an elephant strawberries.

The previous night while the heavy stuff of both sides were sending over their mutual regards he realised that he had not received word from our right forward section which held a pillbox about 250 yards to our right front, so he went out to see how they were fixed. He had gone about two hours and we had come to the conclusion that they had got him when something which I found hard to recognise came crawling in. It was just Jake – that is the name by which we knew him. He looked as though he had been having an argument with a wild cat. His clothes were torn to shreds and he was cut and bruised all over. How he got there and back only he knows because he had the fire of our own troops to contend with as well as Jerry's. I don't suppose he knows the meaning of fear. He never asked a man to do anything he could do himself. He wouldn't talk much about it. He wasn't that kind. It was just another job of work for him.

Another time a platoon of RWF [Royal Welch Fusiliers] came to reinforce us and had been there only half an hour when one of our own mortar bombs dropped right among them. Jake came dashing up, asked me what had happened and then off he went galloping up the hillside to stop the mortar platoon. He didn't even stop to take his steel helmet and he was under fire all the way.

For Sergeant O'Neil, as for Private Irving, his officer was without equal. The VC makes a man incomparable. DSOs, MCs, DFCs, DSCs and all the other awards are commonplace compared with the VC. The VC was to be 'a decoration highly prized and eagerly sought after by the officers and men of our naval and military forces', as well as 'a decoration dependent neither on rank nor long service nor wounds nor any other circumstance or condition whatsoever, save the merit of conspicuous bravery'. Moreover it was to place 'all persons on a perfectly equal footing in relation to eligibility for the decoration'.

The awards of the VC for exploits during the Second World War prove that Queen Victoria achieved her wish.

VC Winners from Australia, Canada, India, New Zealand, South Africa and Fiji

P indicates posthumous award; KIA indicates killed in action at a later date; M indicates murdered by the Japanese after capture.

Australia

	Lieutenant Arthur Cutler, 2/5th Field Artillery, AIF, Syria, June/July 1941
P	Lieutenant Albert Chowne MM, 2/2nd Battalion, AIF, Papua–New Guinea, 25 March 1942
	Lieutenant-Colonel Charles Anderson, 2/19th Battalion, AIF, Malaya, 18/22 January 1942
KIA	Lieutenant Thomas Derrick DCM, 2/48th Battalion, AIF, Papua–New Guinea, 23 November 1943
P	Corporal John Edmondson, 2/17th Battalion, AIF, Libya, 13/14 April 1941
P	Private Bruce Kingsbury, 2/14th Battalion, AIF, Papua–New Guinea, 29 August 1942
P	Corporal John French, 2/9th Battalion, AIF, Papua–New Guinea, 4 September 1942
P	Private Percival Gratwick, 2/48th Battalion, AIF, North Africa, 25/26 October 1942
P	Sergeant William Kibby, 2/48th Battalion, AIF, North Africa, 30/31 October 1942
M	Flight Lieutenant William Newton, RAAF, New Guinea, 16 March 1943
P	Private Arthur Gurney, 2/48th Battalion, AIF, Egypt, 22 July 1942

Private Richard Kelliher, 2/25th Battalion,
  Papua–New Guinea, 13 September 1943

Private James Gordon, 2/31st Battalion, AIF,
  Syria, 10 July 1941

P Corporal John Mackey, 2/3rd Pioneer Battalion, AIF,
  North Borneo, 12 May 1945

P Flight Sergeant Rawdon Middleton, RAAF,
  over the English coast, 29 November 1942

Private Edward Kenna, 2/4th Battalion, AIF,
  Papua–New Guinea, 13 May 1945

Sergeant Roy Rattey, 25th Battalion,
  Solomon Islands, 22 March 1945

Private Leslie Starcevich, 2/43rd Battalion, AIF,
  North Borneo, 28 June 1945

Private Frank Partridge, 8th Battalion, AMF,
  Solomon Islands, 24 July 1945

Canada

P CSM John Osborn, Winnipeg Grenadiers,
  Hong Kong, 19 December 1941

P Sergeant Aubrey Cosens, Queen's Own Rifles of Canada,
  Holland, 16 February 1945

Major David Currie, 29th Canadian Armoured Reconnaissance
  Regiment, Normandy, 18/20 August 1944

Lieutenant-Colonel Charles Merritt, South Saskatchewan Regiment,
  Dieppe, August 1942

P Warrant Officer II Andrew Mynarski, RCAF,
  France, 12/13 June 1944

Major Frederick Tilston, Essex Scottish Regiment of Canada,
  Germany, 1 March 1945

Private Ernest Alvia Smith, Seaforth Highlanders of Canada,
  Italy, 21/22 October 1944

Major John Mahoney, Westminster Motor Regiment,
  Italy, 22 May 1944

Captain Paul Triquet, Royal 22nd Regiment of Canada,
  Italy, 14 December 1943

P Flight Lieutenant David Hornell, RCAF,
  North Atlantic, 25 June 1944

Corporal Frederick Topham, 1st Canadian Parachute Regiment,
  Germany, 24 March 1945

P Lieutenant Robert Gray, RCNVR (1841 Squadron Fleet Air Arm),
  Japan, 9 August 1945

India

P   Jemadar Abdul Hafiz, 9th Jat Infantry,
       India, 6 April 1944

P   Rifleman Sher Bahadur Thapa, 9th Gurkha Rifles,
       Italy, 18/19 September 1944

P   Jemadar Ram Sarup Singh, 1st Punjab Regiment,
       Burma, 25 October 1944

     Sepoy Namdeo Jadhao, 5th Mahratta Light Infantry,
       Italy, 19 April 1945

     Rifleman Lachhiman Gurung, 8th Gurkha Rifles,
       Burma, 12/13 May 1945

     Rifleman Ganju Lama, 7th Gurkha Rifles,
       Burma, 12 June 1944

     Sepoy Kamal Ram, 8th Punjab Regiment,
       Burma, 2 March 1945

     Naik Gian Singh, 5th Punjab Regiment,
       Burma, 2 March 1945

     Naik Nand Singh, 1/11 Sikh Regiment,
       Burma, 11/12 March 1944

P   Lance Naik Sher Shah, 16th Punjab Regiment,
       Burma, 19/20 January 1945

P   Rifleman Thaman Gurung, 6th Gurkha Rifles,
       Italy, 10 November 1944

     Havildar Umrao Singh, Indian Artillery,
       Burma, 15/16 December 1944

     Sepoy Bhandari Ram, 1st Punjab Regiment,
       India, 22 November 1944

P   Jemadar Prakash Singh, 13th Frontier Force Rifles,
       Burma, 16/17 February 1945

     Rifleman Tulbahadur Pun, 6th Gurkha Rifles,
       Burma, 23 June 1944

P   Subadar Netrabahadadur Thapa, 5th Royal Gurkha Rifles,
       Burma, 26 June 1944

     Naik Agansingh Rai MM, 5th Royal Gurkha Rifles,
       Burma, 26 June 1944

P   Naik Yeshwant Ghadge, 5th Mahratta Light Infantry,
       Italy, 10 July 1944

P   Company Havildar-Major Chhelu Ram, 6th Rajputna Rifles,
       Tunisia, 19/20 April 1943

     Havildar Gaje Ghale, 5th Royal Gurkha Rifles,
       Burma, 25 May 1943

     Rifleman Bhanbhagta Gurung, 2nd Gurkha Rifles,
       Burma, 5 March 1945

Havildar Parkash Singh, 8th Punjab Regiment,
  Burma, 6 January 1943
Sepoy Ali Haidar, 13th Frontier Force,
  Italy, 9 April 1945
P Naik Fazal Din, 10th Baluch Regiment,
  Burma, 2 March 1945
Second-Lieutenant Premindra Singh Bhagat, Royal Bombay
  Sappers and Miners,
  Abyssinia, January/February 1941
Subadar Richpal Ram, 6th Rajputna Rifles,
  Eritrea, 7 February 1941
Subadar Lalbahadur Thapa, King Edward VII's Own Gurkha Rifles,
  Tunisia, 5/6 April 1943 (the first Gurkha to win the VC during
  the Second World War)
P Lieutenant Karamjeet Singh Judge, 15th Punjab Regiment,
  Burma, 18 March 1945

New Zealand

P Flying Officer L.A. Trigg, RNZAF,
  Atlantic, 11 August 1943
P Second-Lieutenant Moananvi-A-Kivi, 28th Battalion,
  Tunisia, 26 March 1943
Sergeant Keith Elliott, 22nd Battalion,
  Western Desert, 15 July 1942
Sergeant John Hinton, 20th Battalion,
  Greece, 28/29 April 1941
Sergeant Alfred Hulme, 23rd Battalion,
  Crete, 20/28 May 1941
Sergeant James Allen, RNZAF,
  over Germany, 7 July 1941 (died in a German hospital two
months later)
Lieutenant Charles Upham VC and Bar, 20th Battalion,
VC, Crete, 22 May 1941; second VC, Western Desert 14/15 July
  1942

South Africa

Sergeant Quentin Smythe, Royal Natal Carabineers,
  Western Desert, 5 June 1942
P Captain Edwin Swales, SAAF,
  Germany, 23 February 1945
Captain Gerard Ross Norton (see Italy VCs)

Fiji

P   Corporal Sefanaia Sukanaivalu, Fiji Infantry Regiment,
        Solomon Islands, 23 June 1944

Living holders of the VC in 1997

Name	Country of Residence
AGANSING RAI, Captain, VC	Nepal
ALI HAIDAR, Jem., VC	Pakistan
ANNAND, Captain R.W., VC	UK
BHAN BHAGTA GURUNG, Havildar, VC	Nepal
BHANDARI RAM, Captain, VC	India
CHAPMAN, E.T., VC, BEM	UK
CRUICKSHANK, Flt. Lt. J.A., VC	UK
CUTLER, Captain Sir Roden, VC, AK, KCMG, KCVO, CBE	Australia
FRASER, Lt.-Cdr. I.E., VC, DSC, JP	UK
GAJE GHALE, Captain, VC	India
GANJU LAMA, Captain, VC, MM, PD	Sikkim, India
GARDNER, Captain P.J., VC, MC	UK
GOULD, Petty Officer T.W., VC	UK
HINTON, Sergeant J.D., VC	New Zealand
JAMIESON, Major D.A., VC, CVO	UK
KENNA, Private E., VC	Australia
KENNEALLY, CQMS J.P., VC	UK
LACHHIMAN GURUNG, Havildar, VC	Nepal
MERRITT, Lt.-Col. C.C.I., VC, CD	Canada
NORTON, Captain G.R., VC, MM	Zimbabwe
PAYNE, WO II K., VC (Vietnam, 1969)	Australia
PORTEOUS, Colonel P.A., VC	UK
RAMBAHADUR LIMBU, Captain, VC, MVO (Sarawak, 1965)	Nepal
REID, Flt. Lt. W., VC	UK
SMITH, Sergeant E.A., VC, CD	Canada
SMYTHE, Captain Q.G.M., VC	South Africa
SPEAKMAN-PITTS, Sergeant W., VC (Korea, 1951)	South Africa
TULBAHADUR PUN, Lieutenant, VC	Nepal
UMRAO SINGH, Sub. Major, VC	India
WATKINS, The Rt. Hon. Lord Justice, VC, GBE	UK
WILSON, Lt.-Col. E.C.T., VC	UK

Bibliography

Over the generations since 1855 many books have been published about the Victoria Cross and about individual winners of the award. I list here some of those books together with general histories which deal with the background to campaigns and battles of the Second World War in which VCs were won.

Three books deserve special mention. They are: *For Valour: The Air VCs*, by Chaz Bowyer (Kimber, London, 1978; 1992 edn, Grub Street); *The Victoria Cross at Sea*, by John Winton (Michael Joseph, London, 1978); *The Register of the Victoria Cross*, compiled and researched by Nora Buzzell for This England, Cheltenham, 1981 and 1988.

Bowyer's book, which covers all air VCs from 1914, is the result of exemplary and painstaking research. Delving beyond the citations, Bowyer interviewed VC winners themselves, their comrades, friends and families. In this way he was able to prove, for instance, that Flight Sergeant Arthur Aaron was not shot down and killed by an enemy fighter but by the gunner of another British aircraft. For this revelation he was vilified by the head of the Air Historical Branch, who considered that citations were sacrosanct. He was mistaken; it is an historian's responsibility to find out and tell the truth, and this Bowyer does in *The Air VCs*.

Winton does a similar service for the Navy, by describing in detail the sea actions in which Victoria Crosses were won.

This England's *Register of the Victoria Cross* presents a condensed version of every VC citation published between 1855 and 1982, the most recent date of a VC award. Also, it contains a small photograph of virtually every VC winner.

Crook, M.J., *The Evolution of the Victoria Cross*, Midas Books, Tunbridge Wells, Kent, 1975

Feilding, Rowland, *War Letters to a Wife*, Medici Society, London, 1929

Fraser, George MacDonald, *Quartered Safe Out Here: A Recollection of the War in Burma*, HarperCollins, London, 1992

Fraser, Ian, *Frogman VC*, Angus & Robertson, London, 1957

Gurney, Major Gene, USAF, *The War in the Air*, New York, 1962

Harris, Barry, *Black Country VCs*, The Black Country Society, 1985

Hart, Sydney, *Submarine Upholder (Wanklyn VC)* Melrose, London, 1966

Hastings, Macdonald, *More Men of Glory*, Hulton Press, London, 1959

HMSO, *Victoria Cross Centenary Exhibition 1856–1956*, HMSO, London, 1956

Jameson, William S., *Submariners VC*, Peter Davies, London, 1962

Keegan, John, *The Second World War*, Hutchinson, London, 1989

Kirby, H.L., and Walsh, R.R., *The Seven VCs of Stonyhurst College*, THCL Books, Blackburn, 1987

Kitson, Lt-Col. J.A., *The Story of the 4th Battalion 2nd King Edward VII's Own Gurkha Rifles*, Gale & Polden, 1949

Lassen, Suzanne, *Anders Lassen VC: The Story of a Courageous Dane*, Muller, London, 1965

Macdonald, W. James, *A Bibliography of the Victoria Cross*, pub. by author, Beddeck, Nova Scotia, 1995

Macmillan, Norman, *The Royal Air Force in the Second World War*, Vol. 2, 1940–41; Harrap, London, 1944

Masters, John, *The Road Past Mandalay*, Michael Joseph, London, 1961

Ministry of Information, *Victoria Cross: Stories of VC Awards During the Second World War Up to June 1943*, London, 1943

Owen, Frank, *The Campaign in Burma*, The HMSO official report, 1946

Parrish, Thomas ed., *The Simon and Schuster Encyclopedia of World War II*, New York, 1978

Phillips, C.E. Lucas, *Victoria Cross Battles of the Second World War*, Heinemann, London, 1973

Roe, Frederick Gordon, *The Bronze Cross: a tribute to those who won the supreme award for valour in the years 1940–45*, Cawthorn, London, 1945

Scott, Kenneth Hare, *For Valour*, Garnett, London, 1949

Sims, Edward H., *The Fighter Pilots*, Cassell, London, 1967

Smyth, Sir John, *The Story of the Victoria Cross 1856–1963*, Muller, London, 1963

Sowards, Stuart E., *A Formidable Hero: R.H. Gray VC*, Canav Books, Toronto, 1987

Stevens, Lt-Col. G.R., *History of the 2nd King Edward VII's Own Goorkha Rifles*, Vol. 3, Aldershot, 1952

Turner, John Frayn, *VCs of the Air*, Harrap, London, 1960

Turner, John Frayn, *VCs of the Army, 1939–1951*, Harrap, London, 1956

Turner, John Frayn, *VCs of the Royal Navy*, Harrap, London, 1956

Whitman, J.E.A., *Gallant Deeds of the War*, Oxford University Press, 1941

Index